Presented To:

_____

From:

_____

Date:

_____

THE
DAILY
PROPHECY

DESTINY IMAGE BOOKS BY BRENDA KUNNEMAN

Decoding Hell's Propaganda

The Roadmap to Divine Direction

THE
DAILY
PROPHECY

Your Future
Revealed Today!

BRENDA KUNNEMAN

DESTINY IMAGE® PUBLISHERS, INC.

P.O. Box 310, Shippensburg, PA 17257-0310

"Promoting Inspired Lives."

This book and all other Destiny Image, Revival Press, MercyPlace, Fresh Bread, Destiny Image Fiction, and Treasure House books are available at Christian bookstores and distributors worldwide.

For a U.S. bookstore nearest you, call 1-800-722-6774.

For more information on foreign distributors, call 717-532-3040.

Reach us on the Internet: www.destinyimage.com.

ISBN 13 TP: 978-0-7684-0303-9

ISBN 13 Ebook: 978-0-7684-8783-1

For Worldwide Distribution, Printed in the U.S.A.

11 / 19

FOREWORD

Someone has aptly said, "You will spend the rest of your life in the future." Truer words have never been spoken. In fact, according to the studies and research of scientists and mathematicians, the "present moment" lasts for about seven seconds on average, and then you are in the future. Interestingly enough, the God we serve operates from the future into the present moment, because He "declares the end from the beginning", and He "calls those things that are not as though they are" (see Isa. 46:10; Rom. 4:17). One of our greatest challenges in the journey toward spiritual development is that if we are to walk with the Lord and flow in His Spirit, we have to become reoriented toward the future becoming our now, which is the walk of faith.

God always begins things in our lives with the end in mind and in view. Our greatest challenge as creatures of time, with habitual reactive patterns because of time, is that we can often get stuck in the past, bring the past into the present moment, and then project it into the future. The result is that we continue to relive outdated behavior patterns based on outdated and limiting beliefs that were formed in us, embedded in us, and anchored in us over the course of our journey from childhood to adulthood.

An aspect of the renewing of our minds which is all too often overlooked requires a reorientation to becoming "present to the future" rather than "present to the past". Every decision we make either anchors us to our past patterns and past reactions, or it reorients us to that which wants to emerge in our lives based on the power of God's proceeding word over us. A proceeding word from the Lord releases us into a process that orients us toward the future God intends for us, and when we embrace that process we let go of outdated behavior patterns that hinder our growth and get us stuck in ruts. We unlearn the inaccurate beliefs that have created those behaviors so that we can newly learn and take on the new beliefs and patterns that are congruent with and aligned with God's purpose for our lives.

The apostle Paul makes it clear in First Corinthians that the future belongs to you. In fact, he says everything belongs to you: "Whether Paul or Apollos or Cephas or the world or life or death or things *present or things to come;* all things belong to you, and you belong to Christ; and Christ belongs to God" (1 Cor. 3:22-23 NASB). So, if we accept Paul's exhortation here in the Scriptures, we are acknowledging that "the things to come" as well as "things present" belong to us. The future, Beloved, belongs to you. In fact, God intends for you to influence and shape the future and cooperate with what wants to emerge in your life based on His proceeding word over your life and your cooperation with His Spirit to bring it into manifestation.

For that reason, becoming "present-future" oriented is a part of the unfolding process of the renewing of your mind so that you can agree with God, calling those things that are not as though they are, and walking with God from the present into the future. All too often, we fail to renew our minds in this aspect and get stuck in a "past-present" orientation. Like Phil Connors, Bill Murray's famous character in *Groundhog Day,* we keep reliving our past, and we experience negative confirmations of self-fulfilling prophecies that anchor us to our past and cause us to be reactive learners. We continue to react as we did in the past, causing us to relive our yesterdays instead of influencing our tomorrows. As a result, we never live in the "now" of God.

Isn't it time for you to break free from the reactive learning patterns that have anchored you to the past, and cooperate with the Spirit of God and get anchored to the future God has for you? That begins by taking small incremental steps, one day at a time, and making little shifts here and there—fundamental shifts, shifts that are part of the lifestyle of the renewal of your mind, which includes a fundamental shift of thinking, feeling, speaking, and doing. The scriptural word for that is "repentance." In the Greek it is *metanoia. Metanoia* is a life-long process, and it is an educational process that re-forms us and renews us toward the intention of God, who has created a compelling vision of a completed future for us in His Word.

So how do you break the reactive learning patterns of being oriented in a "past-present" frame of mind, and get reframed toward a "present-future" orientation of faith? You get there one day at a time, one decision at a time, one shift at a time, by using this powerful devotional book of inspiring prophetic declarations, *The Daily Prophecy: Your Future Revealed Today!* It will take you step by step, day by day, decision by decision into a shift of heart and mind that will anchor you to the future by listening to, honoring, and acting on the daily prophetic word you will be reading and receiving from the Lord through Brenda Kunneman.

Pastor Brenda is one of the most effective, powerful, and prolific prophetic voices in the Kingdom of God whom I know of in this current hour. She is a skilled communicator in the Word, a masterful teacher of the truths of Scripture, and someone who is passionately stirred by the glory of the Father to move the hearts of His children in His intended direction for their lives. She will speak into your life in such a way that she will create a hunger in you for greater intimacy with the Father and a greater love for His work and Word in your life.

I am honored to have both Pastor Brenda and her husband Hank as friends and comrades in the Kingdom in this day and season of restoration, revival, and awakening. She and her husband have spoken powerfully into my life and the life of our ministry in such a timely fashion on more than one occasion. I am persuaded she is going to deeply impact your life as you take a 365-day journey with her into the blissful realm of walking in your future now! Enjoy the journey; it will get brighter and brighter with each passing day as you embrace what she reveals daily by God's precious Holy Spirit!

Dr. Mark Chironna
Mark Chironna Ministries
Orlando, Florida

INTRODUCTION

If there is any one thing that is true, it is that everyone is hungry to have a glimpse into their future so they feel confident to make decisions and feel better equipped to manage their lives accordingly. People not only want to know their outcome long-term, but they also want the confidence that they know what the immediate tomorrow holds for them on an ongoing basis. It's the reason secular people seek psychics, the horoscope, fortune-tellers, and similar mediums. Then, while it's often done in fun, the same drive to have a peek into tomorrow is why people read their fortune cookie after a plateful of Chinese food! There is that something that drives us to crack open that cookie and just see if there might be something within that sheds a beam of light into tomorrow.

For believers, while we don't seek after the same mediums the world does, we are still driven to hear a word from God that accomplishes a similar goal. We want to know what tomorrow holds, at least to some degree. We want to know what God is saying about our long-term future and also about our current situation. In that quest, of course we often seek the Scripture. If most believers were to admit it, both preachers and new believers alike, at some point just about everyone has held their Bible in their lap and let it fall open to a random page hoping that the first verse they read jumps out to them as just the very miraculous directive they were looking for.

Believers also look to the ministry of prophets and prophetic insight to know what their future holds for them. People love hearing a word of prophecy that offers some insight into what tomorrow may bring, whether it be on more of a wide scale or a personal prophecy directed for them. While every believer must practice listening to the Holy Spirit for themselves, let's admit that we all appreciate and sometimes need a word from God about our lives that comes from someone else. A certain amount of this is important and biblical. Many people in the

Bible, both Old and New Testaments, received words from God via other believers and prophets. It often proved to be the very thing that kept them from making some wrong decisions and saved them from a great deal of hardship. While hearing God through others—such as prophets, ministry leaders, and even fellow believers—cannot be your sole way of listening to God; it can prove to be a valuable resource and even safety net that helps us in our quest to embrace the Word of the Lord for our future. The bottom line is that we are all hungry and even driven at times to find God's timely voice somewhere, from someone at just the right moment in time.

The Daily Prophecy is one such resource to help you find the Word of the Lord in your daily life. Regardless of your background or walk of life, each daily word offers a balanced, biblical piece of insight from God. It is written with the goal to edify your heart and help give you a sense of direction as to what God may be saying in your life today. As you read each daily word, may you find it to be one of those unexpected, miraculous resources that you can't see any other way but supernaturally. May it also be used to confirm some of the things the Holy Spirit may already have put in your heart. Each day is communicated in such a way that it brings the Bible alive as God speaking to you personally. Each word is coupled with Scripture, a short balanced teaching, and a prayer declaration.

Countless thousands of readers of *The Daily Prophecy* have found it to be a lifeline for embracing God's next steps and for receiving that key word of consolation in a world where everyone wants to feel confident about their future and where believers are on an ongoing quest to hear God's voice. May the Holy Spirit use *The Daily Prophecy* to open His direction for you step by step as your future is revealed *today!*

New Strength and Ability Released

"In those areas that you have tried and tried to fix and get right, God says, release your willing heart once again to Me, and I will release new strength and ability for you to succeed this day."

Prophetic Scripture

If ye be willing and obedient, ye shall eat the good of the land (Isaiah 1:19).

We all have times when we feel like no matter how hard we try, we keep failing at the same old things. Then we question if God is angry at us because we have messed things up—yet again. However, God's ability can make up for our shortcomings, but it begins with *willingness*. God isn't impressed by our human ability. God looks for the willing heart who wants to obey Him and rely on *His* ability. It means doing whatever He asks you. It might mean you have to give up a few things, change some attitudes, or perhaps choose some new friends. When you are willing to follow Him no matter what, it releases you to walk in His divine ability. Be willing to obey and follow His Word closely today. You will find yourself succeeding at things that you once failed at and it will cause you to operate in a new ability from the Lord today!

Prayer

Dear Lord, I give You my life and my heart today. I commit all that I have into Your hands. I am willing to do all that You ask of me. Lord, I believe that You are releasing a fresh impartation that causes me to succeed and not fail. I declare that new strength and ability is released into my life right now! In Jesus' Name, amen.

My Healthcare Is Yours

"The Spirit says, know that as My child I have provided you a healthcare benefit. My healthcare system makes miraculous healing available. Healing grace is in your hands and healing power is available to benefit you this day!"

Prophetic Scripture

Bless the Lord, O my soul, and forget not all his benefits; who forgiveth all thine iniquities; who healeth all thy diseases (Psalms 103:2-3).

As a born-again Christian, you are a citizen of a new Kingdom. Just like in a natural kingdom, in God's Kingdom there are benefits provided for its citizens. For example, in many workplaces or nations, healthcare, among many other benefits, is made available for employees or citizens. As a citizen in God's Kingdom, you have been provided with a benefits package. Included in the package is healing. God has always had a healing provision for His people. When Israel was delivered from Egypt, God promised them that if they served Him, He would be their Healer (see Exod. 15:26). In Christ, we also have a healing benefit (see Isa. 53:4-5; Matt. 8:16-17; Acts 10:38; 1 Pet. 2:24). Healing is for the whole person—spirit, soul and body. It doesn't matter if you need spiritual, emotional, or physical healing. It is available! Let today be about receiving God's healing benefits!

Prayer

Dear heavenly Father, I thank You that as a citizen of Your Kingdom, I have healing benefits today. Those benefits not only heal me, but cause me to live in divine health. As I lay hands on myself, I decree that Your miraculous power goes into me—spirit, soul, and body. I call upon Your unfailing healthcare system today and I thank You, Lord, that it is working in me now! In Jesus' Name, amen.

Help Is Here!

*"So what is it that I can help you do this day? says the Lord. I am offering
My strong arm of help to you. Ask Me to help you do something impossible.
Ask Me to help you overcome the obstacles in your way. Ask of Me, for
help is here!"*

Prophetic Scripture

*For I the Lord God will hold thy right hand, saying unto thee, Fear not; I
will help thee* (Isaiah 41:13).

Sometimes we forget that the Lord wants to participate in everything
that we deal with. He wants to be included in the smallest, most
seemingly insignificant things of our lives. I am amazed at times when
out shopping how many incredible deals and savings I get when I ask the
Lord to help me find the sales! We often forget that the Lord wants to be
involved with the everyday things. It's easy to fall into the trap of only
talking to God about the issues that are predominantly surrounding our
problems. Yes, God will help us with those things, but by getting Him
involved in the everyday things, we more readily expect His help to be
available during those trying times when it's harder to feel as confident.
Ask Him to help you today. Get Him involved because the Lord can
do things you could never do on your own. He is waiting; ask for His
help today!

Prayer

*Dear heavenly Father, I receive Your supernatural help today! Lord, I believe
Your promise that You are holding my hand and helping me in everything.
I **will** come out in victory because You are doing the impossible for me. I
specifically ask You to help me with _____.
I know I cannot fail because Your help is here! In the Name of Jesus, amen!*

A Door Is Before You

"See today that I am opening doors that man cannot open or close. There are divine appointments and connections that I am setting up for you. For a door to destiny is before you this day, says the Lord of Hosts."

Prophetic Scripture

...Behold, I have set before thee an open door, and no man can shut it... (Revelation 3:8).

I am certainly not a marketing professional, nor do I want to liken the Lord to a marketer, but He does know how to set up just the right divine appointments. Sometimes we get too busy to notice the doors and opportunities the Lord is setting up for us. It might be a missed opportunity to pray with someone who needs healing or making a key phone call. Sometimes we miss divine appointments that may have the potential to open cities and nations to the Gospel. What if Philip the Evangelist had ignored that impression of the Holy Spirit to go speak to the man from Ethiopia because he was late to an appointment or something? (See Acts 8:27-40.) To this day, Phillip's ministry is marked by this great event. Look for divine appointments and open doors today. Perhaps, if you expect them, they will open even more. When you do, no man will be able close the divine doors that are before you today!

Prayer

Father, open my eyes to the doors You are setting before me today. Help me to slow down and see them clearly. Place people in my path, set up appointments, and create divine connections. I believe that as I walk through divine doors, I will see destiny unfold before me. Thank You Lord! In the Name of Jesus, amen!

A Day of Singing

"Sing today and let My praise be upon your lips. For as you sing and rejoice, your heart will be glad and your mind will become steadfast in Me. It will cause the noise of confusion around you to become still. For I say to you, this is the day to sing!"

Prophetic Scripture

O come, let us sing unto the Lord: let us make a joyful noise to the rock of our salvation (Psalms 95:1).

We all know something about the power of song and music. Think about what people do on a noisy airplane. If you travel much at all, you definitely appreciate the power of music in your earphones! When passengers want to tune out the noise, they quickly scramble for their headset.

I think it is the same in the spirit. When we sing to the Lord, our song can drown out the noise of life around us and interrupt those thoughts trying to get us down. When I don't play my music on the plane, I hear all the noise, conversation, and crying children. That environment can produce stress and irritation. But when the music plays, the noise level moves to the background of my mind. If life has presented you with a lot of noise today, sing to the Lord. As you sing, it will cause you to see the Lord as your Rock, rather than feel the stress that comes from hearing all the noise. Sing to Him today!

Prayer

Father, I choose this day as a day of song. As I sing to You, cause my heart to be reassured in You. I sing to the Rock of my salvation. I sing praise no matter what things are trying to speak into my mind. Lord, let my song of praise to You be a sweet melody to Your heart and let it give me rest today. I worship You with all my heart. Amen.

The Cloud of His Glory

"Begin to look for My glory in places and at times that you least expect it. For I desire to manifest Myself upon you as fire and light. Expect to sense My glory as you go about your routine, and know that it shall descend upon you like a cloud!"

Prophetic Scripture

Behold, he cometh with clouds... (Revelation 1:7).

When you think about how many times in the Bible God's glory descended upon His people, it makes you feel a sense of awe. When Moses met with God on Mount Sinai, the cloud of glory covered the mountain (see Exod. 24:15). The same cloud filled the temple in Second Chronicles 5:13. When Jesus was transfigured before His disciples, the cloud of glory overshadowed them (see Mark 9:7). Not only did the glory of the Lord appear as a cloud, it appeared as a bright, fiery light. The shepherds at Jesus birth experienced it in Luke 2:9. Saul experienced it on the road to Damascus (see Acts 9:3). We also know when the day of Jesus' glorious return comes that He will arrive in the clouds of God's glory according to Revelation 1:7 and Matthew 24:30.

We see all through the Bible that God's cloud of glory manifested in unexpected places, on unexpected people, and in unusual ways. We shouldn't only expect to experience the glory in a church service. It can manifest upon you anywhere and in any location. I believe you should expect the glory to manifest at any moment upon you today!

Prayer

Father, I ask that Your glory would manifest upon me today. I expect it anytime, anyplace! Let Your glory change me and make me a new person. I ask that as Your glory descends upon me, I will receive insight, revelation, and a fresh touch of Your power. Lord, show me Your glory! In the Name of Jesus, amen.

Extend Your Hand

"So the Spirit says, extend your hand in prayer today for someone else. Dedicate this day as a day for others. For your prayers for others are as seeds of giving, and the harvest of answers to your own prayers and needs shall burst forth on every side!"

Prophetic Scripture

Knowing that whatsoever good thing any man doeth, the same shall he receive of the Lord, whether he be bond or free (Ephesians 6:8).

Often when we speak of giving, we think of giving finances. That is one of the most important forms of giving, because Jesus said our heart and our money are connected (see Matt. 6:21). Simply put, we reap what we sow, or you get back whatever you give (see Gal. 6:7).

Yet consider today another form of sowing and reaping that will encourage you in those areas where you are needing answers. It's sowing seed in prayer for someone else. Jesus sowed this type of "prayer seed" when He prayed for His disciples in John 17. Jesus prayed this amazing prayer for *others* while facing His own time of personal challenge prior to His death. His prayer seed produced a blessing in return—not only as a harvest of souls, but it prepared the way for His glorious resurrection!

Sowing prayers for others, especially during your own times of trial, will reap a harvest of answers to your own needs. Give someone the seed of prayer today and watch what God will do for you!

Prayer

Dear Lord, I pray for _____ today. I ask that You will move powerfully on their behalf. I ask You to meet their needs and keep them safe and protected. I pray they would experience a fresh touch of Your presence, fresh revelation, and complete peace. In Jesus' Name, amen.

My Covenant Is Yours

"Know this day that I am the God of promise, and what I have declared I shall make good. I have a covenant of agreement with you that I will never break. So expect the promises of My covenant to be yours this day!"

Prophetic Scripture

God is not a man, that he should lie; neither the son of man, that he should repent: hath he said, and shall he not do it? or hath he spoken, and shall he not make it good? (Numbers 23:19)

We have all come to learn that people will let us down. Combine that with any of the numerous challenges we face and one could unintentionally lump God in with the myriad of disappointments. Most of us could probably recall a time when we questioned God or asked Him the all too famous question, "Why God? Why?"

Of course, the "why" question cannot always be easily answered. What is important to know is God never lies or makes a mistake. His promises are true and unchanging. It's during those times when you cannot answer "why" that you need to dig your heels into God's promises. That is when you say to yourself, "God will never lie! His covenant promises are true no matter what!"

I encourage you to make this a day all about reaffirming His promises in your life. Take your eyes off all the things that don't seem to be working out and declare, "God's promises are mine today!"

Prayer

*Heavenly Father, I thank You that Your promises are always true and never change. Today, I stand upon these promises: _____.
I affirm that they are true because Your Word declares them to be so. I make a solemn decision to take my eyes off the adverse circumstances and I place them on what You have already declared. Thank You Lord! In the Name of Jesus, amen.*

Enter into the Spirit

"Know that there is a place by Me where you can experience My presence in a way that is custom designed uniquely for you. For as you pray in the spirit, it shall be opened to you, and you shall be refreshed, says the Lord."

Prophetic Scripture

For with stammering lips and another tongue will he speak to this people. To whom he said, This is the rest wherewith ye may cause the weary to rest... (Isaiah 28:11–12).

Many people want to have a supernatural experience with God in the spirit that transcends them from the everyday. But in order to enter *into the spirit*, we need to first pray *in the spirit*. Praying in tongues acts as a doorway to the supernatural glory of God. The early apostles walked in supernatural power *after* they experienced the Day of Pentecost when tongues of fire sat upon them.

Imagine what could take place in your experience with the Lord today if you prayed in the spirit throughout the day. You can pray in tongues as you drive in your car or get ready for work. You can pray under your breath as you lay down to sleep or even doing chores around the house. By increasing time praying in the spirit, we will have a greater measure of supernatural encounters in His presence that will refresh our walk with Him. There is power when we pray in tongues!

Prayer

Lord, as I pray in the sprit today, I am expecting experiences in Your presence that You have reserved just for me. I believe I shall have an increase of divine encounters and experiences in Your glory. Even now, as I pray in the spirit, I shall be refreshed! Amen!

JANUARY 10

Make Your Request Known

"God says, I am imploring you to let your requests and desires be known to Me! I wait for your supplications to come before My throne. What do you need? Ask it of Me and I will work on your case and do things that human power could not have accomplished."

Prophetic Scripture

Be careful for nothing; but in every thing by prayer and supplication with thanksgiving let your requests be made known unto God (Philippians 4:6).

Here the Bible is telling us to make our requests known to God. It isn't telling us to shy away in the belief that God thinks our requests are ridiculous. Instead, we are told to ask and make our needs boldly known.

The funny thing is that God knows exactly what we need before we ever ask! He already knows what we desire! Yet, even though God knows our needs and already knows what we are going to pray about, He still wants us to make these requests.

It's because God wants to hear us come in agreement with Heaven and use our faith. He wants to hear you express your belief in His faithfulness and goodness! God is a Father and He loves when you come to Him as Papa God and ask Him to meet your needs. What good father wouldn't want to hand his children good things? (See Matthew 7:11.) Your loving Daddy loves to hear your own unique voice, so don't be afraid to just ask Him. He will provide all you need and *wants* to do impossible things for you!

Prayer

Dear Heavenly Father, You are my Father. I let my request concerning _____ be known to You today. I know You love to hear me ask You for things. Therefore, Lord, I ask you to meet my needs. I thank You, Lord, for answering me and being such a wonderful Father! I love you Lord, amen.

Joy and Laughter

*"I say that it is time to laugh! Yes, some things look as though it is impossible to laugh, but laugh says the Lord, laugh anyhow. Step out and **make** joy and laughter happen in your situation and I will **make** joy and laughter bubble up from within you and it will change your situation forever!"*

Prophetic Scripture

…Weeping may endure for a night, but joy cometh in the morning (Psalms 30:5).

One cloudy morning, I was driving to my office feeling somewhat blue. I was thinking about all the things I had before me to deal with. Not long into my drive, the sun began to peek through the clouds and my spirits began to perk up! I started singing and thinking about how great life is.

I was reminded how easily we let something miniscule like a cloudy morning change our perspective. Often what looks like the impossible mountain is impossible because we allow it to be so in our own minds. Even the real trials require us to keep the right perspective if we are ever going to gain victory.

Laughter is a great way to get a new perspective. It can change your mood and make you forget your problems. You can be having a tough day, but then someone tells a funny joke and you forget everything! Laughter gave you a new outlook, just like the sunshine did for me driving in my car. I believe laughter is like sunshine. It will brighten your day. Laugh today; you may be surprised how your laughter will become a real force of power!

Prayer

*Hallelujah, Lord, I laugh today! I **make** it a day of joy and laughter. I choose to laugh in spite of all my circumstances. Ha! Ha! Ha! Lord, let me experience an overwhelming force of joy in Your presence today that gives me a new perspective! In Jesus' Name, amen.*

The Highly Exalted Name

"Exalt My Son, exalt His Name! For Jesus is raised to the highest exalted position above the most formidable forces of evil. Exalt the Name of Jesus, and see your foes lose their foothold all around you."

Prophetic Scripture

Wherefore God also hath highly exalted him, and given him a name which is above every name. That at the name of Jesus every knee should bow, of things in heaven, and things in earth, and things under the earth (Philippians 2:9-10).

The sound of the Name of Jesus can change the hardest of hearts while at the same time cause the most rebellious person to retaliate in anger. The early apostles were threatened for declaring His Name. The Pharisees hated that multitudes praised His Name. Jesus' Name is the most controversial but most powerful and most spoken name on earth. To our horror, it is also the only name used for swearing and cursing.

If you search the name *Jesus* online (including *Christ* and *Jesus Christ*), you will learn it is the most searched name above any other public figure. The Bible also remains the bestselling book worldwide, topping out at more than 6 billion sold since its first known publication date in 1451. (http://home.comcast.net/~antaylor1/bestsellingbooks.html)

Regardless of resistance, hatred, and every attempt to stop it, the Name of Jesus and His Word continues to gain every form of attention known to humankind. Nothing can resist His exalted Name! Know that His Name is higher than anything you are dealing with today, large or small. Just speak the Name of Jesus and it will cause every enemy in your life to tremble.

Prayer

Lord Jesus, I exalt Your Name above all else in my life today. All my fears, problems, sicknesses, pains, and challenges must bow down to the Name of Jesus. I declare that Jesus' Name reigns and the powers of darkness must bow their knee! Amen!

JANUARY 13

Done by the Finger of God

"Know that the season is upon you when men and women across the earth shall see My miracles and wonders working in you and through you, says the Spirit. Ha! Ha! For they shall surely say that this can only be done by the finger of God!"

Prophetic Scripture

But if I with the finger of God cast out devils, no doubt the kingdom of God is come upon you (Luke 11:20).

Over and over the Pharisees questioned whether Jesus did legitimate miracles. They even accused Him of casting out demons by the power of the devil! Today much of society wants to explain away the power of God to some scientific phenomenon. However, there comes a point when that becomes impossible. In Exodus 8:19, the magicians of Pharaoh imitated the miracles of Moses through sorcery and trickery. Yet, there came a point when they could not explain away Moses' miracles anymore! They were finally forced to admit that it was the finger of God! I see prophetically that we are going to step into such a realm of the supernatural that people will know the miracles are done by the finger of God. If Jesus and even the early apostles did it then so shall we. As a result, people will see it and not be able to explain it away. As this happens, the world will know the Kingdom of God has come upon them!

Prayer

Father, I ask You today to do miracles through me! Let them be so powerful that those I meet will know it is by Your power they are done. Help us, as the Body of Christ, to position ourselves for that level of power and teach us how to walk in it. Through us, let the world know that Your power has come to touch them. In Jesus' Name, amen.

A Word in Your Mouth

"I shall touch your mouth this day, says the Lord. Don't worry about who you shall speak to or what you shall say. I shall give you the words and your hearers shall encounter My presence upon your lips!"

Prophetic Scripture

Then the Lord put forth his hand, and touched my mouth. And the Lord said unto me, Behold, I have put my words in thy mouth (Jeremiah 1:9).

The Lord must have known that we get concerned over having the right words to say at the right times because there are so many accounts in Scripture where the Lord encouraged people not to be concerned over what they were to say in difficult situations. The Lord reminded Moses that He would provide him the right words when he was to speak to Pharaoh (see Exod. 4:10-12). Jesus reminded His disciples that they didn't need to be concerned with what to say when they were falsely accused (see Mark 13:11). He also reminded them that their words would be so supernatural to the point they wouldn't even have to pre-plan what to speak! They were to expect a miraculous divine utterance.

The Bible says not one of Samuel's words fell to the ground (see 1 Sam. 3:19). That is because God divinely put His Word in Samuel's mouth.

If God could put the right words in the mouths of these people, He will do the same for you. Expect God's Word to come from your mouth today, and when you speak, God's presence will be upon your words!

Prayer

Father, I thank You that Your words are in my mouth today. As I speak to those who I must communicate with, I am asking that divine utterance will come from my mouth. Place Your hand upon my lips and let me speak under the anointing of your presence in everything I say! In Jesus' Name, amen.

Increase of Angels

"Yes, the time is at hand; an increase of angelic activity is here. For spiritual reinforcements have been sent to help My church handle the present time and season. So expect this day for angels to help you."

Prophetic Scripture

Are they not all ministering sprits, sent forth to minister for them who shall be heirs of salvation? (Hebrews 1:14)

There is no doubt that the countless prophecies of Scripture regarding end-time events are unfolding. If you were to look at things from a natural or earthly perspective, you could feel a sense of fear. However, we need to know that God has an army of helpers who aren't going to leave us to face this hour alone. In addition to the Holy Spirit, God's angels are on assignment to help the church.

As you drive your car, they are protecting you. As you pray and decree, they are making things happen for you. Angels are working to keep harm from coming near you (see Ps. 91:10-11).

We are in a time when we should expect more angelic activity. Some may see them, others may sense them or dream about their operations. The key is knowing they are around and are working for you. You can even speak and commission your angels to help you by speaking God's Word (see Ps. 103: 20). They listen to God's Word when it is spoken from our mouths. Expect good things to happen today as angels work for you and help bring God's will for your life into existence.

Prayer

Father, I want to say thank You that angels have been sent from heaven to watch over my life and help me. I expect to see the supernatural results of the work of angels. I decree that angels shall help me in the area of _____. Thank You Lord! In the Name of Jesus, amen.

Call for a Breakthrough

"Call today for one particular area of breakthrough, says the Lord. Be specific, for I go before you to break down walls of resistance and to open a gate this day."

Prophetic Scripture

The breaker is come up before them: they have broken up, and have passed through the gate, and are gone out by it: and their king shall pass before them, and the Lord on the head of them (Micah 2:13).

We know that all throughout the Old Testament Israel fought many various battles. If you look at them all collectively, you could easily think, "Wow that is a lot of fighting!" But when you look at each separate battle and think about how powerfully God overtook their enemies, you feel an incredible sense of victory in your heart.

Instead of trying to obtain breakthrough for all the various areas of your life, call for a breakthrough in just one area. The devil wants you to spend so much time looking at the big picture of challenges before you until you feel defeated. Instead, I believe the Spirit of God wants to give you a different approach today. Stay on one area and don't give up until it breaks. Once you see God's miracle power break through in that one area, faith will arise in your heart for the next area and so on. Stay in prayer and God's Word and don't forget—you have a mighty God working with you and leading you into a breakthrough today!

Prayer

Dear Lord, I know that You are the Breaker who leads me into complete victory. I call for a breakthrough regarding _____.
Through the eye of my faith, I see You, Lord, leading me through the gates of resistance and I declare this area of my life experiences a miracle of break-through right now! In the Name of Jesus, amen.

Water from the Rock

"Expect provision and resources to come from the most unusual places. For blessing is about to be poured out in unlikely locations and from unexpected sources. For you will say that you didn't know it could come this way!"

Prophetic Scripture

He opened the rock, and the waters gushed out; they ran in the dry places like a river (Psalms 105:41).

All of us will say that God is powerful. However, far fewer people can confidently say that God will use His power for them when they need it. Sometimes we limit our confidence in God to things that are humanly possible. Yet, the verse above reminds us that God brought provision from a most unusual place that was not humanly possible. He showed His power from a place where people probably weren't looking because it wasn't something they could have produced. Of course, water coming from a rock is also a prophetic picture of Jesus, the Rock. In other words, all provision comes from Him. It comes from a miraculous source. Instead of just looking to your job or some rich uncle to come through, perhaps it's time to refocus on Jesus. He will bring what you need in the way you least expect, just like He did for Israel when the water came from the rock. They were in a desert of what looked to be ultimate destitution, but suddenly a rock opened for them! You can be certain of one thing—His provision might come from an unexpected place, but it will always be what you need, right on time!

Prayer

Father, I receive supernatural provision today. I call upon heavenly resources and I expect the unexpected blessings of God. I place my eyes on Jesus, my Rock and provider today! Blessings and provision, you must come to me now! In the Name of Jesus, amen!

It's Payback Time!

"This is the time, yes it is payback time, says the Lord! Know that all your work shall be rewarded and what the enemy has tried to steal from your hand shall be brought back to you in its full measure during this season!"

Prophetic Scripture

The Lord recompense thy work, and a full reward be given thee of the Lord God of Israel, under whose wings thou art come to trust (Ruth 2:12).

That is the prophetic sound for this season in the Spirit. God's prophets have been speaking "payback time." That means it's time to get in on the blessing you need—claim it for your own life. Start getting up each morning and saying, "This is my day of reward; it's my payback time!" It doesn't matter what things look like; what matters is knowing that God is paying us back for what the enemy has stolen. Why does the Lord do that? It is because God is a God of justice and when He sees that we have done righteously and the devil has come into our lives to steal, kill, and destroy, God tallies up the final score. The Lord always finds the devil without another hand to deal. The devil loses. The righteous always win out over evil. Be confident today that it is payback time in the spirit and your full reward is upon you!

Prayer

Dear Lord, I declare payback, payback, payback over my life today! I trust You and know that You are rewarding me for following You and putting Your Word into practice in my life. So, I tell the devil today, "You bring back everything you have stolen! I command _____ to be brought back to me right now, in Jesus' Name! Amen.

Forgive and Release

"Know that miracles and forgiveness are attached together. For as you forgive and release those who have bruised and misused you, then shall answers to prayer and miracles be released to you in this hour."

Prophetic Scripture

And he kneeled down, and cried with a loud voice, Lord, lay not this sin to their charge... (Acts 7:60).

Remembering the story of Stephen, the first martyr, the Bible says that he had a mighty miracle ministry (see Acts 6:8; 7:58-59). However, I am convinced that one of the greatest miracles that should be credited to Stephen was the salvation of the apostle Paul. At his death, Stephen cried out for the forgiveness of his murderers, and it was shortly thereafter that Saul was converted. I believe the two are connected. Jesus taught in John 20:23 that those whose sins you remit, they are remitted, but those that you retain, they are retained. When Stephen remitted the sins of Saul for condoning his death (see Acts 8:1), I believe it released Saul to receive salvation, not only because he may have heard Stephen verbalize forgiveness, but also because it released Paul spiritually from that bond of indebtedness.

Begin the practice of forgiveness today. Sure we need to draw godly boundaries (see 2 Cor. 6:14-17) and build trust with people, but it progresses to unforgiveness when we cannot get free from the internal bitterness or repeated discussions regarding the things they did.

Your forgiveness may be the very thing someone needs in order to open their heart to God and be free. Make the choice to forgive the people who have hurt you today!

Prayer

Heavenly Father, I forgive _____ today. I release them from everything they did wrongly to me and ask that You would bring them into a renewed relationship with You. I hold nothing against them. I thank You, Lord, for the amazing, supernatural power of forgiveness. In Jesus' Name, amen.

Increasing Your Measure of Anointing

"Watch as I increase your measure of influence, even today, says God. I will cause you to have an effect on people that you did not seem to have before. For know that the measure of anointing is increasing upon you."

Prophetic Scripture

For he whom God hath sent speaketh the words of God: for God giveth not the Spirit by measure unto him (John 3:34).

When the Lord sent Jesus into the world as a heavenly spokesman, the Spirit of the Lord was upon Him without measure. Jesus walked in unlimited power, but the Bible says He grew into a man of full spiritual maturity (Luke 2:52). God could anoint Him without limits because Jesus learned the ways of God and was able to handle the power of God on such a level.

For us, God wants to increase the anointing on our life too, as we become His ambassadors in the earth. He wants to increase our measure of power as we learn God's ways and can handle the anointing properly. When the measure of anointing on your life increases, you will have new boldness, confidence, and ability to manifest God to people in a way that is beyond human capability. So position yourself today for an increase of anointing by growing, drawing close to God, and asking for it. When you do, I believe by this time next year you will be amazed at how much stronger the Holy Spirit's presence will be upon your life! God is increasing your measure today!

Prayer

Dear Father, I ask You for an increase in the anointing. Teach me how to handle Your power correctly and with maturity. I submit myself to You and those who You have placed in my life to help me mature. I expect my measure of anointing to expand today. Hallelujah! Amen.

Up from the Death Shade!

"Even in times when it would seem that certain destruction is near, I will bring you up from the shadow of death. For light is being cast upon the shadows of evil and you will come to a place of sure deliverance."

Prophetic Scripture

Yea, though I walk through the valley of the shadow of death, I will fear no evil: for thou art with me; thy rod and thy staff they comfort me (Psalms 23:4).

The phrase *shadow of death* literally means "death shade." The best way I can describe it is like a Pink Panther cartoon I once saw. Pink was going about his business when a little rain cloud appeared above him. Everywhere he went it kept raining, but only on him. He tried to escape, but it just followed him everywhere, keeping him under a dark cloud.

That is what the shadow of death is like. It is as if you are under the cloud of impending disaster. However, Psalms 23:4 says that we don't have to fear a death shade because of God's presence. Remember two things: First, it's only a shadow. Shadows can't hurt you, they just indicate that something is there. Know that if the devil has been limited to mere shadow-casting then something is preventing him from actually touching you! Second, remember that shade always disappears when light is cast upon it and the Lord is casting light on those shadows today. Stand with confidence in the light of God's presence and watch those shadows of death disappear!

Prayer

Dear Lord, I thank You that I am free from the shadow of death. I know that Your presence is with me, casting a light on every situation, and nothing is able to harm me. I come out from the death shade in the Name of Jesus and I refuse to be fearful any longer! Amen!

Gifts Are in Thee

"The Spirit says that I am manifesting a special gift and endowment of power upon you. It is ready to operate with divine inspiration and it shall set a change of events in motion!"

Prophetic Scripture

Wherefore I put thee in remembrance that thou stir up the gift of God, which is in thee... (2 Timothy 1:6).

The Holy Spirit makes the gifts of the Spirit available to empower us. They provide divine utterances, perform miracles, and do mighty exploits. Too often, when ministering to others or even when dealing with our own lives, we leave out the spiritual gifts and endowments the Holy Spirit has provided (see 1 Cor. 12:4-10). These divine gifts are available to benefit us whenever there is a need. Our job is to expect and stir up those gifts. A key way to do that is to pray in tongues, because praying in tongues is a faith-builder (see Jude 20). Another way to stir up the gifts is to just step out by faith. You could compare that to how Peter stepped out of the boat and walked on the water (see Matt. 14:28-31). Peter took the first step and then expected the power of God to be available.

Take small steps as you learn to flow in these gifts. Perhaps if you are ministering to someone, just give them a short, polite word of encouragement regarding what you believe the Lord is saying to them. You can even prophesy this same way to your own situations. The key is to know that divine gifts and manifestations are available. Just stir your faith to believe and take a step.

Prayer

Dear Lord, I stir the gifts of the spirit through faith today. I declare that miraculous gifts shall operate through me, not only for others, but for myself. Holy Spirit, I thank You that circumstances shall be changed today by Your power and supernatural gifts! In the Name of Jesus, amen.

Insight and Wisdom

"Know that I am bringing a divine revelation concerning your circumstances. Prepare your focus and expect My Spirit to impart unto you new insight and wisdom that you have yet to consider."

Prophetic Scripture

That the God of our Lord Jesus Christ, the Father of glory, may give unto you the spirit of wisdom and revelation in the knowledge of him (Ephesians 1:17).

There is a vast difference between natural human wisdom and supernatural wisdom from God. Of course, we need natural human wisdom, which was given by God to govern our daily lives. Examples of such would be things like "don't touch a hot stove, because it will burn you," or "keep an organized budget so you will be better equipped to live in financial stability."

However, there is supernatural wisdom that God gives into situations, especially when all the best human efforts can't solve the problem. His wisdom can sometimes sound foolish to natural wisdom. Sure, you can try to solve your financial problems with careful penny pinching. However, in God's wisdom there is the principle of *giving away* finances that acts as the road to financial increase.

Sounds foolish to natural wisdom, but divine wisdom cannot be explained.

Expect a divine impartation of wisdom today and that the Lord will give you a key piece of insight that will help you solve some tricky situations with divine inspiration. James 1:5-8 tells us to have faith for that kind of wisdom. Start declaring, "God's wisdom is in me today and I know exactly what to do!"

Prayer

Dear heavenly Father, I ask You for divine wisdom concerning _____. Reveal to me things I need to do differently and provide me a key piece of insight in this area. I receive it and will respond today like I know Your divine wisdom is upon me! In Jesus Name, amen.

Decree a Blessing

"Decree a blessing over what you seem to lack. For what doesn't seem to be enough, says the Lord, shall become more than enough when you bless it and it shall multiply for you!"

Prophetic Scripture

And he commanded the multitude to sit down on the grass, and took the five loaves, and the two fishes, and looking up to heaven, he blessed, and brake, and gave the loaves to his disciples, and the disciples to the multitude (Matthew 14:19).

We know the story of Jesus and how He fed the multitude with only five loaves of bread and two small fish. Yet, we often overlook the part about how Jesus took something that was insufficient and how His words caused it to become sufficient. Jesus took what was *not* enough, and when He spoke a blessing over it, suddenly it became more than enough. There is no doubt that when Jesus decreed a blessing over that handful of food He knew His words carried power to produce a miracle.

Your words have power today. Begin speaking a blessing over something in your life that feels insufficient. Declare that what isn't enough becomes more than enough. Perhaps it is your finances or something in your business. Maybe you are lacking in some measure of self-confidence or self-worth. Start reversing it by speaking a blessing about who you are and who God had made you. If there is something that you are lacking today, speak a blessing over it and expect what isn't enough to become supernaturally more than enough!

Prayer

Father, I decree a blessing over _____. I declare that I have more than enough. I decree miraculous multiplication and I say that I shall live in overflow. I have divine supply to meet every need. I say, I bless it and I know that provision is multiplied for me on every side today! In the Name of Jesus, amen.

Visions Shall Be Seen

"Forget not that the era of visions, dreams, and prophetic inspiration is now. For I am giving visions into the Spirit for those who walk by Me and follow My commands."

Prophetic Scripture

And it shall come to pass in the last days, saith God, I will pour out of my Spirit upon all flesh: and your sons and your daughters shall prophesy, and your young men shall see visions, and your old men shall dream dreams: and on my servants and on my handmaidens I will pour out in those days of my Spirit; and they shall prophesy (Acts 2:17–18).

This Scripture in Acts 2 is talking about the last days we are living in. As we watch Bible prophecy unfold and as the days become more evil, we need visions and dreams from Heaven more than ever. Visions, dreams, and prophetic utterances have been given by God to help us walk through the challenges of the last days.

Begin to expect visions and dreams to operate in your life. Of course, I am not encouraging us to become spacey and goofy with visions and overly focused on them, but they *do* have their proper place. The Lord will use them to keep us one step ahead of the devil and to gain Heaven's perspective on many of the countless modern-day issues we are facing. If we want these manifestations, the key is to walk humbly and close to God and be accountable to other believers. Then from there, begin to believe in your life that visions from God shall be seen!

Prayer

Dear heavenly Father, I ask You to reveal spiritual visions and dreams in my life. Teach me how to handle them correctly and tastefully. I open my faith to these manifestations and I believe that I will speak prophetic utterances at a new level in this hour. In Jesus' Name, amen.

Draw Me Deeper, Lord

"Let me pull you into the deeper place today. Let me bring you into the inner chamber of revelation. Launch out into that deep place and I will bring you into uncharted rooms in the dwelling of My Holy Spirit!"

Prophetic Scripture

...Launch out into the deep, and let down your nets for a draught (Luke 5:4).

Growing in the Lord means you are willing to allow God to take you into unfamiliar spiritual places. They are not new to God, but they are new to us. God wants us to experience the depths of His heart, His thoughts, and His plans, but it takes faith and commitment to go into unfamiliar territory in knowing the Lord.

When Jesus told His disciples to launch out into the deep, most of our normal responses to that request would be much like theirs. "But Lord, we tried that and it got us nowhere, and besides now we are tired of trying." That is a rough paraphrase, but Jesus was beckoning them back into the deep waters. Instead of responding as if it is just "over your head" or too deep for you, respond with a willing "Yes, Lord, draw me into the deep place." Sure, the deep places in the Holy Spirit require adjusting our schedule and being willing to stretch our level of spiritual understanding, but it's worth it! Go ahead, ask the Lord to draw you into the deeper places of knowing Him today!

Prayer

Lord, I come to You with a willingness to enter the deeper places of the Spirit. Draw me, Lord, where I might experience all that is on Your heart. I want to know You in a new and a fresh way, and I lay down my own time and agenda today that I may go deeper in You! In Jesus' Name, amen!

Weapon of the Light

> *"I make you this day a weapon of light against the darkness of this hour. Rise up and act as the light and expect the darkness and evil that would come near you to dispel."*

Prophetic Scripture

> *The people which sat in darkness saw great light; and to them which sat in the region and shadow of death light is sprung up* (Matthew 4:16).

Everywhere Jesus went, He brought light. Of course, not everyone loved it as He brought light to people who had been sitting in darkness for some time. Have you ever watched how people respond to the light after several hours in the dark? Think of a time when you were asleep and someone flipped on the light. Your eyes needed time to adjust!

When God's light shines where there has been a lot of darkness, there may be an initial adjustment period and some may try to hide or resist. But in Jesus' ministry, He continually kept bringing the light, and eventually multitudes responded positively.

We are the light of the world (see Matt. 5:14). That means that wherever we go, we bring the light of God with us like Jesus did. Expect someone to respond to the light of God that is in you. Don't be discouraged if there is a period of shock or even resistance. Just do what you do best—keep on shining! You are a weapon of light and those who are living in darkness will begin to respond in a good way!

Prayer

> *Dear Lord, I thank You for making me a weapon of light! I will let my light shine through my actions, character, words, and attitude. As people see me, let them see You, Lord. I have faith that someone will respond to Your light inside of me and receive a touch from You that will change them forever! In Jesus' Name, amen!*

A Touch of Love

"Let Me love on you this day, says the Lord. Let Me give you a revelation of how much I care for you. Set aside those things in your mind that would make you doubt My love, for you are the apple of My eye."

Prophetic Scripture

But God, who is rich in mercy, for his great love wherewith he loved us (Ephesians 2:4).

Every believer needs to continually reaffirm in their heart a revelation of God's love for them. When we go through trials, the devil is always there to make us feel forgotten and unloved.

To gain a better perspective of how much God loves us, we need to look at life through eternal glasses. *God loved me enough to give His own Son to die on my behalf.* In fact, Romans 5:8 says that God gave us this kind of incredible love when we were still worthless sinners!

Still many will ask, "Yes, but where is God's love in this painful situation I am in right now?" Sure, we could speculate about why God hasn't seemed to relieve us of certain situations, but perhaps we don't get relief simply because we don't have faith in the love that He has already shown in Jesus. When you are confident that someone loves you, you will expect them to do anything possible to help you. Know that if God loved you enough to save you from eternal judgment, He loves you enough to walk you through your present challenges. You are the apple of His eye! (See Psalms 17:8.) Just let Him love on you today!

Prayer

Precious Father, I thank You for Your wonderful and eternal love for me today. Forgive me for ever doubting Your love. Help me understand and have a renewed faith in Your love for me. I believe Your love will see me through every trial into victory! I love You Lord! Amen!

Peace of Mind Comes Now!

*"Command your mind and even your thoughts to be at peace. For many are losing control of these things, but this is your day to speak and say to yourself, my peace of mind comes **now**!"*

Prophetic Scripture

Casting down imaginations, and every high thing that exalteth itself against the knowledge of God, and bringing into captivity every thought to the obedience of Christ (2 Corinthians 10:5).

With the way things are going in the world today, we have to make a determined choice to keep our minds and our thoughts in check. We cannot just let our head think whatever it wants! If you do, you will find yourself running down all sorts of wrong mental paths. You will jump to wrong conclusions about people, situations, and events that go on around you. The best way to keep your mind in check is to tell it what to do. Speak to your mind and tell it to come in line with God and His Word. The word *casting* in the verse above literally means to demolish in a violent way. Now that doesn't mean you do this by literally beating your head against a wall! We exercise spiritual violence against sin and evil with words. You must command your mind to be at peace when thoughts of fear try to come at you. Speak to your mind today and tell it to be at peace in the Name of Jesus! Then fill your mind with thoughts about the goodness and peace of God today!

Prayer

Dear Lord, I know that You have given me power over my thoughts today. So I speak to my mind today, in the power of Jesus' Name. "Mind, you be at peace, in the Name of Jesus. You think upon thoughts of peace and God's goodness, right now!" Father, I worship You and give You glory in my thoughts today! In Jesus mighty Name, amen!

The Scent of Prayer

"Know that your prayers are held in precious regard. The things you pray are not lost, but kept before Me. They are to Me as the scent of sweet perfume. Let the scent of your prayers come to Me this day, says the Spirit of the Lord."

Prophetic Scripture

And when he had taken the book, the four beasts and four and twenty elders fell down before the Lamb, having every one of them harps, and golden vials full of odours, which are the prayers of saints (Revelation 5:8).

We have all experienced times when it feels like our prayers aren't accomplishing much. Sometimes prayer can even feel mundane. In fact, for many people prayer has become nothing more than a religious ritual. It lacks any true faith and power. Yet, the Lord loves our prayers.

We have to resist this tendency and think of every prayer we utter as a fresh mist of sweet perfume or cologne before the Lord. If you have ever sprayed on your favorite scent in the morning, you know how its smell often becomes unnoticeable by the end of the day. For many of us, prayer is the same. We tend to forget that beautiful scent of prayer by the end of the day. Then if we aren't careful, the next time of prayer is either not a priority or we treat it no different than the next list of things to do on our agenda.

Press into prayer today. The Lord treats your prayers as precious perfume and the scent of them always stays fresh before Him.

Prayer

Heavenly Father, I press into prayer with fresh fervor this day! I know that my prayers are held before You and that You love to hear them. Revitalize my prayer life and ignite the times I spend with You! I know that because You hear my prayers You are answering me with miracles and blessings! In Jesus' Name, amen.

The Testimony of Prosperity

"Today, I declare that you are called 'The Testimony of Prosperity!' All provision, all help, and all supply is raining upon your life, even today!"

Prophetic Scripture

And keep the charge of the Lord thy God, to walk in his ways, to keep his statutes, and his commandments, and his judgments, and his testimonies, as it is written in the law of Moses, that thou mayest prosper in all that thou doest, and withersoever thou turnest thyself (1 Kings 2:3).

Following God closely in your life is always connected to prosperity. In other words, when you serve the Lord, you cannot help but walk in blessing. You become a testimony of His blessing. Prosperity doesn't just apply to finances, even though money is included. Prosperity simply means that you are living every area of life to the fullest. Prosperity speaks of wealth, but that wealth may be emotional wealth. It may be wealth in your family relationships. With so many things attacking the family today, we need our families and home lives to prosper in a fresh way. Prosperity can be in regard to God's anointing upon your life to serve Him powerfully in the Kingdom. God caused the ministry of mighty men like Moses, Joshua, and Elijah to prosper, and of course monetary provision was always connected to it. Know today that if you stay close to God and obey Him, you cannot help but become a Testimony of Prosperity, right now!

Prayer

Dear Lord, it is a privilege to serve You. Cause me to prosper in the area of _____. Help me walk in Your commandments each day, and I believe that I shall live my life as a testimony to You and as a testimony of Your prosperity so that the world will know that Jesus is alive! In Jesus' Name, amen.

Sudden Intervention!

"In the moment you think there is no solution, look to the One who knows no boundaries or limits. For I will show My power with sudden intervention as you lift your voice this day, says the Spirit of the Lord!"

Prophetic Scripture

And suddenly there was a great earthquake, so that the foundations of the prison were shaken: and immediately all the doors were opened, and everyone's bands were loosed (Acts 16:26).

In Acts 16, Paul and Silas were in prison with their feet and hands in stocks, while their backs were bleeding from a beating they had received earlier for preaching Christ. Without a doubt, they were uncomfortable and in a lot of pain. While their situation may have appeared hopeless, they didn't complain and question God as to why He allowed them to go through this trying time. Instead, they chose to worship the Lord in the middle of their pain, in the middle of their darkest moment. When all hope seemed lost, they praised the Lord with joy! Instead of looking at the chains and prison walls, they saw a God who is not bound by prison doors! Because of that, God stepped in with sudden and immediate intervention. Stop seeing your prison walls today. Stop seeing your impossibilities and look to a God who can deliver you from your most trying situations as you praise Him. Praise Him today and every day, then see the power of God's sudden intervention!

Prayer

Dear heavenly Father, I worship You today. I praise You and rejoice that You are a God of sudden intervention. Forgive me for the times when I complained instead of praising You. Move in my life, just as You did for Paul and Silas. I believe Your power will come into my situation with sudden intervention even when I least expect it! Thank You, Lord! In Jesus' Name, amen.

Leaders upon the Land

"God says, I am raising up a fresh wave of leaders as a sign that I am healing the land. For I shall give you ministers and pastors who have My heart, and they shall lead you into My glory."

Prophetic Scripture

And I will give you pastors according to mine heart, which shall feed you with knowledge and understanding (Jeremiah 3:15).

The prophet Jeremiah spoke of a wave of leaders coming who would have God's heart. He follows up in Jeremiah 3:16 by talking about a season of multiplication and increase. The rise of quality leaders in the church always connects us to increase, multiplication, and revival. Without them, God's people get off course. We see this in Judges 5:6-7. The Bible says that it was time when the people were experiencing decrease and apparent recession. They got off the main road, which is a picture of people who are off course. Yet Deborah rises up, declaring that these things happened until she arose as a leader in Israel. When she took her God-given place, the people got back on track and their depressed conditions ceased.

God is looking to send a fresh wave of revival, and it will take godly and anointed leaders to help facilitate it and keep it on course. Pray for godly leaders to arise. Ask God to anoint and appoint His vessels who shall have the character and stamina to lead God's people. It's time for a new wave of glory.

Prayer

Dear heavenly Father, I am hungry for a fresh wave of glory among Your people. I desire to see revival, so I pray for Your leaders and ministers today. Place Your grace and strength upon them that they may rise up to the task at hand. Protect them and anoint them for the call You have placed on their lives. In Jesus' Name, amen.

Desires Fulfilled

"Say not that the longing of your heart is far off, says the Lord. But behold now, the time of your deepest desire comes, so let your hope be renewed and believe once again that the season of fulfillment is upon you."

Prophetic Scripture

Hope deferred maketh the heart sick: but when the desire cometh, it is a tree of life (Proverbs 13:12).

There are things we know God has promised us, but because they haven't manifested as quickly as we hoped we can become discouraged. Hope is a desire for something that we see in the distance. It isn't directly upon us, but we see it coming. It's like a kid looking at a piece of candy through a store window. He can see it, almost taste it, and he knows that all it takes is for a few things to happen before the candy is his!

I believe the Lord wants to turn those delayed hopes into the reality of fulfilled desire. Hebrews 11:1 tells us that faith is what makes the thing we are hoping for a reality. It becomes the physical evidence that it's ours, rather than the seemingly long distance between us and our desires. We often have more "faith" in the distance between us and our desires than we do in God's supernatural ability to fulfill them. Refresh your hope today and let it cause the fulfillment of your heart's deepest longings to seem closer than ever before. Believe the time is upon you.

Prayer

Dear heavenly Father, I believe that You are fulfilling the desires of my heart today concerning _____. I see it by faith and I declare that delay is broken over me and I shall experience my promised land and it shall be a tree of life to my soul. I say the season of fulfillment is upon me! In Jesus' Name, amen.

Disease Has No Power

"Remember that disease has no power over you. Whatever pestilence they may say is spreading like fire, it shall not harm or injure you who remain steadfast in My Spirit, which lives on the inside of you!"

Prophetic Scripture

Surely he shall deliver thee from the snare of the fowler, and from the noisome pestilence (Psalms 91:3).

Recently, I saw an article about the outbreak of disease epidemics. Many scientists feel that widespread, deadly disease could easily break out worldwide. As I read the article, I immediately thought Psalms 91:3. It says that the Lord will deliver those who stay close under His protective hand. He will deliver us from the noisome pestilence. The word *noisome* means destructive or deadly. That means the diseases that medicine cannot heal and that kill masses of people. Yet God already has a remedy for His people to escape deadly disease, even if that disease is spreading in your own hometown. Psalms 91:1 says you are covered with His wings. Stay close to God and trust Him and be careful how much you listen to the news channel or the scientists' reports. We need to listen in this day to what God has to say above all else. Also notice that this verse above says *surely*. In other words, you can be assured that it *will* hold true if you stay close to God and listen to Him instead of all the world has to say. If you listen to the world's reports long enough, they are what you will believe and expect. No matter what deadly diseases may plague this planet, rest assured that surely He shall deliver thee!

Prayer

Lord, I thank You that I am safe under Your protective hand. I expect to be completely delivered from all communicable diseases, deadly viruses, and infections. None of these things shall touch me or my family, in the Name of Jesus. Thank You, Lord! Amen.

Sounds of His Voice

"So tune your ear this day to the sound of My voice. Listen for Me in multiple places and in multiple ways. Listen, says the Lord, and I will teach you to know My sound that I may fellowship closely with you."

Prophetic Scripture

Behold, I stand at the door, and knock: if any man hear my voice, and open the door, I will come in to him, and will sup with him, and he with me (Revelation 3:20).

If we want a deeper level of fellowship with the Lord, we must learn the art of hearing His voice. The Bible says that God's voice comes in multiple ways. Revelation 1:15 says His voice is as the sound of many waters (see Ps. 29:3). However, Elijah heard Him as a still small voice (see 1 Kings 19:12). As Jesus was teaching about His upcoming death, God's voice was like thunder and people heard it (see John 12:28-29). In fact, His voice is most commonly described as thunder throughout the Bible (see Job 37:5; 40:9; Ps. 18:13; Rev. 4:5). God's voice was also found in the fire and clouds when He spoke to Israel (see Deut. 5:22-24).

These examples help us know that God's voice can take on many forms, but we have to learn how to recognize it. This begins with making a practice of listening to Him all day. Job 37:2 says, "Hear attentively the noise of his voice, and the sound that goeth out of his mouth." His sound may come in many different expressions, but if you stay attentive to hear Him, you will learn which sounds are genuinely Him. Be confident that you can hear His voice today!

Prayer

Lord, I ask You to train me how to hear Your voice today. I make a conscious decision to be attentive for You to speak to me. I thank You, Lord, that as I learn to hear You more, I will have greater fellowship with You in the days ahead! Amen!

Day of Lifted Hands

"So lift your hands this day, says the Spirit, lift them up over your head. For as you hold them high in praise and faith, the tests before you shall become very low this day!"

Prophetic Scripture

Wherefore lift the hands that hang down, and the feeble knees (Hebrews 12:12).

The above verse is written in context of God's correction, but why would we want to lift our hands at that time? Lifted hands represent two things: They are a universal sign of surrender, and they express praise. First, when God is dealing with you, lifted hands are an expression that you are submitted to His will. Second, lifted hands show your thanks that He is a good Father. No child wants to lift a hand of praise to his dad right after he is disciplined. Yet one day when the child realizes that his father's loving discipline kept him from harm, he will throw his arms of thanks around his father.

When we lift our hands to the Lord to thank Him for being a good Father even when we don't feel like it, our problems take on a new perspective. Maybe that is what happened when Moses lifted his hands over the battle that day in Exodus 17. When our hands are up before the Lord, battles are won, but when our hands hang low we forget how good the Lord is! Lift your hands and praise the Lord today, no matter how you feel, because He is such a good and loving Father!

Prayer

Dear heavenly Father, I thank You for being such a good Father. I choose to lift my hands of surrender to You right now. I want to lift my hands of praise just to thank You for Your caring love to correct me and guide me every day of my life. Keep me, Lord, in Your ways and I lift my hands in Your Name! Amen!

Internal Injuries Healed

"I am the God who heals the wounded soul and the broken heart. For that which would have tried to scar your life and cause emotional bleeding, I have come to treat every internal injury of your soul."

Prophetic Scripture

He healeth the broken in heart, and bindeth up their wounds (Psalms 147:3).

Maybe the devil has worked overtime to try and inflict some internal wounds in your life. The good news is that Jesus paid for all aspects of healing in the plan of redemption (see Isa. 53:4-5). The Bible says in Luke 4:18 that Jesus was sent to heal the brokenhearted and set at liberty those who are bruised. Bruises and a broken heart speak of an internal injury that bleeds. Many of us don't realize that perhaps the reason we respond negatively to certain things is because something in our soul is still bleeding. Continual bouts of things like anger, depression, manipulative control, or panic can be a sign that a wound has continued to bleed and needs to be treated.

While it is important to learn new life skills so that we don't habitually respond according to these wounds any longer, we also need an anointing from Heaven to stop the bleeding. Jesus is anointed to heal these injuries of the soul and supernaturally treat these internal injuries. He wants to treat the wounds deep inside your inner person and keep them from the continual bleeding that deprives you of peace and joy. Call upon Him with faith today and expect Him to heal your wounds.

Prayer

Heavenly Father, I thank You that healing power is available for my whole person. I ask that You would treat every wound in my soul and inner person that is bleeding. Help me respond correctly to life and to others in a Christlike manner. I ask You for a healing anointing to heal every internal injury. In Jesus' Name, amen.

Your Nehemiah Season

"Even as Nehemiah asked Me to remember him for good, so I call you to ask Me to remember your good. For what you have sown in righteousness, you will reap in joy in this season, for I am the Lord your reward."

Prophetic Scripture

Think upon me, my God, for good, according to all that I have done... (Nehemiah 5:19).

When Nehemiah led the effort to rebuild the wall of Jerusalem, he put his life on the line to take a stand. Not only did he rebuild the wall, he also helped restore the people from the effects of financial hardship and unfair taxes imposed by cruel governors. Every imaginable enemy rose up against him, yet he persevered to finish his righteous task.

Many Christians right now are much like Nehemiah. They are fighting every imaginable enemy in an effort to stand up for what is right. They are putting their lives on the line, not only to spread the Gospel, but also to separate themselves from the wickedness of this day. That task is becoming more difficult to do, especially when many so-called Christians, friends, and family members are selling out to false and worldly ideals. We are having to make greater sacrifices than ever before to stand up for Jesus and His Word.

On multiple occasions, Nehemiah asked God to remember and reward him for his good deeds that cost him a great deal (see Neh. 13:22,31). We need to call on God for a "Nehemiah season" right now. Ask God to look on your deeds of righteousness today and reward you with good!

Prayer

Father, I am asking You to reward my righteous actions with good today. Cause blessing to come to me in ways I couldn't have imagined. I believe that my season of reward is upon me and I decree this is my "Nehemiah season!" I call it into manifestation right now! In the Name of Jesus! Amen.

A Room Prepared

"I am preparing you as a room for My Spirit to dwell and manifest in power. Yes, the anointing is preparing you to bring the meat of my table to the nations of the world and you will bring my wonders to many lost souls. For I have prepared you for this time!"

Prophetic Scripture

And he will shew you a large upper room furnished and prepared: there make ready for us (Mark 14:15).

The upper room was more than just a physical location. It had prophetic significance. It was where Jesus shared communion with the disciples and a preparation place for the coming of the Holy Spirit. In Acts 1, we find the people gathered there anticipating the arrival of God's Spirit. Every believer should be an "upper room" believer. That means we make our spirit a preparation place for the Holy Spirit's presence.

We prepare our "upper room" by making our heart a place of communion. That could be the literal communion meal, but it also is a place of communion with the Father in prayer. Then, like the people in the book of Acts, we wait for the move of the Holy Spirit in our lives. The word *wait* in Acts 1:4 means to stand in a place of prayerful expectancy! In other words, you are doing whatever is necessary for the power of the Holy Spirit to be on your life. If you will commune with the Father and wait for the Holy Spirit this way, you will become an "upper room" believer prepared to bring the wonders of God to a dark and needy world!

Prayer

Dear Lord, I make my spirit a room for Your Spirit today. I open my heart so that I may manifest Your anointing to the world. Prepare me as I wait for You. Teach me, Lord, how to commune with You in the "upper room" of my spirit. In the Name of Jesus, amen!

Clothed in Power!

"So as you shed the ways of the old man and clothe yourself with the new, so shall you increase in divine knowledge this day, says the Spirit of the Lord."

Prophetic Scripture

...Seeing that ye have put off the old man with his deeds; and have put on the new man, which is renewed in knowledge after the image of him that created him (Colossians 3:9-10).

Every day is about decisions. We wake up each day and either choose to walk with God or choose to walk after something else. Avoiding the things that try to get us distracted begins with the daily decision to follow Christ. Following Christ begins with the decision each day to put on His character and ways, just like you do your clothing. It's a simple decision to put on your clothes, but you routinely do it every day. Putting on Christ and our new man is very much the same.

Make a decision each day to put off your old habits and put on new ones. Much of the New Testament is built around this pattern. We literally "put off" the old things and "put on" the new. If you think of it as part of your daily routine, like putting on your clothes, it helps you break it down into an attainable goal. It's through this continual habit that we experience a powerful renewal in the spirit. This is the long-term way to overcome sin and evil. It clothes you in power! Begin the habit of putting on the new man today.

Prayer

Dear Lord, I make a decision today to put on the image of Christ and the new person that You have made me to be. I choose to put off my old habits and am choosing new ones. I thank You, Lord, that I am clothed with supernatural power and I am growing in the knowledge of You. In Jesus' Name, amen.

Safe in Dangerous Times

"As you see the day of evil approach, know that even as I sustained Elijah the prophet, I will sustain you. I will feed you, care for your family, and watch over you in all things. Yes, I am your Lord, and I have covenanted Myself with you to keep you safe."

Prophetic Scripture

The fear of man bringeth a snare: but whoso putteth his trust in the Lord shall be safe (Proverbs 29:25).

The Bible tells us emphatically that this is a dangerous day (see 2 Tim. 3:1-7). We can look around and get easily focused on all the bad that does happen to so many people worldwide, and we can unknowingly start to believe that something bad might happen to us or our loved ones one day. However, our safety is in the Lord! Yes, but some might say, "I realize that, but something bad *did* happen in my life before." Well, perhaps in one short paragraph we can't answer all the reasons for that. Yet, one big reason we experience bad things even when God's promise is protection and safety is because we *believe* more in the possibility for bad to occur than we believe in God's promise of safety and good. If you were to think it over, you will probably find there are times that has been true in your life. Be confident in the protection of the Lord today. Stop being afraid of people and all the things in this world, because God's promise to you is protection and safety, even when the day is evil.

Prayer

Father, I know that Your promise is protection from harm. I believe that promise and I refuse to accept anything otherwise. I dwell today underneath the safe shadow of Your wings and I trust in You for my good. Thank You, Lord, that I live safe in Your arms today. In Jesus' Name, amen!

New Strategies

"In the areas where you feel as though you have lost your way, I am helping you get relocated and on the right path again. I am giving new strategies, and you shall experience a new sensation of divine direction in all you do."

Prophetic Scripture

Now God himself and our Father, and our Lord Jesus Christ, direct our way unto you (1 Thessalonians 3:11).

Sometimes when things don't seem to be going right, you can get the feeling that you have gotten off the beaten path somewhere. Sometimes we actually have gotten off track, but other times, like Paul, we just need help from God in reassessing our game plan. We come to a point where we need to call on God for a new strategy. Paul experienced one problem after another (see 1 Thess. 2:18), but there was finally a point when he needed God to give him a new sense of direction. He asked God to direct his way. He was saying that he needed divine guidance and power to help him figure out what to do and give him a new and successful game plan. We all have those times when we feel like we have come to a dead end and need to reassess our location and develop some new strategy. It's just like trying to follow directions in our car. When we realize we missed our turn, we have to stop and reassess how to get back on track again.

If it appears you missed a turn somewhere in life, ask the Lord to help get you redirected. If there are some sin areas, repent of them and get back to God, then know that He is helping you map out some new strategies today!

Prayer

Father, I believe that You are directing my way just like you did for the apostle Paul. Help me to experience a new sense of guidance from You. Show me how to adjust my strategy where necessary. I believe it and receive it! Hallelujah! Amen!

Wealth and Riches in Your House

"Know that I shall give wealth to the righteous, says the Lord. Expect the manifestation of financial provision. For I will see to it that your present monetary needs are covered."

Prophetic Scripture

Wealth and riches shall be in his house: and is righteousness endureth for ever (Psalms 112:3).

Through the Bible, we find that living in righteousness and financial blessings go together. When Abraham committed to God by faith, God promised financial blessing (see Gen. 15:1 AMP). Deuteronomy 28:1-15 lists blessings for those who are committed to righteous living.

Perhaps you're wondering if you have made too many mistakes to qualify, but never forget that our righteousness is through Him. We can't ever do enough good deeds for God to view us as righteous. We have to rely on the blood of Jesus and His righteousness (see 2 Cor. 5:21). However, our job is to press into a lifestyle of "right living" so we can remain under the canopy of His righteousness and grace (see Heb. 10:26-27; 12:15; Rom 6:1-2). To do this we are to follow the lifestyle parameters seen throughout the New Testament. While this doesn't earn our righteousness, it reflects that God's righteous grace is truly written upon the tables of our heart (see 2 Cor. 3:3). Then, when we do make mistakes, through repentance Jesus' blood and provision of grace covers us (see 1 John 1:9).

Through God's grace, you are a candidate for financial prosperity! Expect wealth to come to your house and that your financial needs will be covered because God has made you righteous!

Prayer

Father, I thank You that I have been made righteous by Jesus blood and I am a candidate for provision and prosperity today. I ask You to provide for every financial need and I am confident that you will cover every need that I have because You always bless the righteous! Thank you, Lord, for provision! In Jesus' Name, amen!

Acts of Kindness

"This day in all you do, do it with kindness. For it is in kindness and tenderhearted love that I am found. Reach out through acts of kindness and I will be found of you."

Prophetic Scripture

And be ye kind one to another, tenderhearted, forgiving one another, even as God for Christ's sake hath forgiven you (Ephesians 4:32).

I once heard about a group of Christians who formed a committee to criticize and bring a lawsuit against a particular ministry because they didn't like some things. Now, I don't know all the details of the story, so this is not to say who was right or wrong in the situation. However, what I do know is that when we lash out in anger or backbiting and create attempts to tear down one another, we are missing one important ingredient—kindness. God isn't interested in our great position on the issue when promoting our opinion requires us to resort to hateful gestures. Instead, God looks for kindness, especially when we don't feel like being kind. We should find tenderness in our hearts rather than be cold and harsh, especially when we think we are right. Decide how it would feel if others treated you the way you treat them. It's always good to err on the side of kindness, because one day you may be on the side of needing the kindness. Do something kind for someone today. Without question, you will find God right there participating in it with you.

Prayer

Dear Lord, teach me how to walk in kindness today. I ask You to forgive me for treating others unkindly at times. Give me a tender heart today and show me how to be a person who is kind. I know that if I sow acts of kindness, I will reap the same. I thank You, Lord, for that truth today. In Jesus' Name, amen.

Tears of Rejoicing

"If you could comprehend what I am doing even now, you would begin to rejoice. For the foundations of your very destiny are being laid, and as it unfolds it will cause you to experience tears of great rejoicing!"

Prophetic Scripture

But many of the priests and Levites and chief of the fathers, who were ancient men, that had seen the first house, when the foundation of this house was laid before their eyes, wept with a loud voice; and many shouted aloud for joy (Ezra 3:12).

Every one of us has a calling. Through time, the Lord puts that calling together like a house, piece by piece. During the tedious and sometimes lengthy process, we can sometimes lose sight of our call by thinking it will never fully unfold. Perhaps we do so by forgetting about a prophetic word received or forgetting about those powerful Scriptures that once came as promised revelation. In the Book of Ezra, when the people began to take on the rebuilding of the temple, it seemed like a huge undertaking, but when destiny finally began to unfold there came a time when they suddenly experienced tears of rejoicing because they finally saw the foundation come together.

Don't lose sight of your call today. The foundation is coming together. Try and comprehend a moment when you will be so excited about what takes place that you will not know whether to laugh, shout, cry, or dance. The key is to keep your eye on God's plan and you will soon find your eyes filled with overwhelming tears of rejoicing!

Prayer

Dear Lord, I rejoice in the many things You have destined for me. I expect each one of them to manifest in my life in a divine way. I know that they are already working and my life is being transformed. Thank You, Lord, that I shall become everything You have for me. In Jesus Name, amen.

Fear of Failure Broken

"You have not been created for failure, says the Lord. Even this day, the fear of failure would try to tell you that you will never succeed. Rise up now and break the fear and that voice of failure in your life!"

Prophetic Scripture

This book of the law shall not depart out of thy mouth; but thou shalt meditate therein day and night, that thou mayest observe to do according to all that is written therein: for then thou shalt make thy way prosperous, and then thou shalt have good success (Joshua 1:8).

The fear of failure is one of the greatest obstacles that people have to overcome. Most often we fear failure because of a previous negative experience when something didn't work out the way we planned. Maybe it was a prayer that we didn't receive the answer we wanted. Perhaps it was a project or business endeavor that didn't produce the desired results. Whatever your circumstance, these things can plant a failure mentality in us. Then as you step out in faith again, your mind will try to tell you, "Remember what happened the last time?" If we aren't careful, then we find ourselves less willing to take steps toward the success God really intends.

However, the verse above tells us that our road to success is found by meditating on the Word of God. A daily focus on God's Word will give you God's perspective and destroy the voice of failure. You have the power to speak to those thoughts of failure and tell them to leave in Jesus' Name. Rise up and break the fear of failure trying to enter your life today!

Prayer

Dear heavenly Father, I know that You have created me to be successful. I set my attention upon Your words today. I will not fail in the area of _____ and I command all fear of failure to leave my life right now! In Jesus' Name, amen!

Moved by the Holy Ghost

"The Spirit says, get ready, for I am about to inspire you in an unusual way. Yes, even the gift of faith will operate and you will be compelled to speak and do things as you are moved by the Holy Ghost."

Prophetic Scripture

For the prophecy came not in old time by the will of man: but holy men of God spake as they were moved by the Holy Ghost (2 Peter 1:21).

When many people read verses like this one above, they assume that the only ones who were candidates of this level of divine inspiration were the people of the Bible. Of course, it was an incredible measure of divine inspiration that moved these men of God to pen the Scriptures.

While we aren't writing the Bible today, we definitely need divine inspiration and power to do God's work. We need to be moved by the Holy Spirit at a high level in this hour. We are in a season in which we will be unmistakably compelled to do amazing things as we are pressed upon by the Spirit. I see it being at a higher level than before. I see a new wave of the gift of faith in manifestation for us to operate in miracles in our efforts to reach the lost. Expect things that once intimidated you to feel conquerable as you step out and address them. We are in the season to be moved by the Holy Ghost!

Prayer

Dear Lord, I thank You for divine inspiration of the Spirit today. Move upon me with the anointing and cause me to step out with divine utterance and ability. I am asking You to do great things through my life today and cause me to be used as a powerful vessel for Your Kingdom. In Jesus' Name, amen.

Multiplied Peace

"So expect My infinite power to defend you, even causing some who are against you to be at peace. For even as you serve Me and separate yourself for Me, many around you will begin to tremble at My name."

Prophetic Scripture

Then King Darius wrote unto all people, nations, and languages, that dwell in all the earth; Peace be multiplied unto you (Daniel 6:25).

When King Darius realized that Daniel could not be destroyed in the lion's den, he was forced to acknowledge the Lord and ceased from any further actions against Daniel. He even made a decree that the only God to be feared was the God of Daniel. For this secular king, this was truly a divine moment.

In Daniel 6:25, at the opening of his public speech, he made an interesting statement. He used the phrase, "Peace be multiplied unto you." King Nebuchadnezzar used the same phrase at the opening of his own public concession speech after a similar encounter at the fiery furnace (see Dan. 4:1-3). It's obvious that their declaration of peace indicated that they had to come in contact with divine power that caused them to change their actions.

Paul commonly opened his letters with the phrase "grace and peace be unto you" or "grace and peace be multiplied" (see Rom. 1:7; 1 Cor. 1:3; 2 Cor. 1:2; Gal. 1:3; Eph. 1:2; Phil. 1:2; 1 Thess. 1:1; 2 Thess. 1:2). It seems clear that he was ever reminding believers that God was multiplying peace that would cause those the devil was using against them to declare a truce. Perhaps Paul had a deep personal revelation of this, because he once was such a person until his own divine encounter.

Proverbs 16:7 says, "When a man's ways please the Lord, he maketh even his enemies to be at peace with him." Declare today that peace is being multiplied to you and that it will even cause those who persecute and come against you to come to peace and drop their harmful intentions.

Prayer

Dear Lord, I ask that peace would be multiplied to me today. I believe that Your power is causing my enemies to come to peace with me and as a result it will cause many people to fear Your Name. In Jesus' Name, amen.

You Shall Live!

"So let it be known to you this day that I have spoken life to your blood! Yes, you shall live! For by My own blood, I have cleansed your blood from sin's dominion, and your mind and body are made alive!"

Prophetic Scripture

And when I passed by thee, and saw thee polluted in thine own blood, I said unto thee when thou wast in thy blood, Live; yea, I said unto thee when thou wast in thy blood, Live (Ezekiel 16:6).

This prophetic Scripture in the book of Ezekiel is a beautiful picture of our new lives in Christ Jesus. It is so powerful how the prophet depicts God's rescue of His people lost in their own polluted condition. God has declared over His beloved, *"Live!"*

When the Lord spoke the word *live*, He was speaking to our whole person. This not only includes your spiritual person, but also your mind and body. It includes your mind because Hebrews 10:16 says, "…I will put my laws into their hearts, and in their minds will I write them." Then it also includes your physical body because Romans 8:11 says, "…shall also quicken your mortal bodies by his Spirit…." Of course, all these promises will be fulfilled one day in Heaven, but they also apply to our lives on earth. Stand today upon this promise in Psalms 118:17 which says, "I shall not die, but live, and declare the works of the Lord." Trust in that promise and know that God is giving you an escape from the agents of evil that try to pollute and shorten our lives, and His decree for you today is *live!*

Prayer

*Dear heavenly Father, I come in agreement with Your declaration of life over me today. I say to my whole person…**live**! I shall not die bound by sin, of a premature physical death, or from any form of mental bondage. I shall **live** and not die, in the Name of Jesus! Amen.*

Houses and Lands Returned

"Know, says the Spirit, that I have made a promise that I shall return lost homes and lands that you have given up even for My Name's sake. I will restore lost properties in a multiplied way, so expect it in this time."

Prophetic Scripture

And Jesus answered and said, Verily I say unto you, There is no man that hath left house, or brethren, or sisters, or father, or mother, or wife, or children, or lands, for my sake, and the gospel's, but he shall receive an hundredfold now in this time, houses, and brethren, and sisters, and mothers, and children, and lands, with persecutions; and in the world to come eternal life (Mark 10:29-30).

Giving up our possessions for the Lord is one of the most powerful ways to show God our commitment. Yet, it is the very thing that releases God to express His commitment back to us through multiplied blessings. Sure, there are times that it may feel like we will have to do without some important things and yes, there are some things we may have to give up permanently. However, we must also know that if we give up something for God, He always has something better to replace it. Jesus promised it would be restored a hundredfold in this lifetime.

Many who lost properties and businesses during the recession years are going to receive back more than what they lost. We need a faith revival in God's payback system, especially in this current economic landscape. Trust today that the Lord is already arranging for you to receive "houses and lands" with a greater value than what you had.

Prayer

Heavenly Father, I know that the things I have given up for the Gospel are being restored into my life a hundredfold. I fully trust that I shall receive back greater possessions than I previously had and it shall hold an eternal reward for me as Jesus promised. Thank You, Lord! Amen.

Out of the Ashes

"Rise up, says the Lord, and leave the ashes of past disappointments behind. Know that ashes are all that remains and I call you in this hour to step out of the ashes so your past shall have no further hold on you."

Prophetic Scripture

To appoint unto them that mourn in Zion, to give unto them beauty for ashes, the oil of joy for mourning, the garment of praise for the spirit of heaviness; that they might be called trees of righteousness, the planting of the Lord, that he might be glorified (Isaiah 61:3).

Many people feel like they are living in the ashes of past challenges. Everything around them represents burnt rubble. If that's you today in some area or another, just realize that ashes are a sign that something is over. Ashes may be a constant reminder that something happened, but it's over nonetheless. That means it's time to dust yourself off and see yourself for who the Lord has made you rather than what the past tried to make you. Begin by making a firm decision that you won't keep rehearsing what happened. You won't keep talking about it to friends and family. There comes a time to make the decision to move on.

When you choose to do so, instead of ashes always reminding you of the past, God will supply you with an anointing that will replace the ashes with something beautiful. Those ashes will eventually disappear altogether and you will find yourself living in a whole new way of life!

Prayer

Heavenly Father, I make a step of faith today to place all my past experiences and disappointments behind me. I come out of the ashes and I fully believe You are going to help me receive a special anointing so that I can begin to respond better to circumstances in life. Thank You Jesus! Amen.

Change of Direction

"The Spirit says that it's time for fresh direction and a fresh focus. So turn your attention away from those things that have prevented you from progressing. Yes, it's time to change your direction."

Prophetic Scripture

And the Lord spake unto me, saying, Ye have compassed this mountain long enough; turn you northward (Deuteronomy 2:2-3).

Sometimes our biggest hindrance to progress is ourselves. We can blame the devil and other people, we can even get mad at God, but when you feel like you are going nowhere, it's time to take a look inside. During their time in the wilderness, the children of Israel circled around Mount Seir for many days. In fact, what should have been a short journey through the wilderness took 40 years of circling! The problem wasn't God, it was them. Not only could they not quit rehashing their problems, they couldn't seem to get focused on the right things.

Perhaps you need to focus on some new things today. Maybe it's time to stop focusing on the current mountain before you. There comes a time when you need to change direction. Think of the areas in your life today that you have circled around for far too long. For some that means some major decisions, changes in occupation or even location. Maybe you don't even need to make changes that radical, but perhaps you just need to focus on a new set of goals or just quit worrying about the present mountain so much. Decide today what things are preventing you that you have focused on long enough. It's time for a new direction!

Prayer

Heavenly Father, I thank You that You are leading me in the right direction. I ask You for divine direction today. Show me in what area I need to change my focus and help me to plant my attention in the direction of heaven. I thank You for giving me a fresh focus today. In Jesus' Name, amen.

Rain from on High

"When the rain of My Spirit falls upon you, it will reverse desert conditions, and where there has been minimal growth there shall be exponential growth. Let Me rain upon you, even once again, let Me pour My Spirit upon you from on high."

Prophetic Scripture

Until the spirit be poured upon us from on high… (Isaiah 32:15).

There are many things we can all do in the natural realm to better our lives, families, finances, ministry callings, occupations, and more. We need to be faithful and responsible people naturally speaking; however, we can't put forth our best efforts and think that it is the answer. The verse above in Isaiah was written about Israel in a time when things were lacking, but then when the Spirit rained upon them, fruitlessness became fruitfulness! Their dry places suddenly became a forest!

We need the outpouring of the Spirit to fall upon us afresh. When the anointing of the Holy Spirit rains upon you, everything begins to grow in a supernatural way! Your job begins to succeed, a church of 50 doubles to 100, then 250, then 500, and so on. People you have witnessed to get suddenly saved. Unexpected checks start to show up. Promotions at work happen. Creative ideas begin to open up to you. Ask the Holy Spirit to pour His rain upon your life. Don't hinder Him by believing your hard work is your payout. Instead, look to Him and expect His Spirit to pour upon you from on high and watch what begins to bear fruit!

Prayer

Holy Spirit, rain upon me today! I ask You for a fresh outpouring upon everything in my life that isn't bearing fruit as it should. Give me a fresh anointing today and let the waste places be turned into a lush forest! I expect exponential growth in the area of _____. Thank You Jesus! Amen.

Never Alone

"See that I have made the way for you to be near Me. So think not that you are ever alone. I am there beside you, so just call to Me, for I am very near unto you this moment and you are near to Me!"

Prophetic Scripture

But now in Christ Jesus ye who sometimes were far off are made nigh by the blood of Christ (Ephesians 2:13).

It is so powerful to realize every day that the blood of Jesus created a supernatural way for you to come close to God and stay there. It makes you as close to God as the breath of His mouth. It is a lie from the devil to ever believe you are alone! When you made Jesus the Lord of your life, and asked His blood to wash away your sins, you were brought directly into the presence of God! You were given heavenly access to a Father who loves you. Perhaps today you don't feel like you have the people close to you whom you expected to be there for you, but God wants you to know that He is close to you. Just because people left you alone doesn't mean God has! Make yourself learn to trust in that fact today. There might have been a day when you were far away from God's help, but you have been made close to Him now, so stand confidently today and know that you are never alone!

Prayer

Lord, I thank You that I am near You right now. I am not alone in my situation or at any time in my life. Forgive me for ever doubting that because I know You are near me at this very moment. I declare that I am not lonely or without help because the Lord my God is with me and I am never alone! In the Name of Jesus, amen.

Plans of the Heathen Overthrown!

"Fear not, the raging sound of the heathen and how they boast dark things. For I have said already that the efforts of the heathen shall fail and their kingdoms shall be overthrown. And they shall not overpower My chosen ones, for My people shall go forth in miraculous victory!"

Prophetic Scripture

And I will overthrow the throne of kingdoms, and I will destroy the strength of the kingdoms of the heathen; and I will overthrow the chariots, and those that ride in them; and the horses and their riders shall come down, every one by the sword of his brother (Haggai 2:22).

I remember one time driving though an office park with an upscale neighborhood nearby it and saying to the Lord, "Lord, it bothers me that the heathen have all this, but your people and churches seem to have small, beat-up buildings, houses, and few facilities." Now, I do know that not everything is that way, but I do believe God wants us to remember that all the kingdoms of the heathen will eventually fail no matter how fancy they look right now. The heathen may appear to prosper on the outside for a period of time, but without God's endorsement they live every day on shaky ground. When Egypt seemed like they had everything going for them and the children of Israel as their slaves had nothing, things were not as they seemed. The chariots of Egypt were on shaky ground and about to be overturned! Know that in today's world the chariots of the heathen are about to be overturned. God will always cause those with a righteous cause to prosper and will create doors of opportunity for them to do so! Know today that God more than ever before is helping the cause of the righteous and defeating the strength of the heathen!

Prayer

Lord, I ask You today to prosper the cause of the righteous and make us strong. Unite Your people together in this hour. I declare that the kingdoms of darkness will not prosper against us, and I thank You that the chariots of the wicked will be overturned in this present time! In Jesus' Name, amen.

A Sharp Sword!

"I am making you into a polished instrument to be used for Me. Your words shall be as arrows that shall declare My grace. Watch as many acknowledge what I have formed you to be in My hand, even this day and in this time."

Prophetic Scripture

And he hath made my mouth like a sharp sword; in the shadow of his hand hath he hid me, and made me a polished shaft; in his quiver hath he hid me (Isaiah 49:2).

God is a master craftsman. He perfects everything He makes, and when it comes to perfecting us for His use, He takes His own "sweet time." The Lord does this because He has the intent of using every one of us to represent the Gospel so that we may win others to Christ. He wants to polish us to perfection, so when we open our mouths to speak God's Word, it is done with precision and boldness along with taste and grace. God doesn't want our ministry to be tainted by self. He wants our mouth to be a sharp sword against the devil!

Perhaps you are hungry for God to use you in a powerful way. You might feel lost in the shuffle right now, but God is hiding you in His "workshop." He is polishing you so that when you come out, your mouth will be a sharp sword in the anointing, and because of it lives will be changed for the better. We need this preparation process, because the time is upon us when it will require us to be poised vessels for God's work. Time is short and we must come forth as God's ambassadors, polished and ready so we can minister in this season with pinpoint effectiveness!

Prayer

Lord, I thank You for making me a sharp sword. I give You the liberty to mold me as a polished shaft in Your hand. Remove from me all areas that are hindrances to being an effective vessel for the work of Your Kingdom. I thank You for perfecting me this day, in Jesus' Name, amen.

Favor in Business

"Watch this day, for I will favor you in the sight of the world and I will place a spirit of increase over you, and many people shall suddenly pour resources into your hands so that in all your business dealings you will know that I have placed multiplied provisions over you!"

Prophetic Scripture

And the Lord gave the people favour in the sight of the Egyptians. Moreover the man Moses was very great in the land of Egypt, in the sight of Pharaoh's servants, and in the sight of the people (Exodus 11:3).

Whenever God asks you to do something, He always provides the needed resources for you to accomplish it. When God asked Moses to lead the people out of Egypt, He provided the needed resources. He didn't send them empty, but sent them fully supplied. However, the unique part was the way in which the Lord supplied for them. Notice He first caused them to receive favor from the Egyptians. Think about the magnitude of what that entailed! Here Moses had been threatening their leader Pharaoh for days, plagues were everywhere, the people were preparing to escape the country, and they still found favor in the sight of the citizens of Egypt! Talk about amazing! In other words, God granted them favor when favor didn't seem possible.

Do you know that God wants to give you favor in your dealings too? Even when it may seem like the economy is down or there are no openings for you to find a job, God gives supernatural favor when favor seems hard to find! Whatever business, talent, ministry, or call you have been anointed for, your season of increase will come on the wings of God's favor. Then you will be filled with more than you ever dreamed!

Prayer

Dear heavenly Father, I activate my faith for unprecedented favor in all my business dealings today. I declare new doors of opportunity and blessing will open unto me. Resources shall come into my hands in the most supernatural ways. I expect favor to follow me everywhere I go today, and I thank You, Lord, for anointing me for favor now. In Jesus' Name, amen!

New Zeal

"Look to the days ahead as I place a new zeal for righteousness upon My people, and there shall be a new and clear dividing line between those who shall walk in the spirit and those who do not. For those who keep My ways, they shall stand out and I will place a visible fire and anointing upon them."

Prophetic Scripture

My zeal hath consumed me, because mine enemies have forgotten thy words (Psalms 119:139).

We are in a prophetic season where God is stirring the spirit of many of His people to take a greater stand for righteousness. While some are content to go with the flow of the world and accept many of its mind-sets, there is a remnant that is about to shine forth like never before. In fact, the more the world displays the works of unrighteousness, the more God's remnant will take a stand in this hour. Isaiah 37:31-32 says that the remnant of the Lord will dig its roots deep in the land and bear fruit as a result. All of this will happen because a spirit of zeal is stirred in the Lord as well as in His people. God's zeal is being stirred up right now and so is the zeal of His people. So whenever darkness and compromise are evident, zeal will only increase. I believe the church is in a time when the evil all around us will only act like a spiritual "fertilizer." In other words, when evil is raging we will refuse to blend in or become discouraged; we will only get more determined for God! This action among the people of God will automatically draw a line between the righteous and the unrighteous. Never think we are just in a time when things are becoming more gray. No, they will be black and white, because God's people will define which side they are on.

Prayer

Dear Lord, I ask that You will stir up the spirit of zeal within me. I pray that You will grant me boldness to stand up for what is right in this hour. I pray this for all Your people. Stir up our zeal, Lord, that we will take a greater stand for You. Let us bear much fruit for righteousness in the land in this hour! Thank You Jesus! Amen.

Time of the Dove!

"It is the season of the dove, says the Spirit, when My presence shall cover the face of the earth. My Spirit is moving in the supernatural, and My people will say across the globe, the sighting of the dove is here, for it's the sign that His presence is upon us now!"

Prophetic Scripture

And Jesus, when he was baptized, went up straightway out of the water: and, lo, the heavens were opened unto him, and he saw the Spirit of God descending like a dove, and lighting upon him; and lo a voice from heaven, saying, This is my beloved Son, in whom I am well pleased (Matthew 3:16-17).

We often find through Scripture that when the Spirit of God was resting on something, an actual dove descended. I have noticed so many people reporting that they are seeing doves more often than normal. In fact, one weekend I noticed a pair of doves just outside the back door of our house. Then, just two days later, my husband saw a dove outside his hotel room window in South America. While he was there, a relative of mine told me a story about someone who saw a dove as a miracle was taking place in their life. These are just a few examples of people encountering doves regularly. Now we don't want to be extreme and start a new "dove sighting" craze. However, I know that when God is doing something miraculous, He will often couple it with certain prophetic signs. I believe that as people everywhere seem to be seeing doves repeatedly, God is just reminding us that the Holy Spirit is manifesting. This is the season of the Holy Spirit, the season of the dove!

Prayer

Dear Lord, I am so grateful today for the presence of the Holy Spirit who is working mightily in the earth today. I thank You, Holy Spirit, for Your supernatural presence that is working in me personally. Have Your way, Holy Spirit, and manifest upon Your people with signs and wonders in this hour! In Jesus' Name, amen.

Barrenness Is Over

"I decree that barrenness is over because you are pregnant with fruit and vision and I will bring forth the offspring I have put in your heart. So prepare now by rejoicing and expanding your surroundings, for it shall come forth in due time!"

Prophetic Scripture

Sing, O barren, thou that didst not bear; break forth into singing, and cry aloud, thou that didst not travail with child... (Isaiah 54:1).

God is not the author of barrenness in any form, whether it be spiritual or natural. When God made Adam and Eve, He told them to be fruitful and multiply. When God met Abraham, He immediately promised him offspring. When Rachel wanted a child, God gave her Joseph (see Gen. 30:22-24), who God used to overcome a barren famine for Israel. When Hannah prayed for a child, God gave her Samuel (see 1 Sam. 1:20), who ended a prophetically barren season. Jesus spoke against spiritual barrenness in John 15:1-6 by saying that branches that don't produce fruit are removed to make way for new fruit.

Isaiah 54:1 was a prophecy to Israel about the coming Messiah, foretelling the birth of spiritual sons and daughters. However, if you read the chapter in which it was written, we find a clue to help us transition from barrenness to fruitfulness. Verse 2 begins with the word *enlarge*. Sure, God prophesied for the Messiah to come, but someone had to get ready (see John 1:23). If we want to overcome barrenness, we need to prepare. We need to enlarge our place to make room for the coming fruit.

Think of what you can do today to get ready for a season of fruitful living. Perhaps there are some natural preparations, or maybe there are spiritual ones. Either way, the key is get ready and expect your barrenness to be over!

Prayer

Heavenly Father, I expect to bear fruit for the Kingdom today. I make a decision to prepare myself by _____. I speak to all areas of barrenness in my life and I command fruit to be birthed right now, in the Name of Jesus! Amen.

Declarations from the Throne!

"I have already declared your beginning and ending, says the Spirit, and nothing can interfere if you will believe Me. Yes, you are set to prosper, so receive now your many declarations of blessings that have come from My throne!"

Prophetic Scripture

Thus saith the Lord the King of Israel, and his redeemer the Lord of hosts; I am the first, and I am the last; and beside me there is no God. ...Fear ye not, neither be afraid: have not I told thee from that time, and have declared it? ye are even my witnesses. Is there a God beside me? yea, there is no God; I know not any (Isaiah 44:6,8).

When something is declared from the throne of a king, you should be confident that what is said will not be taken lightly. People will have to change their plans, habits, and perhaps entire lifestyles to adjust to the kingly word. In the verses above, the word "declared" simply means a published announcement. God, the King of the universe, has made a published announcement of blessing that applies specifically to your life. The devil tries to make us fearful about how the future may turn out, so he fights against your commitment to keep believing what the King has said. That is how Satan deceived Eve in the Garden of Eden (see Gen 3:1). He began with the words "hath God said?" Then he used circumstances and surroundings to make them question the word of the Lord. Stay with what God has declared for you. It has come straight from His throne and cannot be altered, if you will believe it. Align your faith today with the King's declaration of blessing and watch the increase of God unfold all around your life!

Prayer

Lord, I thank You that I serve the King of all kings today. I receive in my heart every word that has been declared from Your holy throne! I align myself with these decrees. I speak to my future and command every word from God to come to pass! In Jesus' Name, amen.

Unto the Lord

"All you do this day, do it for Me. Look not for the praise of man, and know that each good deed, each gift given, and what is done in My Name is carefully recorded in heaven as an eternal reward for you."

Prophetic Scripture

With good will doing service, as to the Lord, and not to men (Ephesians 6:7).

Many of us have forgotten that we are not to spend time looking for man's praise. I heard a story of someone not too long ago who was angry with his church and decided he wanted all the offerings he gave the church to be returned to him. I am sorry to say that man did not give his offerings to the Lord, and therefore those gifts will not be recorded in the eternal record books of Heaven. How tragic! Why would someone want to give up an eternal reward for a few thousand dollars and a grudge? Even a million dollars isn't worth it!

Think of how many things we do that we are somehow expecting our proper dues to be given! Of course, it's okay to be pleased when rewards are given, but we can't let that motivate us. Human praise and affirmation cannot make us who we are and thus determine how much we will do and won't do. No, instead we have to do good deeds and obey the Bible even when no one is handing out compliments. What we do is for the Lord, and no matter what people do with our efforts, the proper motive is going to gain us an eternal reward!

Prayer

Dear Lord, check my motives today. I make a commitment before You to do everything as a service to You and not to man. Cause me to become content with Your approval alone and not be motivated by the affirmation of people. I repent of any time when my good works were done to man and not to You. In Jesus' Name, amen.

Divine Wisdom and Solutions

"Even as you deal with people this day, I will give you divine wisdom. I will grant you answers, ideas, and key input that will astonish those you speak with and give unarguable solutions."

Prophetic Scripture

And no man was able to answer him a word, neither durst any man from that day forth ask him any more questions (Matthew 22:46).

You could say Jesus had a way with words. People came to Him with some of the most challenging questions, sometimes with the motive to try and trap Him. Jesus was presented with so many scenarios that were difficult to answer, but He always had the kind of response that left people astonished! When they thought there was no legitimate solution to the question posed, Jesus always had an unarguable answer.

We also see how God used both Joseph and Daniel this way when the kings of their time came to them for answers. They were given divine wisdom that brought insight and solutions that others couldn't provide (see Gen. 41; Dan. 2).

I believe this is what God wants us to have. Colossians 4:6 says, "Let your speech be always with grace, seasoned with salt, that ye may know how ye ought to answer every man." The Lord grants us divine wisdom in dealing with difficult things that have no easy answer. Our job is to let our speech be graceful (kind and mannerly) and also to be full of God's Word (seasoned with salt). From there God will give us answers, ideas, and wisdom for things when others found themselves void of solutions. God is giving you divine wisdom today!

Prayer

Dear Lord, I receive divine wisdom to challenging questions today. I am asking You for solutions to the things I am presented with, large and small. Let my wisdom move those I speak to and give them the answers they need. In Jesus' Name, amen.

Christ Maketh Thee Whole!

"Know that wholeness is yours this day, says the Lord. For yes, Christ maketh thee whole, so it's time to believe it, respond to it and know that it's yours!"

Prophetic Scripture

And Peter said unto him, Aeneas, Jesus Christ maketh thee whole: arise, and make thy bed. And he arose immediately (Acts 9:34).

In Acts 9:32-35, the Bible tells a story of a man named Aeneas who had the palsy for eight years. Peter commands the man to get up from his bed of sickness for which he receives an instant miracle. The miracle got so much attention that it caused two cities to experience revival. Acts 9:35 says, "And all that dwelt at Lydda and Saron saw him, and turned to the Lord." The only ingredient we find that led to the miracle was Peter's command of "Christ maketh thee whole" coupled with his command for Aeneas to get up and make his bed. The man must have believed it, because he obeyed the command and got up, even while he looked bound to the bed! His one act to believe he was whole caused him to get up and it resulted in an outbreak of revival!

Jesus Christ is making you whole today in whatever area needs it— physically, emotionally, or spiritually. What could potentially happen if you believe in the wholeness Jesus is giving you and decide to "get up"? Loved ones, co-workers, or even a town of people may come to the Lord when they see your miracle. Like Aeneas, it may look impossible for you to get up today. But like Aeneas, it's also time to believe Jesus Christ maketh thee whole and respond in agreement with that wonderful command!

Prayer

Father, I thank You that Jesus Christ makes me whole today. I choose to get up from my places of sickness and brokenness and I walk in wholeness. Lord, use the miracle of my wholeness to reach people with the miracle of the Gospel, in Jesus' Name. Amen.

Calling the Prodigal

"The Spirit says, call out for your lost loved ones, and call out for your prodigal children. For even as you call, I shall place divine encounters in their lives that shall be used to propel them to Me."

Prophetic Scripture

For this my son was dead, and is alive again; he was lost, and is found. And they began to be merry (Luke 15:24).

God loves families and He wants our loved ones saved even more than we do. In the story of the prodigal son, it was the boy's father who had the most excitement when his son came home. No one feels greater pleasure than God when our loved ones get saved or return to the Lord. Second Peter 3:9 says God wants *all* men to come to repentance.

While we can't change a person's will, we can call upon the Holy Spirit to set up things in their life so that it will put them in the best possible position to submit to repentance. Sometimes as family members, we try everything in our own ability to get them saved. We nag and preach to them. Sometimes thinking we are loving them, we enable their sinful lifestyle. At times, we try so hard that we are actually standing between them and God! Sure, we need to share the Gospel with our loved ones and we need to express love, but in the end we really need the Holy Ghost to draw them through prayer. Ask the Lord to arrange divine appointments and events that will propel them to God. Then step back and let it happen! Call on the Lord to draw them today.

Prayer

*Heavenly Father, I know that You want my loved one saved just as much as I do. So today, I call out to You on behalf of _____.
Set up divine encounters. I will not get in Your way, Lord, and I ask You to show me how to trust you for their salvation. In Jesus' Name, amen.*

Scatter Thy Seed

"Your ability to be furnished with abundance is found through the scattering of your financial seed. For as you give in an ongoing way, here a little and there a little, your continual planting will result in continual a return."

Prophetic Scripture

As it is written, He [the benevolent person] scatters abroad; He gives to the poor; His deeds of justice and goodness and kindness and benevolence will go on and endure forever! (2 Corinthians 9:9 AMP)

The verse above uses a key word regarding financial giving. The word is *scatters*. Farmers know that they stand a better chance at reaping a productive harvest when they have a lot of seed in the ground as opposed to just a little. There is a difference between planting a few seeds and scattering seeds. Scattering speaks of planting in lots of places. It is ongoing planting, not just occasional. Throughout Second Corinthians 9, Paul teaches the principle that in order to be furnished with financial abundance you must not just plant seed, you must scatter seed (see 2 Cor. 9:9 AMP). You must be in the habit of giving of your finances for the Gospel all the time. The end result is that your seed will go on forever. In other words, the harvest that comes from your practice of "scattering" becomes so large that it can't help but be ongoing! That is what the Bible means when it says the plowman will overtake the reaper (see Amos 9:13). The harvest becomes so plentiful that you can barely get more seed in the ground before a new crop is coming in!

Look for places to keep scattering your financial seed. In fact, sow a seed somewhere *today!* Before long, your continual sowing will become continual reaping!

Prayer

Dear heavenly Father, help me build the habit of being a continual giver. As a first step of faith toward that, I plant a financial seed right now to _____. Let this seed bless them and cause me to be furnished with abundance! In Jesus' Name, amen!

Prayer for the Nations

"It is time again, says the Lord, to increase prayer over the nations. Even as prayer without ceasing interrupted Herod from killing Peter in the days of the early church, so shall many demonic plans against many nations be interrupted by your prayers!"

Prophetic Scripture

God be merciful unto us, and bless us; and cause his face to shine upon us; Selah. That thy way may be known upon earth, thy saving health among all nations (Psalms 67:1-2).

Prayer, unlike anything else, can go places that we often cannot go. Why else do you think the apostle Paul coveted the prayers of the Christians as he traveled the nations? Because he knew that prayer would prepare the ground for his preaching. It was committed prayer that rescued the apostle Peter from being beheaded in Acts 12.

Right now, we need to cover the nations in prayer like never before. We need to stir up the lull concerning global prayer because there is so much unrest brewing around the world. We need to water the ground in prayer once again and ask for God's protection. We need to declare that angels would be sent to deliver the righteous and that the Gospel would find an open door. The committed prayers of the saints can be the key to abort certain tragedies and evil uprisings. God wants to drive back the darkness so the nations can see the light in this hour. We must be the ones who pray fervently so God's saving power can bring life and health to the nations of the world!

Prayer

Dear Lord, I make a fresh commitment to pray for the nations that You lay upon my heart. I ask that Your presence would begin to rest upon those countries. Cause open doors for the Gospel to be preached and that the believers who live there would prosper and be protected. Cause the people of _____ to hear the word of the Lord and live in safety. I ask You to bless the nations afresh today! In Jesus' Name, amen.

Eyes of Mercy

"My eyes look at you from the mercy seat, for there your communion with Me is found. Yes, child, I deal with you from the place of mercy, says the Spirit of Grace."

Prophetic Scripture

And there I will meet with thee, and I will commune with thee from above the mercy seat... (Exodus 25:22).

Notice that the place God chose to commune with Moses was from above the mercy seat. The mercy seat in the Old Testament was a fixture of two angels atop the golden Ark of the Covenant. It was a natural fixture that symbolized God on His holy throne. One angel (or side) on the fixture represented God's mercy, while the other represented God's justice. In between was to be the representation of God's throne called the mercy seat. These angels were always facing the mercy seat (see Exod. 25:17-22; Exod. 37:7-9). When the Old Testament priests atoned for the sins of the people through the blood sacrifice of an animal, they placed the blood upon the mercy seat as a sign before God that the death penalty for sin was paid. However, when Jesus died and rose again, His blood became the final death sacrifice to be placed on the mercy seat. His blood would wipe away all our sins in God's eyes if we would believe it (see Heb. 9:1-12). The fact that the angels were to face the mercy seat represents that God is always communicating to us through that mercy plan. To commune with Him in return, we must continually reaffirm trust in that mercy plan. When God chose to meet face to face with Moses in the location of this wonderful mercy seat, it was a beautiful picture that God looks at us through the eyes of mercy. He is communing with you today through mercy's eyes.

Prayer

Dear Lord, I thank You for seeing me through the eyes of mercy. I ask that You would give me a fresh understanding of how to fellowship with You under the power of Your great mercy today. In Jesus' Name, amen.

Covenant Friendships from God

"I desire to provide you covenant friendships with trustworthy people who shall help enhance you. Set aside those relationships that would drag you down this day and let me provide the right ones for you."

Prophetic Scripture

Iron sharpeneth iron; so a man sharpeneth the countenance of his friend (Proverbs 27:17).

When David was being threatened and pursued by King Saul, the Lord gave him a trusted friend in Jonathan (see 1 Sam. 18). Of course, our first and most trusted source for friendship must be the Lord, because people aren't perfect in their reliability. We get into trouble when we make human relationships our source of security over God. However, keeping things in biblical perspective, God does provide key relationships and friendships with people at certain times in our lives, just like he did for David during one of his most fierce trials. The verse above in Proverbs shows us that God uses other people to lift up our countenance during trying times. That is because God uses people for His divine purposes and being a friend to someone happens to be one of those purposes.

The early church fellowshipped with each other on a regular basis because they understood the power of key relationships with people who are equally committed to God (see Acts 2:42; 4:32). If you need quality friendships with people who help enhance your walk with God, begin by being a friend to someone else who needs just such a friend (see Prov. 18:24). Then ask the Lord for friends in return. If God tells us that the right kind of friends can lift up our countenance, then trust Him for them today.

Prayer

Dear Lord, I ask that You would provide me friendships that will draw me closer to You. Keep me from those who would drag me down. I make the decision to choose friendships with those of like-minded faith. In the Name of Jesus, amen.

MARCH 12

His Voice in the Morning

"Know that I wait each morning to bring you peace and a promise, says the Spirit. For even as the day breaks around you, so shall My voice come unto you this morning."

Prophetic Scripture

And in the morning came the word of the Lord unto me... (Ezekiel 12:8).

There is something special about mornings. Now I personally have never considered myself a morning person. I fumble about until that first cup of coffee before I can wrap my brain around the day! However, mornings have a unique power to them that no other time seems to have when it comes to encountering the supernatural presence of God. Growing up, my mother always talked about the power of mornings. She always met God in the morning. She had developed a list of Bible verses on a piece of paper that she would rehearse each day which she affectionately nicknamed her "morning-things." She would read her list every morning and she always said, "No matter what I dealt with the day before, God's peace always returns to me each morning."

Countless Bible figures had these same morning experiences. Jesus rose early in the morning to pray (see Mark 1:35). The word of the Lord came to Ezekiel in the morning (see Ezek. 12:8). Moses met God early in the morning on Mount Sinai (see Exod. 34:4). David received the word of the Lord from the prophet Gad in the morning (see 2 Sam. 24:11). Then Psalms 30:5 emphasizes the power of mornings by saying that joy comes in the morning.

Prepare to encounter the power of God this morning. He has something to speak and impart to you, so get ready and let His peace flood your heart!

Prayer

Father, it is a new morning. I receive Your peace this morning. Speak to me, for Your servant is listening. I rest in Your promises for me this very special morning. In the Name of Jesus, amen.

The Great Instructor

"Those things that you have struggled to know and understand in the past shall become easy to learn now. For I long to teach you carefully and instruct you in deeper things. Yes, I will teach you with supernatural anointing so your enemies will not prevail."

Prophetic Scripture

Teach me thy way, O Lord, and lead me in a plain path, because of mine enemies (Psalms 27:11).

Here David is actually asking the Lord to teach him. Sometimes we assume that God is teaching us automatically, and that is true. The Holy Spirit lives inside of us and He is our teacher. However, it is also important to ask God to teach us, especially in the specific areas of our lives where we need help. For example, if you need help with parenting, begin by asking God to teach you the skills necessary to become a good parent. You can look for good Christian resources to help you, but it is important to ask God so that He is involved in the process of learning right from the beginning. Sometimes we don't learn as quickly because we don't purposefully make God a part of our learning endeavors. When God is a part, He will provide supernatural instruction that will take you far beyond what you could learn just through human study and effort.

David, in the verse above, asked God to teach him because he knew that there were many enemies out there who wanted to trap him and use his mere human learning efforts against him. Let the Holy Spirit add the dimension of supernatural instruction to your life today, so your enemies will not prevail at anything!

Prayer

Lord, You are truly the Great Instructor. Teach me Your ways and instruct me as I read Your Word. Help me gain knowledge in the area of _____, and I thank You that I will avoid the traps of the enemy. In the Name of Jesus, amen.

No Fear of Man

"Fear not what some might say or do against you. I am standing on your side and have put My hand over you, and their attempts to intimidate or harm you will be fruitless."

Prophetic Scripture

The Lord is on my side; I will not fear: what can man do unto me? (Psalms 118:6)

All through history, the devil has used people to try to intimidate and afflict believers. Yet I love the simplicity of the Scripture above. It doesn't go into a lot of detail nor explain how the Lord will help you escape people's attempt to attack you. It simply says that the Lord is on your side. It's like the times when you were a child on the playground and kids would pick teams to play a ballgame. There was always that one kid everybody wanted on their team. It was thought that if you had that kid on your side, then you could expect a sure win.

When the Lord is for you, the ballgame is decided before the first play. That is why this verse follows with the simple statement, "What can man do unto me?" The answer? Nothing, absolutely nothing! Oh, there may be times when it may look like you are losing the game, but it's not over until it's over. If the Lord is on your team, the win is certain. Now, winning doesn't mean we taunt our enemies. We are commanded in the Bible to love the people trying to put us down, but we don't have to fear them. The peace is in knowing that no matter what anyone tries to do against you, God is for you!

Prayer

Dear heavenly Father, I thank You that You are on my side today. You are for me! I worship You because I know you will be my defense and help. I declare today that I will not be fearful of what man may do to me, because You are my life! In the Name of Jesus, amen!

MARCH 15

Recession Has No Power!

"In the talk of economic recession, I laugh, says the Lord. Know that even as the birds fed Elijah by the river, so will I feed My children and care for them in ways that will baffle the world. So fear not the power of recession, but fear the Living God who brings impossible abundance among you!"

Prophetic Scripture

The thief cometh not, but for to steal, and to kill, and to destroy: I am come that they might have life, and that they might have it more abundantly (John 10:10).

In many economies worldwide, the fear of recession is prevalent. People are concerned about losing jobs, finding work, maintaining a successful business, and so on. Yet our confidence cannot be in our economy or income. Jesus said that on this earth, corruption exists. In other words, a thief called the devil is here to steal from people. Yet when Jesus governs our lives, we don't have to fear living without provision. We find in First Kings 17 that the Lord supplied for Elijah in a miraculous way by sending ravens to feed him. God wants to give us an abundant life of supply, but we will miss out if we keep looking over our shoulder in fear of economic collapse. God laughs at recession because He knows that He is much greater than all of that. When the Lord is your source, you don't have to fear economic ruin even when circumstances look bleak. Like He did with Elijah, God will always supply for His children even in the most unusual and unexpected ways!

Prayer

Heavenly Father, I rejoice that I am part of the Kingdom of Heaven and I do not have to fear economic collapse or recession. I place all my confidence in You today. You are my source of abundant supply and nothing shall be able to harm, steal, or destroy me or my family. I laugh in the face of recession and expect supernatural blessing! In Jesus' Name, amen!

Nights of Restful Sleep

"That which robs the world from sleep in this day shall not be so for you. I shall give you nights of restful sleep and surely I will deliver you from restlessness and the night terror."

Prophetic Scripture

When thou liest down, thou shalt not be afraid: yea, thou shalt lie down, and thy sleep shall be sweet (Proverbs 3:24).

Many people today are suffering from sleep disorders. It seems things like insomnia, sleep apnea, bad dreams, restlessness, and similar sleep problems are on the rise. The stressful world we live in contributes to these issues. We find multiple occasions in Scripture that prove this fact. When King Nebuchadnezzar was tormented, sleep left him (see Dan. 2:1). A lack of sleep also came to King Darius (see Dan. 6:18). King Ahasuerus couldn't sleep in the days of Esther when he was unsettled (see Esther 6:1).

Good sleep is indicative of God's peace. Believe today that God is anointing your times of sleep. The Bible says we should experience sweet sleep. This is sleep that isn't broken up by noises, tormenting thoughts, and even just general things that rob you of rest. The devil loves to use the night hour to bombard you with racing thoughts about currents circumstances and even to paint fearful pictures about future events. He then attempts to use those night terrors as a means to make you too tired the next day to resist the attack. Psalm 91:5 says, "Thou shalt not be afraid for the terror by night...."

Be in complete peace with the Lord tonight and command yourself free of every night terror or anything else that would rob your God-given ability to sleep!

Prayer

Heavenly Father, I believe You are giving me the ability to rest well every night of my life. I command every demon that would try to rob my sleep to depart from me in Jesus' Name. I tell my mind to rest in the Lord, and I decree I shall sleep well according to God's promise for me. Amen!

Patience That Promotes

"The Lord says, there are many in the last days who shall succumb to shortcuts and the easy road. But if you hold onto the quality of patient endurance, surely you shall receive promotion in My Kingdom."

Prophetic Scripture

For ye have need of patience, that, after ye have done the will of God, ye might receive the promise (Hebrews 10:36).

Biblical patience is also longsuffering or endurance. It is the ability to be uncomfortable and put under intense pressure, yet refusing to waver. Special forces in the military are put in combat drill situations, teaching them how to endure adverse situations. They are taught mental and physical endurance that exceeds the endurance capacity of the average person.

Biblical patience doesn't mean remaining smiley after the fifth red traffic light when we are already late to work! No, it's talking about not giving up our beliefs even when severely tempted to do so. It means not diverting from godly principles in the midst of rampant deception and compromise. It's believing Bible promises in spite of those who water them down. It means believing in going to church even when friends are embracing a more "modern" model. The apostle John warns the seven churches of Revelation that it is those who keep God's principles to the end that will be rewarded (see Rev. 2:11,17,26; 3:5,12,21). Patience is committed endurance that doesn't give in to shortcuts, but rather reaches for the prize in the midst of pressure to quit. The apostle Paul reminds us to press in for the prize of the high call (see Phil. 3:14). Press in today and let patience promote you!

Prayer

Lord, I ask that You would help me walk in biblical patience today. Help me to have the endurance needed to overcome the evils of the last days. I make a commitment to develop the kind of patience that promotes me in Your Kingdom. In Jesus' Name, amen.

Look to the Rock

"Look no longer at the dysfunctions of your earthly heritage, but look to the Rock. Look now to your new heritage in Christ, from which you have been brought forth with tender care, for your legacy is brand-new."

Prophetic Scripture

Listen to me, you who pursue righteousness and who seek the Lord: Look to the rock from which you were cut and to the quarry from which you were hewn (Isaiah 51:1 NIV).

We all spend a considerable amount of time rehearsing, reminiscing, or sometimes even complaining about our family ties. We talk about everything—ethnic descent, family traditions, ancestors, and even habits we inherited from our bloodline. Of course, there are always things we inherit that we wish didn't come with the package. For some who come from very dysfunctional backgrounds, these issues often hinder normal life. Regardless of your upbringing, there are undoubtedly things inherited from your bloodline that you would like changed.

Isaiah 51 was a reminder to Israel to focus back on their godly heritage because they had gotten their eyes off where they came from. As Christians, we do the same thing sometimes. We look so much at our natural family tree and its shortcomings that we forget about our new spiritual heritage. While your earthly bloodline doesn't disappear, you don't have to live according to the problems it passed down. Instead, look to Christ the Rock who provided you a new heritage, established with care and meticulous precision. That heritage is the more powerful of the two and can supernaturally remold you into a new person (see 2 Cor. 5:17). Rehearse and study that heritage until it forms your habits. Look to the Rock today and embrace a brand-new legacy!

Prayer

Heavenly Father, I look once again to my godly heritage in Christ. You have called me into a whole new bloodline. I look to the Rock today and ask that a supernatural impartation would take place in me so that I will live according to my new heritage. In Jesus' Name, amen.

Day of Divine Discernment

"Expect Me to give you divine discernment in all things, says the Spirit. For as you keep a teachable heart that will learn of Me, surely I shall keep you in truth in the day of deception."

Prophetic Scripture

But he that is spiritual judgeth all things... (1 Corinthians 2:15).

The Greek word for *judgeth* in the verse here is *anakreeno*. It means to scrutinize, investigate, examine, and discern. In the passage surrounding this verse, we find Paul talking about how natural, carnal people will not make a habit of using careful discernment regarding the things they embrace. Carnal people are at high risk for rejecting the true and embracing the false. Yet the person who is spiritual will make a habit of studying and investigating things while keeping a teachable attitude. True discernment isn't being critical and suspicious! It is being like the Bereans in Acts 17:11-12. Before they scrutinized it, they first received the preaching of Paul and Silas with all "readiness of mind." They started with a receptive attitude, even though they hadn't heard it before. Undoubtedly, the Holy Spirit gave them an initial moment of divine discernment because they were teachable. Then afterward, they researched the Scriptures in an effort to add substance to the initial witness they felt.

I believe the Lord wants to give us these kinds of initial divine moments of discernment that can withstand the deceptions of the day. With so many things being presented, we need the supernatural witness from the Holy Spirit. Then, as spiritual people we need to follow up with God's Word. Ask the Lord to give you divine discernment today, and trust that if you spend time in God's Word with a receptive spirit the Holy Spirit will lead you to the truth.

Prayer

Holy Spirit, I ask You for divine discernment today. Help me not to be critical and suspicious but be open to fresh revelation from heaven. Teach me to walk in truth. Allow it to challenge me and train me to follow You! In Jesus' Name, amen.

Outlasting Glory Upholds You

"Let Me give you a vision of the glory of heaven. Yes, the Spirit says, let not the tests of this present time get you down, for they only last a short while, but My outlasting glory shall uphold you forever!"

Prophetic Scripture

For our light affliction, which is but for a moment, worketh for us a far more exceeding and eternal weight of glory (2 Corinthians 4:17).

The older you get, the more you realize that life doesn't last that long. The Bible says that our time spent on this earth is like the morning fog—it's here for a little time, but then as quickly as it came, it's gone (James 4:14 NLT). This means that even though we can live a full, long life on earth, it will be over before we know it. That gives you a sobering view on how you approach life. It should make you want to keep yourself in check. However, it should also encourage you to remember that today's challenges will only last a short time. It should give you the renewed energy to keep reaching for that eternal glory which will far outlast anything that life on earth has given you.

When we focus too much on this life, we put ourselves at risk for giving up and we forget how magnificent Heaven really is. We need to spend more time looking at the vastness of eternity and how much longer it is in comparison to now. Eternity is forever! Ask the Lord to give you a revelation of it and let it be the propelling force that upholds you today!

Prayer

Heavenly Father, I ask for a renewed vision of eternity today. I make the decision to not put all my focus on this present life. I thank You that everything I am dealing with today is small in comparison to the eternal glory that is mine! Amen!

Ignorant Men Confounded!

"Yes, even as it was in times of old when men and women stood and confounded kings, so shall you confound the foolish acts of this age. Even in media, in workplaces, and in courtrooms, get ready, says the Spirit, as the well-doing of My people across the land silences accusations on every corner!"

Prophetic Scripture

For so is the will of God, that with well doing ye may put to silence the ignorance of foolish men (1 Peter 2:15).

You can't argue with a deed done right! When we make right choices, people around have no answer. It becomes hard for them to laugh about sin at work while you joyfully do what is right. People are tired of compromise and apathy. They want the lines of truth and righteousness to be clearly drawn. The Scripture above says that ignorant and foolish people are put to silence when we draw clear lines and do what is right. We are not here to be self-righteous, critical, nor are we to point fingers. We just have to determine that we will not compromise what is right. God is stirring something in His people that will cause us to rise up as a unified sound in this hour in taking a righteous stand.

Something is about to happen that is going to place the church in a position where the world won't have a good argument to stop our voice. Decide today how you personally need to take a stand through your actions. No matter how small, a righteous choice on your part may change someone's life forever!

Prayer

Father, cause me to be a voice in this hour through my actions. Teach me how to set a righteous standard in love and mercy. I repent for any area where I have compromised. I commit to walk as a light in this hour and I believe lives will be changed as a result! In Jesus' Name, amen.

Tree of Righteousness

"The Spirit says that nothing can hold you, nothing can keep you bound. Listen to My counsel this day and I shall make you like a planted tree, and the fruit of your righteousness will overtake all that would hold you captive!"

Prophetic Scripture

And he shall be a like a tree planted by the rivers of water, that bringeth forth his fruit in his season; his leaf also shall not wither; and whatsoever he doeth shall prosper (Psalms 1:3).

Sometimes we get overwhelmed by our own shortcomings. Even the most dedicated Christians have times when they feel like their failures outweigh their successes. A key principle for overcoming that sense of failure is found in a sermon by John the Baptist in Matthew 3:8 when he said, "Bring forth therefore fruits meet for repentance." He was saying to begin developing character traits that reflect true repentance. Of course, fruit growth doesn't happen all at once. It grows over time, but what makes it successful is the right environment.

The right environment for us to bear good fruit comes by staying in God's Word (see Ps. 1:1-2). His Word will cause us to live according to His counsel, which will develop a stable spiritual root system. With that in place, fruit will grow! Ask the Lord to reveal counsel from His Word today and let it create the environment for fruit-bearing in your life. Watch as the multiplied growth of that fruit gradually begins overtaking all the negatives that have held you back before and your successes start outweighing your shortcomings!

Prayer

Father, I make a fresh commitment to stay close to Your counsel so that fruit will grow in my life. Help me be a fruit-bearing Christian. I thank You that I am able to overcome every bondage that would hold me down! In Jesus' Name! Amen.

Born for Signs and Wonders!

"See that I have created you for the miraculous and am sending you forth this day in signs and wonders. Allow Me to use you in this hour and I will teach you how to operate in things men cannot explain!"

Prophetic Scripture

Behold, I and the children whom the Lord hath given me are for signs and for wonders… (Isaiah 8:18).

God is supernatural, and we are made in His image. That means if God does supernatural things, then we can expect His supernatural power to work in and through us. When Jesus was on earth, He gave supernatural power to His disciples (see Mark 3:14-15). From there, they went about Galilee healing the sick and casting out demons. That first surge of power never left them. In fact, it went to another level after Pentecost. Jesus told them in Acts 1:8, "But ye shall receive power, after that the Holy Ghost is come upon you." Once the Holy Spirit fell in Acts 2, the disciples ministered with supernatural power everywhere they went.

God wants to use His people to perform signs and wonders to a lost generation that desperately needs to see God's power manifest. They are constantly presented with demonic power via television and similar mediums. They need to see God's genuine power. That power can manifest through your words, actions, prayers, and also through various other supernatural manifestations of the Holy Spirit. Ask the Lord to use you in miracles today because you are made in His image. Yes, you were born for signs and wonders!

Prayer

Father, I ask You to teach me how to minister for You with supernatural ability when I speak to people, pray for them, and minister in the gifts of the Spirit. I thank You that You shall perform signs and wonders through me! Amen.

Time Extended

"So shall I extend time for you. Even as you give time to Me, I shall multiply time back to you, and you will surely know that there is more than ample time to accomplish all that is needed."

Prophetic Scripture

And the sun stood still, and the moon stayed, until the people had avenged themselves upon their enemies... (Joshua 10:13).

Topping the charts of extreme miracles ever recorded was the time when Joshua literally stopped the progression of time until he finished defeating his enemy in battle (see Josh. 10:12-14). He spoke to the sun and commanded it to stand still. In fact, the Bible states that there wasn't a time other than this in which the Lord listened to such an extreme demand.

While we don't have any other examples in Scripture of time actually being altered like this, it does stand to reason that the Lord can take time and "stretch" it. In other words, He can enable you to accomplish more than normal in the time you have. God can take the 24 hours before you today and, in a sense, make it multiply so you can accomplish more than you thought possible. The key to receiving this kind of "expanded time" is to first give your time to the Lord, then He will give time back to you. We have all felt that we have more to do in one day than possible, but if we give our time to God, He will make sure we have plenty of time to do what we need. Expect Him to multiply and expand your time today!

Prayer

Father, as I give my time to you this day, I ask you to multiply my time. Not only do I ask You to teach me how to manage my time wisely, but I ask that You will enable me to accomplish more than I expected possible today! In the Name of Jesus, amen.

The Dayspring from on High!

*"My visitation is here and near you now. I am the light in your darkest tunnel. Yes **now**, I am the day that springs forth from on high, and you shall see the way of escape out of every trial."*

Prophetic Scripture

Through the tender mercy of our God; whereby the dayspring from on high hath visited us, to give light to them that sit in darkness and in the shadow of death, to guide our feet into the way of peace (Luke 1:78-79).

The Lord is the day that springs up from the darkness! No matter what you are dealing with or trying to sort through, God is always the light that leads you out of it. The reason we often have trouble following Him out is because we are too busy examining the darkness. We go over our trials, work problems, financial problems, health issues, and family troubles again and again trying to figure a way out. We need to refocus our eyes on the Lord. He is the Light. He is the dayspring. The best part of it is that He is more than willing to shine the light to help you. Not only is He the Light, but He is merciful to give it to us. You may not feel like the light guiding you is very bright today, but you can get out of a tunnel with just a flashlight! It doesn't take much to guide you to safety. Look for the light of God guiding you every day, every moment, and in everything. Mercy is leading you out today!

Prayer

Dear Lord, I thank You for Your mercy that is shining light upon me. Help me to see Your guiding hand in every situation. I make a choice to take my eyes off the darkness right now and I stand in the light of Your mercy! In Jesus' Name, amen!

The Oil of Thanksgiving

"I call you this day to give Me the oil of thanksgiving. And even as you rehearse blessings and what I have done for you, shall you see a greater anointing. For thanksgiving and the miraculous work together to cause increase over you!"

Prophetic Scripture

If one offers it for a thanksgiving, then he shall offer with the thank offering unleavened cakes mixed with oil, and unleavened wafers spread with oil, and cakes of fine flour mixed with oil (Leviticus 7:12 AMP).

When God taught the priests of the Old Testament to bring an offering of thanksgiving before Him, they were instructed to bring it in the form of unleavened cakes mixed with oil. These two elements are key ingredients that have prophetic significance for us in how we offer praise to the Lord today. We know the unleavened bread represented purity and a holy lifestyle (see 1 Cor. 5:6-8). Oil represents the anointing of the Holy Spirit. Notice in the verse above that the unleavened cakes were brushed over with oil.

When we offer thanksgiving to the Lord in the environment of a holy lifestyle, the oil of the Holy Spirit washes over us and our lives literally become covered in the anointing. One of the ways David offered thanksgiving to God all through the Book of Psalms was to rehearse a list of things God had done for him. Rehearse to God the good He has done for you and allow that praise to cause the oil of a fresh anointing to wash over every aspect of your life today. When it does, miracles and blessing will be sure to follow!

Prayer

Lord, I rehearse the good things You have done in my life today. I make a list of these things by remembering when You _____.
Thank You, Lord! Now, even as I thank You, I expect the anointing to increase on me! In Jesus' Name, amen.

My Song Over You

"Yes, in the many times you sing to Me, know that I also sing to you, says the Lord. So listen today for My song and know that through it shall you find Me fighting for the destiny I have created for you."

Prophetic Scripture

The Lord thy God in the midst of thee is mighty; he will save, he will rejoice over thee with joy; he will rest in his love, he will joy over thee with singing (Zephaniah 3:17).

Just as much as we love to sing, the Lord sings and loves music. He is the original Creator of song, so we shouldn't overlook the fact that our Almighty God is an incredible singer! Just as we sing to Him, He also sings to us. In fact, God is so thrilled with you that He breaks into singing when He looks at you! Since God sings over us with joy, it only makes sense to believe that He wants us to hear His songs for us. We can hear the singing of God in many ways. Commonly, we are used to hearing songs of God in the Scriptures, such as in the Book of Psalms. We may also hear songs of God given in prophetic form during a corporate gathering when an individual sings a prophecy.

However, we should also listen to God's songs in our own private prayer times. If we are able to hear His voice speak to us inside our spirit, then why not listen for His singing that way? As you spend time with the Lord right now, listen for His songs over you. They undoubtedly reveal parts of His plans for you and how much He is fighting for your success!

Prayer

Dear heavenly Father, I am thrilled to know that I make You sing! Help me hear Your songs for me today. I love to hear Your voice, and I ask you to teach me how to hear You in song! In Jesus' Name, amen.

Restored in Full

"This day, I am restoring what has been lost. Yes, even what you thought would never be returned will come again. Command restoration to manifest over you and expect all things fresh and new!"

Prophetic Scripture

Restore, I pray you, to them, even this day, their lands, their vineyards, their oliveyards, and their houses, also the hundredth part of the money, and of the corn, the wine, and the oil, that ye exact of them (Nehemiah 5:11).

In the story of Nehemiah, we find the people of God in a desperate time. They had been captive in Babylon with their possessions being stolen unfairly. Nehemiah sees this abuse and decides to put a stop to it. He rises up against their abusers and commands a restoration to be given. It takes that same kind of commanding attitude against the powers of darkness that want to rob us of peace, joy, safety, health, finances, and countless other things. The devil often steals from us simply because we allow him. It's time to decide enough is enough of the devil stealing from you repeatedly. Rise up and command it to stop, in the Name of Jesus!

Of course, restoration isn't just limited to the enemy bringing back the things he stole from you. God restores things that have been stolen at the hand of the devil. Not only does He restore things you lost, but He adds to them so that you come out better than when you started! So command restoration to manifest over your life today and expect this season to be a time when you shall be restored in full!

Prayer

Dear Lord, I know today that You are a God of restoration. I use the authority You have given me in Jesus' Name and I command every evil spirit to stop stealing from me! I now expect a season of full restoration to manifest over my life! Amen.

Family Salvation

"This is the hour to build an ark in prayer for the salvation of your loved ones. Even like Noah, who gave his time for it, commit your time in prayer, says the Spirit. For as you do, even those who have been hard in their hearts, I will draw them by My Spirit."

Prophetic Scripture

By faith Noah, being warned of God of things not seen as yet, moved with fear, prepared an ark to the saving of his house... (Hebrews 11:7).

If you have unsaved loved ones, you know the concerned feeling we all have for the eternal future of our families. Here we see Noah, God's righteous man, leading the way for his family by preparing an ark. Noah's ark represents a place that offers protection from harm. In other words, Noah took the responsibility to recognize the seriousness of the situation and create a place of safety for his family. He didn't delay until it was too late.

Today we can create an "ark" for our families through prayer. We can ask the Lord to protect them, draw them, and send Gospel laborers into their lives. We should also ask the Holy Spirit to make intercession for them as we pray in tongues. Lastly, we should command the evil spirits of darkness to loose their hold on their blinded minds (see 2 Cor. 4:4). God wants our family members saved, but we need to see the urgency of their spiritual condition and begin preparing an ark for them. Let's believe that as we do, the salvation of our family will happen, even this year!

Prayer

Lord, I pray for the following members of my family: _____. I ask You to draw them to You. Send laborers into their life to show them the Gospel. I also command the god of this world to stop blinding the mind of _____, in the Name of Jesus! Amen.

Traps of the Enemy Exposed!

"Know that I shall reveal and expose the plans of darkness against you. For not one effort shall succeed, and I will open your eyes and you shall avoid traps on every side, says the Lord of Hosts!"

Prophetic Scripture

Surely he shall deliver thee from the snare of the fowler... (Psalms 91:3).

During Jesus' ministry, the Pharisees and religious leaders of the day tried many times to trap Him. Mark 14:1 (AMP) says they were using secrecy and deceit to trap him. Yet their repeated attempts to take Him out always failed. Every attempt was somehow either thwarted or exposed. Why? It's because there was an anointing upon Jesus, making them unable to touch Him even when Jesus was plainly within reach. He either knew their intentions or supernaturally escaped their traps. It wasn't until Jesus gave Himself into their hands to be crucified that they were able to lay hold of Him.

As heirs of Christ, we also need to know that the Lord is delivering us from the traps of the enemy. Instead of falling into the subtle traps of deception, sins, false doctrine, and offenses, the anointing causes us to see them in advance and avoid them (see 1 John 2:26-27). The Lord can show you when a trap has been set for you if you are willing and open in your heart to the Holy Spirit. We also need faith to believe that we will supernaturally avoid and overcome the traps we don't see. Trust the Lord today that every trap of the enemy laid in your path will be exposed!

Prayer

Father, I thank You that I am delivered from every trap of evil set against me. I ask that You would cause me to see and avoid these traps. I also ask You to place an anointing upon me that shall deliver me from every snare. In the Name of Jesus, amen!

Your Secure Dwelling Place

"Yes, I shall always provide you a secure dwelling place. Even as you commit your possessions to Me, so shall a house always be provided for you and it shall be kept in safety."

Prophetic Scripture

And they shall dwell safely in it and shall build houses and plant vineyards; yes, they shall dwell securely... (Ezekiel 28:26 AMP).

So many people in recent years have gone through the pain and upheaval of the housing crisis, and many are in a dilemma regarding where to live or simply what their future living standard may become. Some are facing foreclosures, while others are just trying to maintain a secure income so they can pay for some form of living quarters. Another group is perhaps speculating about what they will be able to provide their family. The bottom line is that we are living in some very shaky economic times and nothing in this world is certain.

The good news is that we as believers can rely on the Lord, who will make certain we have a secure living. As those who commit all we have to the Lord, giving our tithes to Him and serving Him wholeheartedly, we can live in a level of safety that the world does not have. Even if you lose a home or job, you can be sure the Lord will provide something else and that you will never be left without provision. God is faithful, so don't allow worry to consume you about where your future will take you (see Matt. 6:28-34). The Lord will see to it that you will always have a safe and secure dwelling place!

Prayer

Father, I thank You that I don't have to live in fear about tomorrow or what will take place in the economy. No matter what happens in this world, You will always provide for me as promised in Your Word. Thank You, Father. In the Name of Jesus, amen.

Marked for a Purpose

> *"I have marked you for a divine purpose, says the Spirit of Grace. Believe that I will use you in a way that will astound some who have mocked you and said it will never be. Yes, stand firm, for My seal of guarantee is upon you!"*

Prophetic Scripture

> *Now it is God who makes both us and you stand firm in Christ. He anointed us, set his seal of ownership on us, and put his Spirit in our hearts as a deposit, guaranteeing what is to come* (2 Corinthians 1:21-22 NIV).

When Jacob wrestled all night with the angel, his thigh was thrown out of joint in such a dramatic way that it permanently marked Jacob's life (see Gen. 32:24-32). It caused him to call the place in which it happened Peniel, which means face of God. Jacob described it saying, "I have seen God face to face, and my life is preserved" (Gen. 32:30). He had an encounter with God that "marked" his thigh, which became the mark of a divine purpose. That purpose was seen when his name Jacob (*deceiver*) was changed to Israel (*God prevails*). He went from being a deceiver to one who represented the prevailing power of God as the offspring that ultimately became the nation of Israel.

God has marked you for a purpose today. He so believes in you that He has placed a seal of ownership on you to show you His guarantee. It doesn't matter what others say you cannot do; even if they laugh at you now, know that God sees who you will be. Stand firm in that today!

Prayer

> *Lord, I know that I am marked for a purpose in this life. Through You, I am going to accomplish great things. You have anointed me, and I ask that You will help me stand confident in who I am in You today! Amen.*

APRIL 2

A Righteous Verdict

"Know today, says the Lord of Hosts, that I have risen up in jealousy on your behalf. I am defending you in every case and I shall cry out a righteous verdict regarding the judgments of those who speak a lie against you!"

Prophetic Scripture

The Lord shall go forth as a mighty man, he shall stir up jealousy like a man of war: he shall cry, yea, roar; he shall prevail against his enemies (Isaiah 42:13).

It isn't enjoyable when situations in life seem to deal an unfair hand, especially when the truth about you is being misrepresented. For some dealing with legal battles, it feels so defeating when things are being presented in court that you know are a twist on the truth. For others, sometimes frustration comes simply because people lie about you and you feel there is nothing you can do to stop others from believing those lies.

Of course, the temptation is always to rise up and defend ourselves, but in reality it often doesn't help matters. That doesn't mean you should never speak up for the truth when the circumstance requires it, but in the end, we really need to rely on the Lord. He shall ultimately destroy the ability that any lie has to harm you and He will establish a righteous verdict. It may not always happen in the time frame we want or in the manner we would prefer, but what we have to know is that God will make sure the truth will win out. It's a day to trust that the Lord of Hosts is rising up like a mighty man to defend you!

Prayer

Dear Lord, I ask that You would be my defense today. Let my integrity be clearly seen, and every lie that would rise up against me, let it be destroyed. I thank You that You establish truth and a righteous verdict regarding me. In Jesus' Name, amen.

An Anointing of Liberty Created

"See that I have broken every chain that would shackle you this day. I am creating power within you so that all which would addict and bind shall lose its strength as an anointing of liberty enables you!"

Prophetic Scripture

Create in me a clean heart, O God; and renew a right spirit within me (Psalms 51:10).

We are creatures of habit. The things we regularly involve ourselves with will ultimately become a regular part of our lives. In essence, we become addicted to them. Some people, perhaps due to being abused, have become dependent on manipulative control tactics to feel successful. Others are bound to substances such as drugs and alcohol. Then, even less recognizable are those addicted to things like materialism, certain fears, jealousy, or even things like fame and the quest for occupational success. Some people are addicted to things like insecurity or loneliness. The list is extensive, but the key is that if you feel shackled by anything at all, you need the Lord to provide a special anointing to be free. Of course, it requires acknowledging the issue and making right choices, but it also takes some supernatural ability from Heaven.

David realized He needed God's ability to be free. In Psalms 51:10 he said, "Create in me a clean heart." He was saying, "Lord I can't do this by myself; I need You to create the ability in me." If there is anything binding you, ask the Lord to create within you an anointing that will liberate you and accomplish what you cannot produce on your own. Ask Him to create an anointing of liberty within you today.

Prayer

Father, I ask You to enable me to be free from all bondage today. Create in me what I cannot produce on my own. I decree I am free today from every shackle and an anointing for liberty is working in me today! In the Name of Jesus, amen.

Children Safe in His Arms

"Know that I have created peace for My children and so shall I create peace for your children. As a child of Mine, you are safe, so ask Me to cause your offspring to be safe in My arms. For I shall surely keep them in peace."

Prophetic Scripture

And all thy children shall be taught of the Lord; and great shall be the peace of thy children (Isaiah 54:13).

Those who are parents quickly learn that kids have a mind of their own. They attempt to do things we know are not good for them while we do everything to protect them. In our effort to keep them safe, sometimes we feel that we cannot do enough. Often their complete safety is beyond our control. As God's child, the Lord has created a plan for your safety today. However, that heavenly insurance plan extends beyond you and covers your offspring as well. Their safety is in His control! Whether you have children right now or hope to have some one day, you can claim God's promise of peace for your kids. Perhaps you are a parent of grown children, or perhaps your children are still babies. Either way, it doesn't matter. Claim the peace and safety of God to rest over your children and that they will always be protected from danger. As God's child, you are safe with Him, so begin to believe that same protection will also rest over your offspring. Declare with your lips today that your children are safe in His arms!

Prayer

Lord, I ask You to place a covering of peace and safety over me and my family. I trust the promise of peace over Your children and I believe that all my children and family members who follow after me shall live in peace and safety. In Jesus' Name, amen.

Your Name Is Known!

"Yes, I know your name, says the Lord. Surely, it is recognized in heaven, and although some on earth may ignore your name, I have noted it. And each time your name is spoken, the angels work to propel you into Kingdom greatness."

Prophetic Scripture

And as Jesus passed forth from thence, he saw a man, named Matthew, sitting at the receipt of custom... (Matthew 9:9).

If you read through the different Gospel accounts of when Jesus called Matthew, His disciple, they each tell a slightly different but similar story. In Luke's account, it records Jesus seeing a publican named Levi (see Luke 5:27-28). Publicans were considered sinners, and the name *Levi* comes from the Hebrew name for the Levites, which means to be twined. It speaks of the intertwining seen between borrowing and lending and obviously the bondage involved with the two. Mark's account of Jesus' call to Matthew is similar in that he is also referred to as Levi (see Mark 2:14). Notice how both Mark and Luke see Matthew as the publican named Levi, which indicates they saw him as an insignificant individual.

However, Matthew's account of himself is much different. Matthew says Jesus saw a man. He didn't see a publican or sinner, He saw a person. Then he notes that Jesus saw Matthew. The name *Matthew* means gift. He didn't see Levi, the person intertwined with problems. Jesus saw a real human being, a gifted individual with great potential, named Matthew.

That revelation propelled Matthew, this one-time publican, into Kingdom greatness. Realize that your name is known in Heaven today and Jesus sees a special person who is being propelled into Kingdom greatness!

Prayer

Lord, I thank You that my name is special in heaven. You know me by name! Even the angels, when they hear my name spoken, are working to help me. Thank You, Lord, for the peace of knowing that my name is always recognized! Amen.

APRIL 6

Anointed in the Heathen Circle

"I shall anoint you to stand in the midst of a secular environment with miraculous strength. And many in the heathen world who are struggling to survive will look up and say, 'Who are you who walks in such grace?'"

Prophetic Scripture

And Jesus returned in the power of the Spirit into Galilee: and there went out a fame of him through all the region round about (Luke 4:14).

Before He entered Galilee, Jesus spent 40 days in the wilderness being tempted by the devil. After 40 days of intense pressure, the Bible says He returned to Galilee in the power of the spirit. The pressure of temptation resulted in Him being able to enter Galilee in power. *Galilee* means heathen circle. Jesus was now prepared and anointed to enter a secular, heathen environment and be ready for any challenge that might be thrown at Him.

Just as the wilderness prepared Jesus to enter Galilee with miraculous power, our own experiences are preparing us to enter our circle of influence with miraculous power. As Christians, we must be prepared to enter our own "Galilee" or "heathen circle." We need take the tests and temptations we have overcome and use them as reference points to deal wisely and powerfully in whatever non-Christian environment is before us. Additionally, the miracles we have experienced during our own days in the wilderness can minister to others. We can help them experience the same miracles we have. Our testimony of victory isn't just for the church circle. It is ready to take you into your "Galilee" today. You are anointed for the heathen circle!

Prayer

Father, I ask You to prepare me to minister for You in a secular environment. Teach me how to bring Your supernatural anointing to the lost, and help me do so with wisdom. I am anointed today for my sphere of influence so they can be touched by the Gospel. Amen!

The Oil Shall Endure

"Prepare and make room for supernatural provision, even that which pays off debt. For even as I provided for My people in days of old, so shall the oil of provision endure for you in this time."

Prophetic Scripture

And it came to pass, when the vessels were full...the oil stayed (2 Kings 4:6).

The story of the widow woman in Second Kings 4:1-7 reveals that God will supernaturally provide for us, even enough at times to pay off debts. Of course, this widow woman didn't just sit around and wait for provision; she prepared and made room for it. First, she prepared the way for provision by going to where spiritual things were available. In her case, it was Elisha. Today, we may or may not be able to go some particular minister of our choosing. However, we can go where spiritual things are available by going to church regularly, getting around anointed Christians, and feeding on God's Word.

When this woman got around spiritual things, she automatically prepared the way for provision. Secondly, she made room for provision by doing what she received in that spiritual environment. She did as the prophet instructed by gathering pitchers and jars. Then oil supernaturally filled them and it was enough to pay off her creditors! We can make room for provision in several ways today. Perhaps if you are trusting God for food, then it's time to clean your cupboards and get ready. If you are needing finances, get your bills in order. Ask God how you can both prepare and make room, because it's time for the oil of provision to endure!

Prayer

Father, I ask You to show me how to both prepare and make room for supernatural provision to even pay off debts. If there are things I need to change, reveal them to me. Lord, I have expectation for the oil of provision to endure! In Jesus' Name, amen.

Times and Seasons Are Known

"Begin to open your eyes, says the Lord. For I am causing My people to know the times and seasons in the Spirit. For as you stay mindful of that which is happening in the spirit realm, the hour shall not take you off guard."

Prophetic Scripture

But of the times and the seasons, brethren, ye have no need that I write unto you (1 Thessalonians 5:1).

The apostle Paul spoke to the Church of Thessalonica as those who were mature examples of people who were very aware of the hour in which they were living (see 1 Thess. 1:7-10). He talked to them throughout both books of Thessalonians in this manner. At one point he reiterated that they didn't even need anyone to rehearse the realities of the present season because their eyes were already open (see 1 Thess. 5:1).

There are constantly changing seasons in the spirit. Some are shorter seasons we need to discern, like those pertaining to special outpourings of the Holy Spirit to emphasize certain truths. One example is the great healing revival of the '50s and '60s when divine healing was being restored. Then are times and seasons pertinent to the sovereign prophecies of Scripture progressing us toward the endtimes. The Holy Spirit wants His church to be aware of the changing times and seasons not only as they pertain to the Body of Christ as a whole, but also to local groups and churches. If you stay mindful of the realm of the spirit, you can recognize the present spiritual seasons so that the nothing takes you by surprise.

Prayer

Father, I ask that You would help me be aware of the times and seasons upon the Church. Help me be mindful of that which is taking place in the spirit so that I will handle it with maturity and spiritual readiness. In Jesus' Name, amen.

Rivers of Deliverance

"Be sensitive in prayer this day, for there are unique rivers of anointing that come forth from your spirit. Even as you pray in the Spirit shall there manifest rivers of deliverance that shall change circumstances and move mountains."

Prophetic Scripture

He that believeth on me, as the scripture hath said, out of his belly shall flow rivers of living water (John 7:38).

From the Garden of Eden a river flowed and separated into four different tributaries, which the Bible describes in detail (see Gen. 2:10-14). That detail indicates that God wants us to see something. I believe they each represent a "river" or expression of prayer. The rivers are Pison, Gihon, Hiddekel, and Euphrates. *Pison* means "increase." It speaks of provision and our physical needs being met. *Gihon* means "bursting forth." It's sometimes described like a long garden hose that bursts forth at the end. This is intercession and travail in birth. It takes time, but then suddenly the miracle bursts forth. *Hiddekel* means "rapid." This is intense white water, and this river was pointed toward the wicked nation of Assyria. It speaks of intense spiritual warfare in prayer pointed at the devil. Lastly, *Euphrates* means "fruitfulness." This is prayer that involves worship and commitment to God that produces Christian fruit in our lives.

The Bible teaches us that there are rivers (plural) that come from our spirit (see John 7:38). They each produce different results. Sometimes the anointing will be upon you asking for your needs; other times it will be warfare or intercession. Be sensitive in prayer today and allow the Holy Spirit to manifest different expressions or "rivers" to produce deliverance!

Prayer

Holy Spirit, I make myself available to the many different expressions and rivers of prayer that You want to flow from my spirit. Help me learn to flow in these prayer rivers with precision and accuracy so the deliverance can come forth. In Jesus' Name, amen.

The Sending Anointing

"See that I have reserved for you a sending anointing, says the Lord. And as you allow Me to develop your character in humility, so shall I send you forth endorsed with apostolic influence."

Prophetic Scripture

Come now therefore, and I will send thee... (Exodus 3:10).

The word *apostolic* simply means "sent." It means God endorses you and therefore is sending you to represent Him for a particular task, just like He sent Moses to Pharaoh (see Exod. 3:10). When Moses encountered Pharaoh, there was no mistake about who sent him because he had several factors in place.

To be apostolic doesn't mean you become an apostle, but it means you carry a "sent one" anointing. We all need to operate under the power of sending. It means we don't rise up and do things on our own, but we wait for certain factors to align. Whether your part in God's Kingdom is ministerial leadership or volunteer support, it needs an apostolic or sent-one anointing upon it. The two key characteristics of this sending anointing are fruit and recognition. If you are truly called to help in a church by working in the sound department or prayer ministry, you will have fruit to show for it. Secondly, your gifts and abilities will be recognizable to other believers and ministry leaders. These factors must be present for those called to full-time ministry as well. Every one of us must be willing to humble ourselves until both legitimate fruit and recognition become evident. God wants you to be endowed with a sending anointing so you can influence people in an amazing way this year!

Prayer

Father, I ask that You would mold me and develop my character. I humble myself and allow You to place a mature apostolic anointing upon me so that I can be a blessing in Your Kingdom. I wait on You for the full manifestation of a sending anointing! In Jesus' Name, amen.

His Eye Is upon You!

"Know that I am watching over your endeavors. Though some would try to disrupt and even wish for your failure, My eye is upon you and your labors shall not be terminated!"

Prophetic Scripture

But the eye of their God was upon the elders of the Jews, that they could not cause them to cease... (Ezra 5:5).

When Israel began the rebuilding of the temple while under the control of Babylonian rule, they had many people who didn't feel they should be allowed to do it. These objectors complained that the Israelites didn't have the proper authority. They created problems and tried very hard to wear them out. Yet in spite of it all, they could not cause the project to cease. In fact, the Bible says not only did the project get completed, it did so with rapid progress (see Ezra 5:8). That is because God was watching over it.

As you serve the Lord, His eye will be upon your efforts. Even those who are in disagreement with your work cannot stop you. The secular world has tried every which way to stop the Gospel from going forth, but it continues to grow and prosper. You cannot fight against that which God endorses and defends. Sure, it may look like the attacks are great and there are moments of seeming defeat, but in the end the work of God will prosper.

Be confident that whatever projects or work-related endeavors you are doing for the Lord shall succeed. Don't worry about the disruptions today, because His eye is upon you.

Prayer

Lord, I thank You that Your eye is upon me and all the things I do for Your glory shall succeed. Let me complete things in record timing today, and I declare that my work shall not cease! Amen.

Thy Kingdom Come

"Decree this day for My Kingdom to manifest and rule over you. For even as you make the declaration now, so shall you walk greater in My perfect will and you will experience greater breakthroughs."

Prophetic Scripture

...Thy kingdom come, Thy will be done, as in heaven, so in earth (Luke 11:2).

This excerpt from Luke 11 is a famous line from what is commonly called the Lord's Prayer. Truthfully, Jesus didn't pray this prayer just so we could repeat it. It is actually a guideline on how to pray and which things to prioritize in prayer. Among them was a call upon God for His Kingdom rule to have the preeminence and that His will would be manifest in our lives. However, the specific words in the prayer, "thy kingdom come, thy will be done," are spoken not as formal requests, but rather as a strong decree. This seems to be the one part of the prayer that you almost want to repeat verbatim. It isn't that you are commanding God, but rather it seems that you should say it in order to command yourself. You are telling yourself that you will live under God's Kingdom rule and that you won't allow yourself to get outside of His will.

Declare today for God's Kingdom rule to manifest over you and that you will walk in His will. Say it many times. There is something about your ears hearing you say it that solidifies its truth in your heart. With God's Kingdom rule upon you and His will being your priority, you can't help but experience breakthrough. His Kingdom is upon you now!

Prayer

Father, I declare Your Kingdom come and Your will be done in my life. I make this decree and say it shall come to pass and cause me to live in breakthrough every day. In the Name of Jesus, amen.

There Is Grace for This!

"My grace is available to empower you. It shall cause you to rise up strong, it shall refresh, and it shall heal. And even regarding your long-time concerns, it is now time to say, 'There is grace for this!'"

Prophetic Scripture

My grace is sufficient for thee: for my strength is made perfect in weakness... (2 Corinthians 12:9).

John 5:1-9 is the story of the lame man sitting by the Pool of Bethesda waiting for a sovereign move of God. He was carried daily to the pool where an angel would appear and stir the waters. Whoever was first into the pool was healed. He never made it into the pool before the others, and 38 years later he was still sitting there until Jesus came along and healed him. Through this instant miracle, Jesus demonstrated that in Christ, grace is available now. Everyone by that pool was waiting for their moment of grace to occur, but one man tapped into Jesus and was instantly healed.

The word *Bethesda* means "house of mercy or grace." *Grace* is the Greek word *charis* which means divine favor. It's the root word for *charisma*, which speaks of supernatural gifts that manifest because of divine favor. Paul tapped into this supernatural grace while dealing with a long-time problem (see 2 Cor. 12:7-10). After asking God to fix it countless times, finally Jesus said, "Paul, My grace is enough!" In other words, "There is grace for this!" In Christ, grace is here now, making supernatural power available. It's what that lame man and Paul both encountered. Whatever you are facing today, just shout it out, "There is grace for this!"

Prayer

Father, I thank You for the grace in Christ that is upon me today. I call upon it for refreshing, healing, and supernatural ability to overcome. I declare today, there is grace for this! Amen.

Make It a Good Day!

"Know that all I have created is good, and even as I have made this day, so let it be a day of nothing but good for you. Come in agreement with Me together, says the Lord, and let's make it a good day!"

Prophetic Scripture

And God saw every thing that he had made, and, behold, it was very good... (Genesis 1:31).

Looking at the many things in creation that God created, we stand in awe at how wonderful they are. We are given the account of the six days of creation, where God listed all the things He made and said they were very good. Yet often overlooked is the day when light and darkness were separated, when God created "day." Sometimes, with all that goes on in the world we approach our day wondering what events may await us. Of course, every person has had what would seem like a bad day. However, God wants us to tap into a truth about how to have good day regardless of what occurs during it. Since the Lord made the day, we need to agree with Him and call it good. Psalms 118:24 says, "This is the day which the Lord hath made." This verse tells us how to make it a good day. It says, "...we will rejoice and be glad in it." What are we to be glad in? We are glad because it's a good day! Not long ago I heard one of my son's football coaches say, "Make today a good day!"

That is how we should live. Challenges can face us on any given day, but because the Lord made this day you can call it good and choose to make it a very good day!

Prayer

Dear Lord, You made everything, including today. I call this a good day by faith and I rejoice in it. I say right now, I shall have a very good day! In Jesus' Name, amen.

The Spirit of Jezebel Is Broken

"Rise up and break the power of a Jezebel spirit that would try to alter what I have spoken and break down your confidence. Don't allow it to change your beliefs. Its power is broken, so tolerate it no more!"

Prophetic Scripture

Nevertheless, I have this against you: You tolerate that woman Jezebel... (Revelation 2:20 NIV)

The Bible says that the Church of Thyatira was tolerating Jezebel. Obviously it wasn't the literal Jezebel of the Old Testament who by now was dead. It was the demonic spirit that once ruled through her. A spirit of Jezebel has two main goals: First, to attack the prophetic Word of the Lord. Literal Jezebel attacked it by killing God's prophets. She threatened Elijah with death (see 1 Kings 19:1-2). It affected his confidence so badly that he ran and hid. Second, Jezebel offers a tainted version of the truth. Revelation 2:20 says she did this at Thyatira. Because they tolerated it, perhaps out of wrong motives or even because of ignorance or fear, they were led astray.

Like Elijah, a Jezebel spirit attacks the prophetic word in your heart and uses circumstances to make you second-guess it. Secondly, it wants to make you question your beliefs so you will compromise, like Thyatira. To break its power, first get alone with God. Elijah got alone and heard again the Lord's voice to regain his confidence (see 1 Kings 19:9-15). Secondly, reaffirm what you believe from Scripture. Had Thyatira done that, they might not have tolerated her. Don't tolerate any hint of a Jezebel spirit. Rise up today and tell it to go in Jesus' Name!

Prayer

Father, open my eyes today to the operation of Jezebel against my life. I refuse to tolerate that spirit. I also reaffirm that I believe the prophetic words spoken over me and I hold fast to my biblical beliefs. I bind a Jezebel spirit, in Jesus' Name. Amen!

Sounds of Transformation

"Begin to watch what I am doing globally now. For there is a transformation taking place in My people. There will be new signs and new sounds, fresh revelation and vision. I am forming My glorious church and will do wondrous things through her."

Prophetic Scripture

This people have I formed for myself; they shall shew forth my praise (Isaiah 43:21).

God is always working to change you for the better and is doing the same in the entire Body of Christ. He will have for Himself a glorious Church. You may feel in your life today that you are not progressing or growing spiritually like you should. Maybe it seems like the Church itself is failing more than succeeding. Regardless of how it appears, God is forming you for Himself and is transforming the entire Body of Christ into something spectacular. You may not see the details now, because healthy growth is hard to notice on a daily basis. So even when you don't realize it, God is growing us. However, unlike we often do, God doesn't throw His hands in the air and say, "Oh, this isn't going to get anywhere; I give up!" No, the Bible says He finishes what He begins. Philippians 1:6 says, "Being confident of this very thing, that he which hath begun a good work in you will perform it until the day of Jesus Christ." In other words, God will not give up transforming His people. He will get what He is after and that is a people who are so transformed that a new sound will be heard in the land!

Prayer

Father, I pray for Your people today. Transform us into a people who will give praise to Your Name. Transform me, Lord, into a testimony each and every day, and I choose to be obedient to Your guidance as Your good work is performed in me. In Jesus' Name, amen.

Stable and Surefooted

"I cause you to stand this day, and I say your hands are strong and your knees are stable, making you sure-footed, so that no emotional or physical weakness shall be able to cripple you."

Prophetic Scripture

Strengthen ye the weak hands, and confirm the feeble knees (Isaiah 35:3).

It's notable that diseases like arthritis are receiving more attention these days. Perhaps arthritis is becoming more common, or perhaps it's that the medical community mixed with media advertising is creating more awareness. Either way, the exposure seems to have a prophetic significance for our time in history. It's a time when we see more believers falling away from their faith and confidence in the Lord. It's like a form of spiritual arthritis where their spiritual limbs feel weak and unable to stand. The prophet Isaiah gives a prophetic declaration over God's people by telling them to strengthen themselves. Obviously, he knew it wasn't something they could do alone, but as we see in the verse above he gives the initial instruction by opening with the word *strengthen*. The understood subject in that sentence is "you." I believe it means that overcoming the arthritic condition described begins with taking the first step and seeing yourself rising above it. From there, the power of God undergirds your decision and adds strength to you.

See yourself standing tall and getting stronger each day through the power of God. Even if you are dealing with actual physical arthritis, you can do the same. Once you see it in your heart, expect God's power to come along and cause you to stand stable and sure-footed.

Prayer

Heavenly Father, I see myself strong and well able to stand today. I command every arthritic condition to leave my life, and I picture myself completely strengthened by Your power—spirit, soul, and body! In Jesus Name, amen.

Rewards are Inevitable

"Have I not already promised blessing for the faithful? says the Lord. Blessings are upon your head for every faithful thing you have done, and you shall abound everywhere you turn. Watch and see it, says the Lord, and say this thing: My rewards are inevitable and shall be all around me!"

Prophetic Scripture

A faithful man shall abound with blessings… (Proverbs 28:20).

The key word in this verse in Proverbs is the word *abound.* To abound in something means you go beyond the normal limits. Of course, this verse didn't place any restrictions as to what part of our lives this abundance applies. We normally associate abundance with material things, and I definitely think that is a part of it. However, when you are faithful, abundance will apply to much more than that. For example, if you are faithful on your job, you may get a raise or promotion. Beyond that, you will gain favor and a good status with your boss. You also get a very good feeling inside when you have worked hard and done what is honorable. Faithfulness in anything we do will promote us into abundance. The same faithfulness toward God and spiritual things will promote you spiritually. You will become mature as a Christian and live with the confidence that you have pleased the Lord. Faithfulness is never a dead-end road. It will always promote you, so be confident that if you are being faithful, you will abound with many blessings from the Lord! Your reward of faithfulness is inevitable! Expect those rewards to manifest in your life today.

Prayer

Dear Lord, I thank You that many rewards are coming toward me today. I know that my faithfulness is paying off. Help me increase my level of faithfulness and I expect abundance to follow in every area of my life. In the Name of Jesus, amen!

Hardened to Difficulty

"Know that even what you overcame this year and the last, has strengthened you against difficulties. And things shall not sway you as before, for you have become an unrelenting warrior of My Spirit!"

Prophetic Scripture

Fear not [there is nothing to fear], for I am with you; do not look around you in terror and be dismayed, for I am your God. I will strengthen and harden you to difficulties, yes, I will help you; yes, I will hold you up and retain you with My [victorious] right hand of rightness and justice (Isaiah 41:10 AMP).

Dealing with the difficulties of life is like exercise. Once you press through it, the next time is easier. Similarly, once you have walked through a particular trial, you tend to respond differently to new challenges. Even though God didn't cause the trial, He still uses these hardships to our advantage. We get tougher in the spirit. We learn to wield our spiritual weapons, use discernment, and become more accurate with the Word of God. Then the next time something comes up you stand there with a new approach. You look at new problems with a hardened attitude and think, "Aww, been there before, done that, and wore the T-shirt!" That's how warriors respond to war—they get a little hardened to the pain of battle. Not because they want to be cold-hearted and mean, but the fierceness of war demands it. We need to look at our past trials and realize that, if we stayed connected to God through it all, these battles have made us stronger in the spirit and hardened to difficulty.

Prayer

Father, I ask You to take everything the devil meant to cause me harm and use it instead to make me a stronger spiritual warrior. Cause me to be fearless and hardened to difficulty so that I will always stand strong in You. In Jesus' Name, amen.

Your Words Are Heard

"Listen this day to what the Spirit says, for there are angels assigned in this hour who await your words. For even as your voice speaks My Word, so are your words heard in heaven and it shall be done even as you say."

Prophetic Scripture

...Thy words were heard, and I am come for thy words (Daniel 10:12).

There is a lot of speaking that goes on in the world in any given day. I think about some of the not so nice words I hear on television or in public, and I imagine how much God must get weary hearing all the bad things spoken every day worldwide. That said, I think God is anxious to hear our words when they line up with His Holy Word. I can picture the heavenly hosts and the Lord Himself just scanning the planet waiting to hear godly, Bible-based speech. In the story of Daniel, there was an angel who was literally assigned and waiting to go get Daniel's words. One reason is that Daniel was one of those who used his words correctly, so Heaven was eager to gather and utilize his words for a good purpose.

Undoubtedly, God and the angels are still waiting for God's words to be spoken through us from the earth (see Ps. 103:20). Words are powerful. God created the world with words. Proverbs 18:21 says that our words produce either life or death and even set nature in motion (see James 3:6). Prayer itself is a series of words. Amazingly, God uses human words to carry out His plans upon earth. Speak some words today that you want the angels to hear so they can be released to move. Remember today that your words are heard!

Prayer

Father, I release words of blessing today as I speak Your Word. Let my words be sweet in Your hearing and cause them to release the angels to bring to pass the things I say. In Jesus' Name, amen.

Faith on the Earth

"I am looking across the earth for faith, says the Lord. Will you be one of those who will exercise faith? Will you be one who will ask Me to do impossible things? For I say, I am looking for those of faith, and there shall be signs following them."

Prophetic Scripture

...Nevertheless when the Son of man cometh, shall he find faith on the earth? (Luke 18:8)

Someone once said, "There is something about God, that will pass by crowds of people, just to do a miracle for the one who will cry out in faith." We see this concept with the woman with the issue of blood in Mark 5:25-34. Weak from her condition, she pressed through a multitude. She pressed even when circumstances made it difficult, but her determined faith got the immediate attention of Jesus. Her faith literally pulled the power out of Him, causing Jesus to pause from the rest of the crowd and zero in on her. The disciples were like many of us and couldn't understand why Jesus took His attention off the multitude and put it on this woman. They didn't realize that Jesus had felt her pull of unrelenting faith!

God is looking across the earth right now for some believers who have unrelenting faith to believe that the power of God is going to sweep nations, cities, homes, and lives. God wants to show Himself strong for us, but He is looking to find some faith. Hebrews 11:6 says that you cannot please God without faith. So declare today, "Yes, Lord, You will find faith in me!"

Prayer

Dear Lord, I pray that I will be one of those in whom You will find unrelenting faith as You look across the globe. I exercise faith to see Your Spirit move in mighty signs, wonders, and miracles. Yes, Lord, you will find faith in me! Amen.

Discouragement Conquered

"Let not your heart be trodden down by anything. For though an enemy would desire to keep you disheartened in some things, I have caused a conquering spirit to rise from your heart, and you shall remove the head of discouragement this day!"

Prophetic Scripture

…But David encouraged himself in the Lord his God (1 Samuel 30:6).

Have you ever wondered how most of us would have felt if we were truly in David's shoes walking out to meet Goliath? We might have been like the rest of the crowd standing on the sidelines, probably thinking that little David was going to get whipped! I have always wondered if there had been even the tiniest bit of doubt trying to hit David's mind to make him have second thoughts as he marched out toward the giant. Perhaps not, but I am sure David, human like all of us, had to overcome some discouraging thoughts. He actually did so one time later when he experienced a terrible invasion by the Amalekites, and all his family members were kidnapped. David wept until he had no more strength to cry (see 1 Sam. 30:4). Yet somewhere that same conquering spirit he once had against Goliath rose up in David. He kept His eyes on God and began to find encouragement once again.

Perhaps there is a "Goliath" or some "Amalekites" attempting to discourage some areas of your life. Get your eyes back on the Lord and expect Him to cause a conquering spirit to rise up inside you. Expect to overcome and remove the source of all discouragement today!

Prayer

Father, I thank You that I have a conquering spirit. I make a choice to cast off the spirit of discouragement concerning _____.
Lord, help me see a new perspective, and I command every spirit of darkness that would try to dishearten me to leave! In Jesus' Name, amen!

APRIL 23

Gifts from the Father

"Watch today as I show you fatherly love. For I am the Giver of gifts and I always have something to bless you with. As your Father, expect from Me a lasting supply of good things."

Prophetic Scripture

Every good gift and every perfect gift is from above, and cometh down from the Father of lights, with whom is no variableness, neither shadow of turning (James 1:17).

Not everyone grew up with a great example for a father. Some had such negative fatherly experiences that it still remains hard for them to relate to a father figure. However, even those who grew up with a positive fatherly experience still only have a limited view of true fathering. That is because all of us on earth can only relate to an earthly father having some measure of human shortcomings. Without divine revelation, none of us can relate fully to the incredible nature and love of our heavenly Father.

Jesus expounded on our lack of understanding when it comes to grasping what a true father is. In Matthew 7:7-11, He talks about asking and receiving, and He says that when you ask you can expect to receive because you are asking your heavenly Father. Then He compares our heavenly Father to natural fathers by saying that if a natural father can give good things and supply all the basic needs for their children, then how *much more* will our heavenly Father give? In other words, our heavenly Father will give far beyond even what the best natural father can do. Ask the Lord to give you a divine revelation of the goodness of your Father today and that He will always supply and give you good things!

Prayer

Dear heavenly Father, I ask You for a revelation of You as my heavenly Father. Give me a true understanding of what that means. As my Father, I trust You for good things and a reliable supply for everything I need. In Jesus' Name, amen!

Generational Curses Shattered!

"The Spirit says, for I have made you the seed of blessing to break the generational stronghold over your bloodline. As you run toward righteousness, so shall the power of the curse against your descendants come to an end."

Prophetic Scripture

Know therefore that the Lord thy God, he is God, the faithful God, which keepeth covenant and mercy with them that love him and keep his commandments to a thousand generations (Deuteronomy 7:9).

Generational curses don't exist because God punishes the children for the sins of their parents (see Deut. 24:16). What happens is that the sins of parents are often picked up by the children, and the effects of sin get passed down from one generation to the next. When a parent has a sinful lifestyle, the children often follow that pattern. Because of this tendency we see God having to punish the sins of families several generations in a row. Typically in Scripture it lasted four generations (see Exod. 20:5; Num. 14:18). We who are born again are literally inducted into a new bloodline through the blood of Jesus (see 2 Cor. 5:17). As we draw closer to Him and choose to shed our old lifestyle, we break the curse from our natural family line (see Rom. 8:1). This becomes the seed of righteousness for our descendants. Then Deuteronomy 7:9 says that God will keep His covenant with us for a thousand generations. This generational blessing is much more powerful than the curse, which only extends to four generations.

To break the generational curse against your bloodline, begin by living a righteous lifestyle. Then speak a blessing over your bloodline and command every curse to be broken. You are a righteous seed for every generational curse to come to an end!

Prayer

Father, I thank You that I am in the bloodline of Christ and am the righteous seed for my descendants. I command every curse over my family line to be broken, and I declare a generational blessing to be upon it. In Jesus' Name, amen!

Walls of Salvation

"Fear not, says the Lord. I have surrounded you with a strong wall of protection and it shall keep out all manner of unforeseen invasion. As you rejoice in My wall of salvation for you, be confident that the forces of lack and disease cannot fall suddenly upon you."

Prophetic Scripture

In that day, everyone in the land of Judah will sing this song: Our city is strong! We are surrounded by the walls of God's salvation (Isaiah 26:1 NLT).

Most of us associate the word *salvation* with the peace in our hearts that comes from knowing the Lord. We also associate it with the fact that we are promised eternity in Heaven. With both of these in our lives, we are saved or have experienced salvation. While salvation includes both of these things, it is even more extensive. In Isaiah 26:1, it is literally the Hebrew word *Yeshua* which is Jesus. It means aid, deliverance, health, well-being, victory, and prosperity. We shouldn't just think of these attributes as something that we will only enjoy someday. This form of salvation is available now because it is who Jesus is! He is in you, so you are surrounded with all the things the word *salvation* describes. However, the verse above says that He (salvation) will surround you like a wall that nothing can invade. We see in the verse above that when this revelation entered the hearts of everyone in Judah, they got so excited they turned it into a song!

Have faith and begin rejoicing that the salvation wall of Jesus Christ surrounds you. This wall is complete deliverance and it prevents every form of evil from invading your life today!

Prayer

Father, I rejoice in the wall of salvation I have in Jesus Christ today! Help me grow my faith in this wonderful truth. I decree that the wall of salvation surrounds me and I am protected from all invasion. In Jesus' Name, amen!

Momentum Shall Increase

"Don't revert back from your place of faith this day. This is not a time to go back or think that all is lost. For as you stay firm in faith, I will even place the wind at your back and momentum shall increase for you."

Prophetic Scripture

Now the just shall live by faith: but if any man draw back, my soul shall have no pleasure in him (Hebrews 10:38).

The reason many people never experience the full blessing of the Lord is because they don't keep pressing into it in spite of resistance. This world is all about resistance. You can't come into success without some hurdles. Thinking of all the times I fly in an airplane, I always think of the resistance it takes for the jet to get off the ground. The level of thrust has to be stronger than the power of gravity. The plane has to push hard to get off the ground before it can ever reach its cruising altitude. For many of us, that push off the ground is the time when we want to call it quits. It seems like the time to change occupations, give up on school, move to a new town, or quit tithing. It seems like the time to quit standing in faith for our answer to prayer

Perhaps we don't need to change any of those things, we just need to stay the course until the momentum kicks in. God will add momentum to our faith, but too many times we draw back before that happens. It's what happened to Israel in the wilderness. They quit pressing into the Promised Land when it looked like their basic necessities were in jeopardy. Don't draw back today even though the resistance may be fierce. God will help you obtain the promise today!

Prayer

Lord, I make a sound decision to press in by faith. I will not draw back away from the promises or the things I know shall come to pass in this season. Help me press in until I gain the spiritual momentum You have for me. Amen.

I Am Anointed!

*"So say this day that you are anointed! For My presence goes everywhere you go, and the Holy Ghost upon you shall liberate the hearts and minds of those who are oppressed. Yes, say this day, **I am anointed**!"*

Prophetic Scripture

How God anointed Jesus of Nazareth with the Holy Ghost and with power: who went about doing good, and healing all that were oppressed of the devil; for God was with him (Acts 10:38).

Exodus 33:11 says Moses met God face to face. It wasn't that he literally saw God's face, because God tells him that no one can see it and live (see Exod. 33:20). It means Moses was communing directly in God's presence. You would think this was the highest possible encounter one could have with God. However, it must not have been, because later Moses begs God to reveal His glory to him (see Exod. 33:18). Why did he act as though something was still missing? Unlike us, Moses had not experienced the glory within him. When he left the tabernacle where God was, he didn't have the same presence there with him. In addition to the glory without, we who are in Christ experience the glory within everywhere we go! Moses would have dreamed to know what that was like. It's what Jesus communicated to the woman at the well in John 4:21-23. It wasn't about going to a particular location to meet God, but rather having God in you everywhere you go. Jesus had that glory and anointing everywhere He went, and it caused the oppressed to go free.

Because Jesus lives in you, you are anointed without and within. That same glory and power goes everywhere you do! So say this today, "I am anointed!"

Prayer

Dear Lord, I thank You that Your glory is within me today everywhere I go. I shall use it to do good and minister to those who need it. I declare today, I am anointed! In Jesus' Name, amen.

Your Heart Is Strong

"I declare that your heart is strong. The Spirit says, I fix your heart, I heal your heart, and I make it strong and stable. With every beat, My glory is empowering your heart!"

Prophetic Scripture

Be of good courage, and he shall strengthen your heart, all ye that hope in the Lord (Psalms 31:24).

Physical heart conditions are a worldwide problem and are a clear sign of a spiritual root problem. People's hearts have trouble standing up under the stress of modern living (see Luke 21:26). The human heart is the life center of the body and your natural heart and spiritual heart are uniquely intertwined. Of course, while things like eating right and exercise are important for having a healthy physical heart, the condition of your spiritual heart also directly affects the health of your physical heart. Among the medical recommendations for having a healthy heart is the need for some form of emotional and spiritual wholeness. Scientists realize that your emotional state, or you could say the condition of your spiritual heart, greatly affects the stress level on your natural heart.

As believers, we can tap into God's ability to strengthen our natural hearts and thereby causing our physical hearts to be strong and healthy. Psalm 31:24 reminds us to be of good courage and to hope in the Lord. This means instead of doing what most of the world does by getting worked up over the stresses of this modern age, we can take a deep breath and rest in the Mighty God we serve.

Relax in the Lord today and let Him strengthen your heart. Feel your heartbeat right now and declare your heart to be both spiritually and physically strong!

Prayer

Dear Lord, I have a strong heart today. I rest in You regarding all that concerns me. Let Your power touch my heart both spiritually and physically with strength and healing. In Jesus' Name, amen.

Throw Your Cares Aside

"Have I not said, throw your cares upon Me? Even this day, throw them My way; I can handle all your anxieties for you!"

Prophetic Scripture

Casting all your care upon him; for he careth for you (1 Peter 5:7).

Most of us, when throwing a baseball, never think to throw it softly. Unless you are tossing a ball to a toddler, you always try to throw the ball as hard and far as you can! When the Lord taught us to cast our cares on Him, this was the picture. Not to sound disrespectful, but God isn't a toddler. He can handle a fastball!

On one of my very first jobs, I worked as a bank teller. At the end of one day, my cash drawer was short a large sum of money. I and my supervisors did everything we knew to locate the error, but couldn't. It was Friday evening, and I left work filled with worry, fearing I would be fired and knowing I had to bear the thought all weekend. I decided to cast the fear on the Lord and determined not think about it over the weekend. That was hard to do, but each time the thought returned, I resisted it. By the middle of the weekend, I thought of something both I and my supervisors overlooked! I told them on Monday, and sure enough another account we hadn't balanced yet was over by the very amount I was short and all the money was accounted for.

I believe casting my care on the Lord gave me the revelation of the answer, enabling me to have a great weekend. Go ahead—throw your worries on the Lord with confidence today! He can handle them!

Prayer

Father, I cast all my fear and anxieties on You right now! I refuse to be worried and I resist every fearful thought. I know You are taking care of me. In the Name of Jesus, amen.

Your Crown of Life

"Know that even as I endured, so I cause you to endure temptation. Let Me show you this day a picture of your crown of life and know that it shall energize you to endure for a victorious win."

Prophetic Scripture

Blessed is the man that endureth temptation: for when he is tried, he shall receive the crown of life, which the Lord hath promised to them that love him (James 1:12).

Temptation is any kind of test that makes giving in to sin and failure hard to resist. It isn't always easy to overcome, but we aren't alone. We see the devil sorely tempting Jesus for 40 straight days in Luke 4:2-13. These wouldn't have been legitimate temptations if Jesus wasn't tempted to give in, and they weren't the only things Jesus was tempted with during His life. Hebrews 4:15 tells us that Jesus was tempted with all the same things we are, yet He overcame them. One of the reasons Jesus was able to overcome temptation was He took His eyes off the temptation and put them on spiritual things. Hebrews 12:2 says Jesus was able to endure the cross because He kept His focus on the prize that was to come afterward. James 1:12 says we, too, are promised a prize for enduring. We have a crown waiting for us, and by looking past the temptation and focusing on the crown we can overcome whatever temptation is lurking out there.

The Holy Spirit wants to give you a spiritual vision of your heavenly crown today. Let that focus energize and empower you to endure and finish in victory!

Prayer

Father, I keep my eyes on the crown that awaits me. Help me to get a glimpse of it so that I can keep my focus on the glorious reward that awaits me. I declare I shall overcome all forms of temptation. In Jesus' Name, amen.

Plant Righteousness in Your Land

"Know that even as I used the prophet Jeremiah over nations to root out and plant, so have I called you to root out that which prevents the move of My Spirit across your land. Yes, root out the strongholds and plant the crop of righteousness with the decree of your mouth."

Prophetic Scripture

See, I have this day set thee over the nations and over the kingdoms, to root out, and to pull down, and to destroy, and to throw down, to build, and to plant (Jeremiah 1:10).

When God called Jeremiah, he was to speak over the nations. God used his words to literally remove wickedness and plant righteousness in those places. In a similar way, we the church can decree and speak over our land through the spirit of prayer. We can root out things preventing the move of God and plant seeds of righteousness. Our decrees over our cities and nations help plow the way for revival and the success of our ministry efforts. In Colossians 4:3, Paul says, "Withal praying also for us, that God would open unto us a door of utterance, to speak the mystery of Christ." He was asking the church to speak into the realm of the spirit so regions would begin to open up and receive his ministry.

Every believer can help prosper the work of God's Kingdom simply by decreeing and speaking in their own prayer times. If you live in a crime-ridden city or neighborhood, decree that violence must leave your streets. Then speak peace and safety and ask God to send Gospel laborers. Let's all do our part in this hour. It's time to plant righteousness in our land today!

Prayer

Lord, I decree that _____ is uprooted from my region/nation and I plant a harvest of _____ that shall always grow where I live. I say the Gospel shall go forth successfully here. In Jesus' Name, amen.

MAY 2

Extravagance and Splendor

"Many of My people ask too little from Me, says the Lord. Surely, I am the Lord of extravagance and splendor who owns all the resources of the earth. Ask even more from Me in this season, so that I may sustain your living and prosper the ministry."

Prophetic Scripture

And the twelve gates were twelve pearls: every several gate was of one pearl: and the street of the city was pure gold, as it were transparent glass (Revelation 21:21).

When you look at the Old Testament tabernacle, even in the temple of Solomon you see structures that were created with such a level of extravagance that it is hard for our modern minds to even picture such splendor. Entire furnishings were made of absolutely pure gold. Most people today can't even afford to buy a tiny ounce of gold, which is about the size of two quarters. Yet God is building furniture with solid gold! But that isn't all. If you take a glance at Heaven, we find the streets paved with gold and the gates covered by large pricey pearls. God has some pretty elaborate things!

A lot of people believe that God doesn't want us to have anything that is too fancy, and yes, the Bible does draw attention to how materialism gets people's focus away from God. However, not everyone is bound to materialism, and there are some good-hearted believers and ministries who will use these resources for God. *Average* has held the Body of Christ back in many things. I believe to help prosper the Gospel, we need to tap into the "extravagance and splendor" side of the Lord. Let's stop asking Him for too little and expect a measure of resources that removes the limitations we have known.

Prayer

Lord, I ask You to provide a new level of resources for Your people. Lord, even as you bless me in a greater way, I commit to make the Gospel my first priority. In Jesus' Name, amen.

Demonstrations Are Here!

"It's time now for My people not to just talk about My power, but to demonstrate it, says the Spirit. Yes, step out in miracles, make a practice of signs and wonders. For the demonstrations of God are here!"

Prophetic Scripture

And my speech and my preaching was not with enticing words of man's wisdom, but in demonstration of the Spirit and of power (1 Corinthians 2:4).

Often we talk about the power of God and how it was displayed so powerfully in the lives of those in the Bible, historical figures, and in books. But God didn't stop these demonstrations with the early church era, or even a few decades ago. He manifests supernatural demonstrations because we are willing to step out on the edge and do something that causes Him to move. The early disciples demonstrated the power of God because they took a risk. God wants to manifest miracles for those who will just step out.

You'll need to start small before you can graduate up to the boldness of the early apostles. They did some bold things in the Book of Acts, but they had lots of practice under the ministry of Jesus first! You can begin with things like just offering to pray for someone who needs healing or perhaps sow a larger than normal offering and expect a breakthrough in your finances. Do something that reveals your confidence in God to act on your behalf. You don't have to wait and wonder if miracles will come. The demonstrations of God are already here! Just step out and watch the Lord display His power. The more you do, the more you will see demonstrations of God in your life!

Prayer

Lord, I believe Your demonstrations of the Spirit are upon me today! I believe for healing, revelation, deliverance, financial breakthrough, dreams, visions, and many wonders of Your power. Teach me how to demonstrate that anointing. In Jesus' Name, amen!

Grow Your Miracle!

"Begin to grow your miracle one seed at a time, says the Lord. Yes, it grows even according to your ability to believe it. So remove unbelief by nurturing one seed of faith from My Word today."

Prophetic Scripture

...If ye have faith as a grain of mustard seed, ye shall say unto this mountain, Remove hence to yonder place; and it shall remove; and nothing shall be impossible unto you (Matthew 17:20).

In Matthew 17:14-21, the disciples tried to cast out a demon but couldn't. They had the power because Jesus had already given it to them (see Matt. 10:1). Knowing this, the disciples were dumbfounded about why it wouldn't work. Jesus explained that even though they had the power, unbelief was preventing it. This is where many believers live. They know they have power, but struggle to produce miraculous results. Jesus gives the key in Matthew 17:20, saying, "If you have faith as a grain of mustard." Jesus wasn't telling them that if you have tiny faith like a mustard seed that is all you need. This doesn't make sense because He already told them that they had unbelief, which the Amplified Bible refers to as "the littleness of your faith." Jesus wouldn't tell them their faith was too little, then say they only needed a tiny bit of faith. He was saying that while a grain begins small, the miracle is not in its size but in its growth potential. The disciples needed to take that tiny bit of faith and grow it for that kind of miracle.

You can take your tiny seed of faith today and grow it by nurturing it and watering it with promises of faith from God's Word. When you do, it will grow up, and before you know it you will have grown a miracle!

Prayer

Father, I take the following verse from Your Word _____ and I water my faith for a miracle in the area of _____. I say today that I shall grow this miracle! In Jesus' Name, amen.

Honored and Exalted

"I look at your efforts toward humility and even all the times when you took the lower position for My Name's sake. So now I am going to honor you publicly on multiple occasions very soon."

Prophetic Scripture

Humble yourselves therefore under the mighty hand of God, that he may exalt you in due time (1 Peter 5:6).

The world teaches you to scramble as hard as you can to make it to the top. Of course, there is nothing wrong with hard work, but our goals should never be to try and gain a big name for ourselves so we can enjoy the praise of man. God does exalt people, but His way of doing so does not come through our own human efforts; it comes because we choose humility. I remember years ago when we were first starting in the ministry, someone gave us a prophecy that said, "I am seeing how low you are willing to bow to see how high I might raise you, says the Lord!" Well, that wasn't the most exciting word we ever received, and we wondered just what kind of bowing down the Lord was really expecting! Well, in the years to follow, we definitely experienced our fair share of humble pie. But I look back on all those years and realize that I couldn't stand in ministry today without those humbling experiences.

You see, God has a place of honor for you today. It may not look like that of anyone else, but He has a plan to exalt you nevertheless. Your choices to humble yourself will pay off eventually, and God will exalt you for His purposes in due time!

Prayer

Father, I make a decision to humble myself today under Your mighty hand. Erase all forms of pride from my heart and help me to handle it well when you honor me, even as promised in Your Word. In Jesus' Name, amen.

Come Out!

"Command now every evil spirit that would try to remain this day to leave, and they will obey you! Wherever demonic power has tried to enter in, tell it to come out! Tell them, says the Spirit, and watch them flee from you!"

Prophetic Scripture

For he said unto him, Come out of the man, thou unclean spirit (Mark 5:8).

There are two keys words to secure your own deliverance from evil spirits. We often say them when ministering deliverance for others, but forget to speak them when demon powers want to meddle in our business. Those simple words are "Come out!" You can command unclean spirits to leave your mind, your body, your finances, your workplace, and wherever else they may be trying to gain access. Too often when we see something wrong in our life or surroundings, we deal with it passively. We casually try to ignore it or even pray a little about it. Yet sometimes you have to just wake up one day and realize that this is the devil! When Jesus met up with the demonized man in Mark 5, He had no trouble recognizing the devil was at work. Of course, sometimes the devil doesn't hang around in an obvious way like that, all dressed in a shiny red devil suit. He comes subtly until you get used to him hanging around. So how do you know for sure it's the devil? Because the devil and evil go together. If it's bad and evil, it's probably got a demon nearby cheering it on! Don't let him set up shop at your house! James 4:7 says to resist him and he will have to flee! Tell that devil to just "Come out!"

Prayer

Father, I thank You that I have authority over the evil one because Jesus gave it to me. I make a choice to resist the devil today. I speak to every demon and command them to leave in the Name of Jesus! Devil, come out!

Prophetic Light

"Ask Me to reveal your steps in a prophetic light, for I have things to show you concerning your life in advance. First you shall sense them, then others will come confirm them, and thereafter they shall come to pass!"

Prophetic Scripture

For with thee is the fountain of life: in thy light shall we see light (Psalms 36:9).

Did you know that God is not purposely trying to keep you in the dark about your life? He not only wants to discuss your present and even future destiny, He also wants you to begin to see things in a prophetic light. Too often God cannot open up the secrets of the spirit realm to us because we are so busy ordering our life only after what we can see all around us. The same thing happened with the servant of Elisha in Second Kings 6 and 7. His servant was so busy looking at his surroundings that he didn't have any prophetic revelation. Notice that God didn't automatically give the revelation until Elisha asked. Sometimes we don't ask God to give us prophetic insight, so we only get a natural perspective. However, once Elisha's servant was able to see into the spirit and get God's view on the situation, it changed everything! He suddenly realized that things were not as bad as they seemed.

Think what could happen if we saw some situations in a prophetic light like that. Like Elisha, we can ask the Lord to open our eyes to see His viewpoint. If you feel like you are in the dark about some things, ask God to shed prophetic light on that situation. Then trust that things around you are going to take on a new outlook!

Prayer

Heavenly Father, I ask You to give me a new prophetic insight. Help me to see the world around me from a spiritual viewpoint, and I expect to see things from this moment forward from Your perspective. In Jesus' Name, amen.

Right on Time

"Be assured that I am working in perfect timing for you. I have set your course and timed each step, so stand now and know that your much-needed answer will not be late!"

Prophetic Scripture

For yet a little while, and he that shall come will come, and will not tarry (Hebrews 10:37).

When you're really desperate for an answer from God, it can be tempting to start thinking the Lord will not respond in time. I once heard someone say a humorous line about the timing of God. They said, "God is never late, but He sure is last-minute!" Sometimes it feels like the Lord is going to miss the window of time for a much-needed miracle. I am sure there were many people in the Old Testament who wondered why it was taking so long for the promised Messiah to appear. After all, couldn't God see all the problems occurring? Without a doubt, many were convinced that the time for the Messiah had to be now! Yet it was to be years before His appearing. They probably were like many of us and thought God had not come through in time.

What we need to know about the timing of God is that God is eternal and sees everything from that perspective. He knows that the events of today are never the final answer. God is not about making you suffer, but realize that the miracle answer will not be late. If you trust that today, your confidence will agree with His perfect timing and you'll realize that things really are well with you. The bottom line is that *He will come* and His answer will never be late!

Prayer

Dear heavenly Father, I thank You that You have perfect timing for every-thing. I trust Your timing and I know that the answer I need will not be late. Thank You, Lord, that You are always right on time. In Jesus' Name, amen!

MAY 9

Ears Be Opened

"I am opening your hearing now, says the Lord. So shall you even begin to hear sounds that you have not heard before. There shall be sounds in the spirit and sounds in the natural, so let your ears be open to them."

Prophetic Scripture

Then the eyes of the blind shall be opened, and the ears of the deaf shall be unstopped (Isaiah 35:5).

The Bible talks a lot about both natural and spiritual hearing. God wants both levels of your hearing to be keen. Jesus regularly cast out demon spirits that caused physical deafness, which is a prophetic indicator that God wants us to hear, not only in the natural realm, but also in the spirit. In Mark 4:23, Jesus said, "If any man have ears to hear, let him hear." He was speaking of our ability to hear into the spirit and know things from that perspective. Jesus continues in Mark 4:24 saying, "Unto you that hear shall more be given." He was saying that he who tunes his spiritual hearing to the spirit will continue hearing these sounds and gain heavenly insight. He continually demonstrated, not only through this teaching but also by healing deaf people, that God wants all facets of our hearing to be opened. The devil wants to impede both levels of our hearing as a tactic to plant a mind-set of deafness on the church.

Make a practice of tuning your spiritual ears to the spirit, and if you have a natural ear condition that hinders your physical hearing, picture yourself with the ability to hear. Command every spirit of deafness to leave all realms of your hearing and expect your ears to be unstopped.

Prayer

Father, I know it is Your will for a spirit of hearing to be upon Your people. I tell both my natural and spiritual ear to hear! I command every deaf spirit to leave all levels of my hearing right now. In Jesus' Name, amen!

Born to Be Radical

"I have not called you to blend in but stand out, says the Spirit. For you have been born to radically represent godliness and the miraculous, and I have put a resounding message in your mouth that I have reserved for this time."

Prophetic Scripture

...Even for this same purpose have I raised thee up, that I might shew my power in thee, and that my name might be declared throughout all the earth (Romans 9:17).

This Scripture was written to Pharaoh in the days of Moses to show that God raises people up for His purpose. Not only does God raise up servants like Moses, but He also raises up other figures, such as Pharaoh, so that His glory might be manifest. God sets up the scene and is in control of who does what. This means that the Lord will always have a vessel of some form ready for whatever the season upon the earth might be.

Even in the days when Jesus was about to make His triumphal entry into Jerusalem, He told His disciples to find a little donkey that was tied up in a nearby town (see Luke 19:30). Sure enough, the donkey was there! Even this little, seemingly insignificant donkey was born for a radical purpose and was in the right place at the right time! If the Lord can raise up Pharaoh and a little donkey, what can He do with us, His vessels of righteousness? You have been born to stand out in a radical way. Your birth was no accident. You have a unique part to play with a unique message that has been reserved for no other time in history! You were born to be radical for God.

Prayer

Father, I know that I have been born for no other time in history. My birth was no accident, and I am a unique message for this hour. Help me to walk it out because I am born to be radical for You! Amen!

Tear the Mountain Down!

"The Spirit says, do not be shaken by the obstacles before you, neither look at the mountain that stands in your way. Know that I am against these things to consume them, so it's time for you to shout aloud and tear the mountain down!"

Prophetic Scripture

Behold, I am against thee, O destroying mountain, saith the Lord, which destroyest all the earth: and I will stretch out mine hand upon thee, and roll thee down from the rocks, and will make thee a burnt mountain (Jeremiah 51:25).

Jeremiah 51 describes how God would rise up against Babylon. While this chapter speaks of literal ancient Babylon, Revelation 17 depicts its symbolic sense, which is that Babylon always represents sin and resistance to God. Jeremiah 51:25 says God will burn the mountain of Babylon. Then in Zechariah 4:7, the prophet also tells the mountain that it will become a plain, meaning that it will be destroyed. Mountains always speak of something considered immoveable, so God destroying it makes the statement that all resistance must bow to Him. The next question is, what method did God use to destroy this resistant mountain? Zechariah 4:7 says the Lord instructed Zerubbabel to shout at the mountain and cry grace to it. This brings more understanding to when Jesus told His disciples they could literally speak to the mountain to remove it (see Mark 11:23-24). He was showing that they had the power to tear the mountain down or remove resistance by speaking.

You have the ability speak to the mountain resisting you. It may be tempting to just keep looking at it and give in to worry, but Jesus gave you the power to speak to it. Go ahead, shout and tear the mountain down!

Prayer

Father, I make the decision to take my eyes off every obstacle that would resist me. I tell the mountain of _____ to leave today. I shout grace and say the mountain shall become a plain! In the Name of Jesus, amen!

Quench Not the Spirit!

"This is not the hour to quench the supernatural manifestations of My hand, nor is it the time to be ashamed of the most unusual things I will do. So be prepared for unusual wonders if you will welcome and acknowledge My Spirit wherever it might work among you."

Prophetic Scripture

Quench not the spirit (1 Thessalonians 5:19).

There are many ways people quench the Holy Spirit, and some have done so out of a well-meaning heart. Often pre-conceived ideas and teachings have caused people to quench the Holy Spirit. They are afraid that they will get mixed up in something false. Still others quench Him because they think some people will not understand or may become fearful of the Lord moving in a supernatural way. However, we need to know that the darker things become in the world, the more we need the power of God to work in a real and tangible way. If the Holy Spirit wants to give us visions or bring about a miraculous healing, then we should welcome it even when it manifests in an unusual fashion. The way to recognize the difference between the genuine work of the Holy Spirit and something false is by comparing it to what God did in the Bible. In the Bible, God did many unusual signs and wonders, so we should not think it odd to experience them today. He used these unusual and undeniable wonders to even convince the most defiant of unbelievers. We find in Scripture that in the last days these manifestations will increase and the church must embrace this work of the Holy Spirit like never before. So don't quench or hide the Holy Spirit's work, but let Him burn like a fire around your life today!

Prayer

Holy Spirit, I welcome the unusual wonders from You today. When I see Your unusual wonders, I will not be ashamed, but I will give You all the praise. Work in my life today. Amen!

Bitterness Uprooted

"It's time to let go of all forms of resentment, says the Lord. Be not like some who have allowed it to take root by holding onto hurts. Release them so the results that bitterness produces will be uprooted from your life."

Prophetic Scripture

Exercise foresight and be on the watch to look [after one another], to see that no one falls back from and fails to secure God's grace (His unmerited favor and spiritual blessing), in order that no root of resentment (rancor, bitterness, or hatred) shoots forth and causes trouble and bitter torment, and the many become contaminated and defiled by it (Hebrews 12:15 AMP).

When you've had a hurtful or tragic experience, bitterness or resentment can grow in your heart unknowingly. Sometimes it's not even toward people, but toward the Lord. Many have this form of bitterness. However, not recognizing any form of bitterness is a danger we all face. It's a resentful poison almost impossible to remove once deeply rooted. Some are so poisoned by bitterness they can't have a normal conversation without spewing venom. While not every form is this bad, all bitterness carries the potential to grow to this level. We can be easily blinded to ourselves, so we need others who can spot when bitterness is trying to take root.

If you can't quit rehearsing the bad that happened, it's likely bitterness is trying to take root. Its effects can be devastating and according to Hebrews 12:15, can even threaten our very salvation. Ask God to help you uproot it, then make every effort to move on. Nothing compares to the peace that comes from removing bitterness from your heart. Let it be uprooted today!

Prayer

Heavenly Father, I ask You to reveal all forms of bitterness that would try to take hold in my heart. Forgive me for letting any hurt or resentment fill my thoughts. I command every root of bitterness to be uprooted from my life today! Amen!

Cured from the Incurable

"What man cannot cure, I shall heal. The incurable heart, mind, and body is to be cured in those who will trust and believe in the supernatural power of Jesus' Name!"

Prophetic Scripture

And Jesus was going about all Galilee teaching in their synagogues, and proclaiming the good news of the reign, and healing every disease, and every malady among the people (Matthew 4:23 YLT).

Notice the word *malady* in the verse above, according to Young's Literal Translation. Webster's dictionary defines the word *malady* as some form of incurable disease or chronic and lingering disorder. Jesus was known for healing lepers, those with palsy, the blind and lame, all of which were incurable conditions. There was no medical solution for healing any of these particular conditions. Therefore, people flocked to Jesus because He had the answer to heal the incurable. Through individual examples in the Bible, we often see that those healed expressed faith in His healing power specifically for themselves. Today, we believe in Jesus' healing power for us specifically through the power of His spoken Name. His Name represents His abiding authority in the earth, and when we speak it with the same expression of faith those in the Bible had, healing from incurable conditions is still available. Countless modern-day testimonies attest to this truth.

In the areas where you need healing in your heart, mind, or body today, the power of Jesus' Name is available. Jesus' Name heals because it is a supernatural name! Begin to see His Name driving incurable conditions from your life and from the lives of those you love today.

Prayer

Lord, I thank You that Jesus' Name heals every incurable condition today. I declare my heart, soul, and body healed. I say that the power of Jesus' Name heals me! Amen!

Hindrances Are Bound

"This day I am binding the power of hindering spirits from creating those aggravating troubles and harassments. Yes, peace is your portion and the chaos comes to a rest, says the Lord!"

Prophetic Scripture

Wherefore we would have come unto you, even I Paul, once and again; but Satan hindered us (1 Thessalonians 2:18).

Paul experienced a lot of trouble against His ministry. Not only was he vehemently persecuted, but it seems that everywhere he went the devil was busy stirring up little problems and aggravating issues to try and prevent the success of his ministry. In First Thessalonians 2:18, when Paul said he was hindered, Strong's Concordance describes the word as an obstacle that blocks what is needed. Paul said it kept happening over and over again. It isn't until First Thessalonians 3:10-11 that we see God remove these hindrances so Paul could get where he intended to go. What finally made the difference? First, verse 10 says his group began to pray intensely, probably because he was tired of the harassment and began to pray some "enough is enough" kind of prayers! Suddenly in verse 11, we see God Himself stepping in with an anointing specifically to remove these hindrances. The divine power of Heaven radically stepped in and brought all the chaos to rest!

If you have felt hindered today by constant little troubles and harassments trying to prevent you from succeeding, God is ready to bring these little fires from the enemy to an end. Begin with determined prayer, but then call upon the Lord for it to stop. If those harassing spirits had to get out of the way for Paul, they shall surely move for you too!

Prayer

Lord, I believe today that You are stepping in the middle of my situation to remove hindering spirits. I declare that every harassment and aggravating form of trouble must stop and that I am going to succeed! In Jesus' Name, amen!

Excess Measure of Blessing

"I shall make good what I have said for those who tithe. Even as I have said and say again that a window opens from heaven to pour out for you an excess measure of blessing."

Prophetic Scripture

Bring ye all the tithes into the storehouse, that there may be meat in mine house, and prove me now herewith, saith the Lord of hosts, if I will not open you the windows of heaven, and pour you out a blessing, that there shall not be room enough to receive it (Malachi 3:10).

I have heard many arguments against tithing (giving 10 percent of your income to God), but I made a personal decision long ago to tithe for two main reasons: First, Hebrews 7:8 says Jesus is alive as the eternal high priest and is still collecting tithes. If that is true, then who am I to argue? Second, I have experienced the excess measure of blessings from tithing that Malachi 3:10 talks about. One time when we were first starting in ministry and didn't have much money, a farmer friend butchered a cow and unexpectedly gave us two coolers full of meat! That was not only a blessing, but we had to go buy a new freezer to store it! It was an excess measure of blessing that was more than we had room for!

I once heard a well-renowned Christian counselor say that in his experience working with marriages, the couples who tithe have far fewer financial problems than those who don't. There is a promise of blessing caused by tithing that cross-pollinates into many areas of our lives, both seen and unseen. Trust the Lord's promise for you as a tither, because an excess measure of blessing is truly yours!

Prayer

Lord Jesus, as my heavenly High Priest, I place the tithe into Your hands. I trust Your promise that I shall live in blessing of excess measure all the days of my life. Amen!

Under His Power!

"These are the days of My Spirit for which many shall be caught up under the influence of My tangible presence. Yes, My people shall be caught up to heavenly realms and enter the spirit more frequently in this season. Watch even those you do not expect, for even they too shall fall under My divine power!"

Prophetic Scripture

I was in the Spirit on the Lord's day, and heard behind me a great voice, as of a trumpet (Revelation 1:10).

Many shy away from supernatural encounters with God that human power cannot control. Yet these occurrences were frequent in the New Testament, so they do have their place today. Many early Christians experienced it, causing their natural faculties to be temporarily suspended under the power of God. During visions, both Paul and Peter experienced a trance-like state (see Acts 10:10; 22:17). Paul and John were both caught up into the realm of the spirit (see 2 Cor. 12:2; Rev. 1:10). We even see the Roman guards fall under God's power when they came to arrest Jesus (see John 18:6). Of course, we should clarify that while we welcome this type of experience, we don't want to go so far overboard that we get off base and begin to behave disorderly. Others get so excessive with "falling under God's power" that they start to borderline on cultish practices. There are always the extremes, but we don't want to eliminate the genuine because of them.

While this kind of manifestation can be unusual at times, if it's genuine you don't have to try and make it happen and it will accomplish miraculous results. We should welcome and expect these occurrences to play a key role in bringing God's tangible presence to the world.

Prayer

Holy Spirit, I welcome the genuine manifestations of Your presence upon people in a very supernatural way just like is seen in the Bible. Manifest in my own life this way, and help lost people to be drawn to You through it. Amen.

Speak to the Wind

"Rise up, and command the wind to blow upon your dead hopes and dreams. For even the things you have given up on in your heart this year, I have prepared a heavenly wind to breathe life upon them again. So speak this day to the wind!"

Prophetic Scripture

Then said he unto me, Prophesy unto the wind, prophesy, son of man, and say to the wind, Thus saith the Lord God; Come from the four winds, O breath, and breathe upon these slain, that they may live (Ezekiel 37:9).

Wind has a powerful symbolism as it is often identified with the Holy Spirit. Of course, there are many types of wind in Scripture—some were winds of destruction (see Mark 4:37; Acts 27:14-15), while others were winds from God that came to breathe life and blessings. One such example was the wind of the Holy Spirit on the Day of Pentecost. This kind of wind typifies the breath of God upon something. In the valley of dry bones, Ezekiel spoke life to the group of dry bones, causing them to come together and form what resembled people (see Ezek. 37:1-10). Then the Lord commanded the prophet to speak to the wind so that the lifeless figures would receive breath. The wind came into them, causing them to live and stand up as a great army.

God has a breath of wind to blow upon the lifeless things He wants raised up in our lives. Sure they may look like nothing more than a group of dry bones right now, scattered across what looks to be a depressing valley. However, today God wants to breathe life on these things that you gave up on. It's time to speak to the wind.

Prayer

*Lord, I speak to the winds of the Spirit and command life to come into my hopes and dreams, which look like they will never live. I say to these dreams right now, **live!** Amen.*

Believe His Prophets!

"It's the hour to listen to the voice of My prophets. For they are speaking on a mass scale to the nations, churches, to kings and individuals who are both within and without My church. So support and believe in them, says the Spirit, for they have been strategically placed to prophesy among you."

Prophetic Scripture

...Believe in the Lord your God, so shall ye be established; believe his prophets, so shall ye prosper (2 Chronicles 20:20).

There are two men in Scripture, both named Saul, who didn't give heed to the prophets God sent them. The first was King Saul of Israel who disobeyed Samuel, causing him to lose His Kingdom and eventually get beheaded by the Philistines (see 1 Sam. 13:10-14; 31:9). The second Saul, who later became Paul, was warned not to go to Jerusalem by a group of prophetic disciples and then also by the prophet Agabus (see Acts 21:4,11-12). The Spirit had even warned him of it during his own private prayer time (see Acts 22:17-18). However, in spite of these warnings, Paul went there anyhow. Like King Saul, he too lost his head.

Jehoshaphat, on the other hand, in Second Chronicles 20:20 valued the prophets and told Judah to listen to them. His wise instruction resulted in the army of Judah defeating the Ammonites in battle.

Think about some prophetic words that you need to believe and follow. God has given them so you can gain insight into His plan and use them to pray and seek His wisdom. You don't need to worry about when they will come to pass, just do your part to respect and believe God's genuine prophets. Then rest assured that doing so will cause you to prosper and succeed today!

Prayer

Father, open my ears to the prophetic words that I have heard and received. I support the prophetic ministry in Your church and thank You that I shall be blessed! In Jesus' Name, amen.

The Finishing Anointing

"This day I am providing you the resources to complete the things I have given you to start. Yes, some situations make it appear as though you will not be able to complete the tasks at hand, but know today that the finishing anointing rests upon you."

Prophetic Scripture

Looking unto Jesus the author and finisher of our faith... (Hebrews 12:2).

I am sure Jesus felt the pressure to quit when He was dragging His cross up Golgotha's hill. Of course, we know He was able to finish because He made the decision to look past the cross and on to the victory awaiting Him on the other side. Yet His press forward accomplished something special for you and I. From Hebrews 12:2, I want you to see a truth that perhaps you haven't considered. It says Jesus is the author and finisher of our faith. This means He stands at both the beginning and end of your running track. He was the one who thrust you off the starting block and He is on the other side pulling you to the finish line! With Christ surrounding you from both ends of the track, there is an anointing stretched out in between enabling and compelling you to finish whatever God has assigned you. You could say there is a finishing anointing present to help you! With that in place, you can have peace knowing that whatever resources, assistance, or strength you need, these things will be made available right when you need them, even when it feels like the opposite is true.

Thank the Lord Jesus for the ability to finish everything with excellence today and every day!

Prayer

Father, I believe there is anointing causing me to finish everything You have given me to do. The power of Christ is supplying me with all I need, and I thank You that I shall not fail! In Jesus' Name, amen.

Wonders in the Heavens

"The Spirit says there shall surely be wonders in the heavens and many shall see them. For it's the time of the latter rain, causing many to be turned unto righteousness. Rejoice, for wonders in the heavens and signs in the earth are visiting you!"

Prophetic Scripture

And I will shew wonders in heaven above, and signs in the earth beneath.... And it shall come to pass, that whosoever shall call on the name of the Lord shall be saved (Acts 2:19,21).

We are in a remarkable period of time. We are beginning to see some of the most supernatural events to be recorded in history. However, signs and wonders may not always appear as you expect them to, and if we aren't careful we can miss them. Isaiah 7:14 prophesied that one of the greatest signs to appear would be a virgin bearing a son. However, religious leaders living at the time the sign appeared didn't recognize it. Supernatural wonders aren't always something everyone will notice. In fact, according to the Bible those who aren't looking for God to manifest may miss Him when He does appear (see Luke 19:44). Isn't that what will happen when Jesus returns? Some will overlook the event as if it never took place. However, God will manifest these wonders because He knows there are going to be those who will see them and respond favorably, just like the wise men when the star of Christ appeared. Not everyone responded, but some did and were blessed!

Expect to see wonders in the Heavens through weather, in government, in nations, through the church, and even via supernatural healings and miracles. We are in the season of wonders and God will use these things to cause many to be saved.

Prayer

Father, I open my eyes to see the heavenly wonders You are displaying in this season. Teach me how to discern them and use them to win many to Christ. In the Name of Jesus, amen.

Self-Worth Restored

"I have come to restore all your self-worth, says the Lord. Let Me show you your value this day. Even the blows that were meant to demean you, I shall make them as though they never were."

Prophetic Scripture

...He shall eat at my table, as one of the king's sons (2 Samuel 9:11).

Mephibosheth was the little five-year-old crippled grandson of Saul who was dropped when his nanny fled with him after Saul's household fell under attack. Long after Saul and Jonathan's deaths, David went looking for someone from the descendants of Jonathan to keep a promise that he would forever show kindness to his family (see 1 Sam. 20:15). A former servant of Saul, named Ziba, told David about Mephibosheth, now grown but still crippled. In Second Samuel 9, when Mephibosheth was introduced to David, he felt completely inferior because of his condition. In Second Samuel 9:8, he responded to David by saying, "Who am I that you would pay attention to a dead dog like me?" It was obvious he had no sense of self-worth. The effects of the murder of his father and grandfather, in addition to his own lame condition, were very visible. Yet, David ignored this and gave Mephibosheth a permanent dinner pass to the king's table! In one day, he went from worthlessness to royalty!

Everyone has experienced attacks on their self-worth, but as an heir of Christ you are given a permanent pass to the table of King Jesus. In spite of life's blows, you have gone from worthlessness to royalty! It doesn't matter how others view you; all Mephibosheth needed was the approval of the king. You have the approval of Christ the King today, and your self-worth has been restored!

Prayer

Father, I receive my place at the table of King Jesus today. I am no longer worthless, and all my self-worth has been restored. I am special, Lord, and I have value. Hallelujah! Amen!

It's Under Your Feet!

"Believe not that anything whatsoever has the power to harm you, for it is time to expect nothing other than every demonic power to be under your feet!"

Prophetic Scripture

Behold, I give unto you power to tread on serpents and scorpions, and over all the power of the enemy: and nothing shall by any means hurt you (Luke 10:19).

Life definitely isn't a problem-free bed of roses! While we know this is true, we also shouldn't expect it to be a bed of poison ivy either! As believers we need to look at our lives and know that we have the ability to overcome the problems that are caused by demonic powers. We shouldn't live in fear of some pending attack lurking around the corner. We need a stronger mind-set that is confident that Jesus Christ will enable us to live in victory above these things. Jesus told His disciples that they could walk over the power of the devil. He reiterated to them that nothing has the power to harm them. This explains why He could escape the hands of His would-be killers early in His ministry (see Luke 4:30). It explains why Peter could be broken out of prison by an angel just before his scheduled execution (see Acts 12). I once heard someone say, "If the devil could kill you, he would have already done so, but the fact that he hasn't means he cannot!"

We need more established confidence today that we have the power to walk over the attacks of demons rather than them walking over us. Know what belongs to you today, because the devil and all his power is under your feet!

Prayer

Lord, I thank You that I have authority over the problems of the enemy. I know that no demonic power has any ability to harm me or my family today! I am covered by the blood of Jesus and I live in victory! In the Name of Jesus, amen!

Pastors Uplifted

"So the Spirit says, pray this day for the strength of My pastors. Help them, for it is they who watch for your soul. Know that I have put pastors over you to keep you in the safety of the sheepfold."

Prophetic Scripture

...Now thy shepherds which were with us, we hurt them not, neither was there ought missing unto them... (1 Samuel 25:7).

I am not sure of the confirmed statistics, but I have heard several shocking reports regarding how many pastors every week are getting burned out and quitting ministry because they can't handle the pressure. While I am well aware that not every pastor handles his or her ministry position honorably, most pastors are quality people and we need to undergird them. Standing on a public platform of evaluation every week isn't easy, and pastors need our support. We can choose to be one less critic on their long list of evaluators.

In First Samuel 25, David attempts to make acquaintance with Nabal, a very evil but rich and influential man. He opens his salutation by drawing attention to the fact that his men who encountered Nabal's shepherds at pasture did them no harm. His point was that when they could have easily attacked them and stole their sheep, they didn't. Their kindness to the shepherds was their way of coming in peace.

One of the best ways believers can show peace and good intentions to the Body of Christ is to treat God's shepherds, the pastors, considerately and realize that they are vulnerable on the front lines of God's pasture. Let's pray and uplift pastors all across the nations today.

Prayer

Father, I pray for Your shepherds today. I ask You to uplift them with super-natural strength to fulfill Your call upon them. Empower them with divine inspiration, and I thank You for placing pastors in our lives to lead us to You. Amen.

Toxins Are Neutralized

"Fear not the toxins and pollutants that would try to filter into you or your surroundings, says the Lord. For even as the poison in the soup was neutralized in the days of Elisha, so shall I still neutralize contaminants around you in this time."

Prophetic Scripture

...And there was no harm in the pot (2 Kings 4:41).

We have heard the many news flashes regarding all the potential toxins reported to exist in the atmosphere, our food, and our overall surroundings. Keeping up with the latest information can be overwhelming, and the truth is it's impossible to implement all the things we are told. While we need to eat right and have responsible living habits, we can't become paranoid of everything that could potentially poison us. In Second Kings 4:38-41, Elisha and his group of prophets were preparing a pot of soup when one of them unknowingly added poisonous gourds. While eating, they realized the soup was poisoned, so Elisha told them to get some flour and add it to the soup. Afterward, verse 41 says, "and there was no harm in the pot." Of course, there weren't any neutralizing qualities to the flour itself. However, flour or meal is representative of Christ's healing power. Elisha was demonstrating that the healing power of Jesus supersedes earthly toxins. Jesus taught this principle regarding those who believe in Him. In Mark 16:18 He says, "...and if they drink any deadly thing, it shall not hurt them." Jesus further reiterated this truth in His demonstration of the communion meal.

Know that whatever toxins exist in the earth today, the healing "meal" of Christ neutralizes them. Trust today that through Him all toxins are neutralized!

Prayer

Lord Jesus, I am thankful for Your healing power that neutralizes all toxins from my body or surroundings. All poisons are neutralized, and I live free from all fear regarding these things. Amen!

I AM THAT I AM!

"Remember this day that I AM THAT I AM. For when they question Your relationship to Me, know that I have qualified you to show them who I AM. Yes, and I will demonstrate to them who I AM on your behalf!"

Prophetic Scripture

And God said unto Moses, I AM THAT I AM: and he said, Thus shalt thou say unto the children of Israel, I AM hath sent me unto you (Exodus 3:14).

When God called Moses to deliver Israel from Egypt, Moses expressed insecurity about His qualifications. We often do the same when presenting the Gospel. While we all have different roles to play, what we need to feel confident about is not our qualifications, but God's ability to qualify us. We assume that a person's educational level, family life, or personality either qualifies or disqualifies them. However, when God told Moses to tell them "I AM THAT I AM" sent him, God was saying, in paraphrase, "Moses, take the pressure of yourself; you just tell them that I am who I demonstrate myself to be." It wasn't about Moses' lack of ability to make the point, it was about who God demonstrated Himself to be before them. Of course, even after all the demonstrations, Pharaoh never submitted in his heart. Our job isn't to be concerned with their response. Not everyone may listen to you, but because you have come in the name of I AM THAT I AM, the anointing will be demonstrated to them in some form. It's not about our eloquence or lack thereof, it's about Him demonstrating who He is. Be confident of this today because you speak for I AM THAT I AM!

Prayer

Father, I know that You are who You have said. As I represent the Gospel to those around me today, I trust that You will demonstrate to them who You are. You are I AM THAT I AM! Amen!

Peace upon You, Israel!

"Command peace to be upon Israel this day, says the Spirit. For even as the eyes of the world rest upon the land of the Hebrews, so is My eye upon it, and I shall defend them before the world once again."

Prophetic Scripture

Pray for the peace of Jerusalem: they shall prosper that love thee (Psalms 122:6).

It seems the secular world should realize there is something unique about Israel, since it is a constant topic in modern-day news. It is repeatedly targeted by Arab nations and has a history that draws international discussion like none other. Israel is also one of the few nations still fighting the controversy of territorial dividing lines. On top of that, just about everyone knows some background about the Jews being God's chosen. With this in mind, most believers also understand that Israel will always be a focus point on the world stage and a gauging tool for pinpointing end-time events. As the next events unfold in Israel's history, we need to keep our prayers at an all-time high. The eyes of the world will be on them, but so will the eyes of the Lord, and we the believers must pray for them.

The Bible teaches us to pray for the peace of Jerusalem; probably, it is mostly for the reasons I have listed above. You can't be that much of a hot topic and not expect controversy. Israel has had its fair share, and undoubtedly that will continue. Pray for Israel and that God's favor upon them would be shown to the nations of the world. Let's declare together today, "Peace upon you, Israel."

Prayer

Lord, I pray for Israel and Jerusalem. I ask that You would not only protect them, but defend them on the world stage. I pray that the people who live there would experience peace and protection in the coming season. In Jesus' Name, amen!

Wells Springing Forth

"I am placing an anointing upon your intellect to help you figure things out that have been difficult for you. I give you the ability to learn and comprehend, says the Lord, and it shall even be like wells springing forth."

Prophetic Scripture

Understanding is a wellspring of life unto him that hath it... (Proverbs 16:22).

Whether you are a student, business person, parent, or wear some other hat in life, you know that there are many things you must really dig your brain into if you want to learn anything. Life is filled with things to learn, some of which take hours of research and investigation to gather all the needed information. The natural learning process is something we can't expect to just fall upon us like raindrops. You definitely have to apply yourself; however, we can certainly depend on the Holy Spirit to help us in the process. The Holy Spirit is a teacher, and He not only teaches us the ways of God but will help us in our efforts to learn the natural things of life that are important. The Hebrew word for *understanding* in Proverbs 16:22 means intelligence. Intelligence is gaining information by the use of our intellect and is accomplished by educating ourselves, whether it be spiritual or natural. As you work hard at expanding your brain power, ask the Lord to help you in that learning process. He can cause you to comprehend with heightened ability.

Whatever is before you in the learning process today, ask the Lord to anoint you for it. With Him helping you understand things, your comprehension will improve until eventually the things you are learning are like wells springing forth.

Prayer

Holy Spirit, help me in the learning process today. Cause me to comprehend the information I need to be educated with and help me correctly absorb even the things that have challenged me the most. Thank You! Amen.

Fatigue Becomes Energy

"Let me boost your energy today and remove fatigue and all its effects from you. See yourself as the mighty and imagine yourself with youthful strength, for so shall I reenergize you!"

Prophetic Scripture

He giveth power to the faint; and to them that have no might he increaseth strength (Isaiah 40:29).

If multitudes of people didn't deal with fatigue and reoccurring tiredness, the beverage market wouldn't be filled with caffeine and sugar-laced drinks to give us that age-old, much-appreciated "kick." Most people probably have experienced the afternoon slump, so we call it, while others deal with a more serious version of fatigue. If you are dealing with ongoing fatigue, it is important to make sure first that you are doing the right things necessary for a healthy lifestyle. However, many people even with the best habits experience some occasions of feeling unexplainable bouts of tiredness. The funny thing is we have more modern conveniences than ever in order to make life easier, but in reality it seems like it's just created more to do! At the fast pace most people run at, we need the Spirit of the Lord to renew our energy.

There is a provision from God for turning fatigue into energy. Isaiah 40:29 says He gives power to the faint. This means that on those days when you feel exhausted, the Lord will give you the physical and emotional stamina to do things you didn't think you could have otherwise. He will take what little energy you do have and cause it to multiply. Sometimes, because we don't feel energized, we talk about tiredness too often. Start talking about God strengthening you today and turning your fatigue into brand-new energy!

Prayer

Father, I ask You for supernatural energy today. Increase my might and stamina. I declare that I am not fatigued, but that I am filled with youthful strength. In Jesus' Name, amen.

Dance and Leap!

"Dance this day, for as you dance shall the raging storms cease. Let Me use your dance of joy to punish the devil, for even as you dance and leap, it shall reverse his works and be a mockery unto him!"

Prophetic Scripture

Let them praise his name in the dance... (Psalms 149:3).

One thing Satan hates most is when we praise God during the attacks he is trying so hard to impose. Nothing feels worse to a would-be attacker than a strategic plan foiled. You can almost picture it—the devil calculates what he is sure will rip the rug out from under you. Right when he is about to do his own version of the victory dance, *you* start dancing to God! You can almost hear him squeal, "What? How can you be dancing? You are supposed to be crying!" This is just about the biggest mockery in the halls of hell. Psalm 149:3 tell us to dance to the Lord, while verse 7 gives the results of it. It says, "to execute vengeance upon the heathen." Now, we don't wrestle against people—we wage warfare with evil spirits. Our dance executes revenge upon demons. Right when they expected victory, you got immediate revenge because they couldn't get you down! The devil knows more than anyone that if he can get you down, your potential to get frustrated with God goes up exponentially. However, he also knows if you praise when it would be easy to feel down, then Jehovah God gets involved!

This is why we don't just dance when things are going great. Dancing to the Lord liberates you, and Satan hates it. Go ahead, dance a little more today and watch the devil lose a foothold over you!

Prayer

Hallelujah Lord, I dance and praise Your Name today! As I dance and leap, I thank You that joy and liberty fill my heart and every work of the devil is destroyed! In the Name of Jesus, amen!

Consumed by His House

"Let the zeal for My house burn within you. For My longing desire is to further My work through ministries and churches. Help My passion, says the Spirit, for I even call you this day to be consumed by a passion for My house."

Prophetic Scripture

And his disciples remembered that it was written, The zeal of thine house hath eaten me up (John 2:17).

Diminishing church attendance and involvement seems to be becoming an epidemic. People have lost interest in getting deeply involved in a local church. Some of this is understandable when people have had a bad experience with church or felt like a ministry mishandled them or others. However, I always like to compare it like this: We don't quit going to doctors or eating at restaurants because of bad experiences. Bad experiences are to be expected with anything, even in Christendom. If you get two people in any room long enough, Christian or not, there will be problems eventually! Bad experiences are par for the course, so we cannot let it excuse us from getting behind God's ministries and local churches. None of them are perfect, but God still has given them a starring role in furthering the Gospel, and we have to support what God endorses.

Friend, the work of God's Kingdom is under siege. The Kingdom of Heaven suffers violence, but it's the violent that take it by force (see Matt. 11:12). In other words, it's the determined warriors of God who, in spite of setbacks or even bad experiences, are going to dig their heals in and get involved. God loves His churches and ministries, so let's defy the odds and let a passion cause us to be consumed for His house today!

Prayer

Father, I pray today for the success of local churches and ministries. I support them and ask You to continually show me how to do my part to have a passion and zeal for Your house. Amen.

Prospered by Prophecy

"Take now every prophecy you have received and rehearse them once again. For there are things within them that I will bring to your attention, even things you overlooked before. Let the words sink within you now, for so shall you prosper through these prophecies."

Prophetic Scripture

...And they prospered through the prophesying of Haggai the prophet and Zechariah the son of Iddo. And they builded, and finished it... (Ezra 6:14).

Under the captivity of Babylon, rebuilding the temple was no easy undertaking. There were many roadblocks, but God saw them through to the end of the projects. While there were many things God did to prosper their project, one key method He used could easily be overlooked, but the Bible makes it very clear. God used prophecy to prosper them. Not only did they take an original word from the prophets, but as the prophets continued to prophesy and the people held onto their prophecies, they were prospered in building, and the Bible says it was the very thing that enabled them to finish the work. First Timothy says, "Timothy, my son, I am giving you this command in keeping with the prophecies once made about you, so that by recalling them you may fight the battle well" (1 Tim. 1:18 NIV).

Think today of prophecies you have received. These can be either personal prophecies spoken specifically over you, or they can be prophecies spoken to a larger audience which you can add faith to and make your own. Either way, war with these prophecies and use them today to prosper your life and help you complete your race!

Prayer

Lord, as I review the prophecies I have heard, I ask that You will draw my attention to the key things You want to show me. Cause these prophecies to create a unique anointing that is key for my success. I thank You for it. Amen.

Relationships Healed

"I have come to heal the relationships that I designed to be in your life because of the fruit they are destined to produce. Know that I shall heal hearts and minds from hurts and misunderstandings so that you are able to agree as one."

Prophetic Scripture

...Holy Father, keep through thine own name those whom thou hast given me, that they may be one, as we are (John 17:11).

Broken relationships, regardless of the reason, are one of the greatest hindrances to human happiness. They are also one of the greatest hindrances to the overall health of the Body of Christ (see 1 Cor. 11:30). While some relationships simply can't be restored due to the hardness of some people's hearts, God does look for those whose hearts are soft enough where He can provide an anointing to bring relationships, including struggling marriages, back together. Of course, not all relationships are designed by God, but at the same time if hearts are open and teachable, God can work with anything and anyone.

We need the relationships ordained by God to be strengthened. If you are part of a broken relationship, then ask God if the relationship is of Him. If you are confident that it is, then believe that the Lord will be involved and help all parties involved come to truth. We can't always fix these relationships through human reasoning. Sure, we can attempt to talk things out and try to decide what needs to be fixed. In the end, we need the Holy Spirit to impart revelation to hearts and minds that creates healing and agreement. Ask the Lord to help you be part of that healing process for godly relationships today.

Prayer

Father, I thank You for all the relationships in my life that You have ordained. Of the ones that are broken, I ask that you would bring healing. Heal my heart of all wounds and help me walk in total love and forgiveness. In Jesus' Name, amen.

Receive the Double!

"Look for the doubling now, says the Lord. For I want to double you, and where there has been shame and you have been looked on with contempt for seeking Me, I will repay each time with a double portion for your sacrifice. Today is your day to receive double!"

Prophetic Scripture

For your shame ye shall have double; and for confusion they shall rejoice in their portion: therefore in their land they shall possess the double: everlasting joy shall be unto them (Isaiah 61:7).

God always gives back to us when we give to Him. This becomes even more powerful when we give to God from a place of great sacrifice. Sometimes the sacrifice is being ridiculed by family and friends for what you believe, but God will stand up for you. He won't let you be accused or mistreated for serving Him without bringing a payback blessing into your life, and those blessings come with a double price tag attached to them! God pays double when we are willing to be shamed for following His ways. God considers your work for His Kingdom important, and while we do it joyfully with gratitude God does see how much effort you put into it. While we don't arrogantly expect payback from God because He has already given us everything, we know God is a giver. He first gave Jesus, and then we give back to Him through our love and heart of unconditional service. For that service, God then gives to us again, and the cycle keeps going! His promise is that you will not suffer shame without possessing a double blessing in your life. So get ready, the double blessing is coming your way.

Prayer

Father, I receive Your double blessing for my life. Thank You, Lord, for giving to me, and I ask that You will help me find many ways to give myself and my possessions sacrificially back to You. I love You, Lord! In Jesus' Name, amen.

None Can Withstand!

"Let it be known again that I rule over all the kingdoms of this world. For might and power are in My hand to save you, and what evil would try to come your way, none can withstand even the slightest breath of My mouth!"

Prophetic Scripture

And said, O Lord God of our fathers, are not thou God in heaven? and rulest not thou over all the kingdoms of the heathen? and in thine hand is there not power and might, so that none is able to withstand thee? (2 Chronicles 20:6)

It's a good feeling to remember that God is in control of everything. He is our great, big Daddy! If you watch the television, it might appear like the kingdoms of the world are in control as they try to take prayer out of school, remove the Ten Commandments from public buildings, and eliminate the Name of God from record books. It can be discouraging sometimes, because it seems like evil is prevailing. However, God is the one who rules over the kingdoms of the heathen, and they may all think that they are succeeding at eliminating God from things right now, but they have overlooked that all power is in His hands. In the end, nothing can withstand the power of God. If you feel today like the evil around you is prevailing in some way or another, then call on the hand of God to intervene and save you from harm. Remember, no matter what happens in the world, nothing will be able to withstand the hand of the Living God. Stay close to Him today and He will be your strength to succeed!

Prayer

Lord, I am ever reminded that nothing can overcome Your power. You are in control of everything, and I rest underneath Your hand of power. Lord, protect Your people today and let Your mighty hand be upon me, for I know that nothing can withstand You! In Jesus' Name, amen!

JUNE 5

Your Eyes Can See

"Let me open your eyes now to perceive things about your future destiny. I will even open your eyes of discernment to give you sharper vision. So command your vision in the spirit and even in the natural to be 20/20, says the Lord."

Prophetic Scripture

...One thing I know, that, whereas I was blind, now I see (John 9:25).

When Jesus healed the man born blind in John 9, the miracle was so extraordinary it couldn't be explained or reasoned away. By applying intense pressure, Jesus' adversaries tried to get the man who received his sight to question its reality. However, the man didn't reason it away like they wanted him to. Instead, he stuck with his bottom line story. Basically, it was that he didn't know how or why it happened. He didn't know what made it occur or why his sight came the way it did, all he knew was this: I once was blind, but now I see.

The Bible likens eyesight or blindness to spiritual revelation or lack thereof. When we come to revelation on something, the experience is much the same way. It's like someone suddenly turns the light on. You don't know how it happens or why, but suddenly something clicks. That is how divine revelation comes. All you know is you were blind, but now you see. When that happens, you are able to perceive and discern things you couldn't before.

The Lord wants you to see. Command your eyes, natural or spiritual, to see. Ask God to increase your clarity of vision and live everyday expecting to have "eyesight." Have faith today that your eyes can see!

Prayer

Lord, I declare that I receive my sight today. I receive spiritual vision and discernment to know Your plans for me. I say today, my vision is 20/20! In the Name of Jesus, amen!

Embracing the New

"Don't stay limited only to what you have learned thus far or to old methods that shouldn't be considered any longer. For in the next few years ahead, I am going to bring fresh input, but it shall require a flexible and teachable heart so you can embrace the fullness of the good plan I have for you."

Prophetic Scripture

Remember ye not the former things, neither consider the things of old (Isaiah 43:18).

Accepting change can be tough. It's why some people attend dead churches, listen to dry sermons, and refuse to open their heart to anything fresh. Sometimes we get stuck with what we are used to because it feels safe. When God began to prophesy to Israel about their coming Messiah, He told them that there were some methods under the old covenant that were going to be abolished. When Jesus came, they had a hard time accepting Him because He came in a package different from what they were used to. They got so used to a certain method and preference that they couldn't see God in anything outside the limitations they created.

We often do the same thing. We like certain music, preachers, and types of churches, and often when God begins to raise up fresh voices and expressions, we can't flow with them. That doesn't mean we accept anything that comes along, but combined with proper discernment, we need to realize that God isn't going to do everything according to our preferences. Don't get stuck in the former today, and ask God to teach you how to embrace the fresh things He wants to bring so you can walk in the fullness of what He has for you!

Prayer

Father, teach me how to flow with the fresh things You are bringing into my life. I choose to be open to change and pray that You would help me discern the new and not be limited by the old that I may walk in Your plan for me! Amen.

Let Love Abound

"Know that your needs shall be upheld in the atmosphere of perfect love. When many would allow godly love to grow cold, choose in all things to let love abound. For love shall overcome the impossible and create an entrance for the supernatural."

Prophetic Scripture

And the Lord make you to increase and abound in love one toward another, and toward all men, even as we do toward you (1 Thessalonians 3:12).

Jesus said that one of the biggest temptations of the last days would be that our love for each other would begin to show signs of growing cold (see Matt. 24:12). He said it would wax cold, like a candle that has burned out. The wax then becomes cold, hard, and provides no warmth or light. You see, the way the world will know that we are genuinely Christians is not by how many people attend our churches or by our good music or preaching. They will know we are true followers of Christ because of one simple fact—that we love each other unselfishly. When the world would rather revert to backbiting, gossip, betrayal, and finger-pointing, we choose to stay in unity and love! The ability to do that will make them stand up and take notice, because it is a truly supernatural act in a world filled with hate. To win the world, we need love toward one another in our churches, families, marriages, and ministries. It is in that atmosphere of love that the presence of God will abide, and you can be certain that wherever God abides there will be no hindrance to miracles, answered prayer, and blessings. Love will release the supernatural, so let your love abound today!

Prayer

Heavenly Father, I ask that You would help me to walk in love today with all my fellow believers and all people. Forgive me, Lord, for the areas where I have not chosen to walk in love. Cause Your love to abound in me today! Amen.

His Good Will for You

"See that I have extended My good will to you. For I have placed My stamp of approval upon you that I may show favors innumerable. Watch for even the smallest expressions of My good will to surround you today."

Prophetic Scripture

Glory to God in the highest, and on earth peace, good will toward men (Luke 2:14).

Many believe God is out to strike people with lightening every time they make a mistake. If you listen to some people's concept of God, you could wonder if God is ever in a good mood. Every time there is a hurricane or earthquake, people blame God. Many insurance policies call these disasters, "acts of God." Yet, the first thing the angels brought at the birth of Jesus was an announcement of peace and good will. God isn't out causing natural disasters because He is mad at the world. In fact, Romans 8:22 says that "the whole creation groaneth and travaileth in pain together until now." In other words, the ever increasing natural disasters are the result of sin taking its toll on the planet. Often for the same reason, people have bad things happen to them. It's not because God is judging them, but rather they are reaping the results of sinful behaviors (see Rom. 1:27). Other times it is the devil causing trouble so people will erroneously believe God is behind it. God, because of His righteousness, will eventually have to judge a world that refuses His hand of good will through Jesus, but in the meantime God is offering peace on earth.

Expect God to show His good will toward you today, even in the smallest ways, and know that He has extended His hand of peace.

Prayer

Lord, I receive Your hand of good will for me. Open my eyes to notice even the smallest expressions of Your good will, and I thank You for favors innumerable upon my life. In Jesus' Name, amen.

Your Reputation Exalted

"The Spirit says, I desire to exalt My Church before the world and make her reputation great. Let Me use you in this season to set a pattern of righteousness and cause your reputation to be exalted so that prosperity will be your portion."

Prophetic Scripture

So that you may bear yourselves becomingly and be correct and honorable and command the respect of the outside world, being dependent on nobody [self-supporting] and having need of nothing (1 Thessalonians 4:12 AMP).

The world needs to see the church rise up in integrity and be different from them. Actually, they are hoping we will be different so they will know that what we have is real. Proper behavior and integrity have many benefits. Not only does integrity give you the peace that comes from doing the right thing, but it makes it more difficult for people to accuse you. Sure, some will falsely accuse just like they did with Jesus, but with Jesus they couldn't even find any evidence to pin on Him. Psalms 25:21 says integrity will preserve you. That means it will save your life! Not only will integrity help you avoid a lot of problems, it will cause people everywhere to talk very highly of you. It will cause your reputation to be exalted. When that happens, it causes a chain reaction and sets you up for a life of prosperity. First Thessalonians 4:12 says that honorable behavior will cause us to live without having lack in anything.

God wants to give us a good name in front of people today. Do something that will make the people around you respect you and feel confident about their relationship to you. God has a plan to prosper you by exalting your reputation today.

Prayer

Father, I ask You to help me live every day in integrity. Count on me to be one of those in Your Church who will set a righteous standard, and I have faith that prosperity shall follow me everywhere! In Jesus' Name, amen.

JUNE 10

Harvest of Mercy

"Begin to plant seeds of mercy, says the Lord. Refuse vengeance and the temptation to settle the score with those who have hurt you, and know that a future harvest of mercy shall be available for you on the day when you need it most."

Prophetic Scripture

Blessed are the merciful: for they shall obtain mercy (Matthew 5:7).

Mercy is the opposite of vengeance. Vengeance is to retaliate against someone so that person will experience the same hurt you did when they hurt you. It looks for ways to get even. Sometimes it's as simple as returning a hurtful word just to get a sense of satisfaction. Based on nothing more than a personal grudge, vengeance wants to settle the score somehow. Mercy, on the other hand, does just the opposite and chooses not to retaliate. When verbally attacked, mercy responds kindly or not at all. When given the power to inflict a wound, mercy lays its weapons down. Of course, being merciful doesn't mean not setting boundaries with those whose behaviors threaten your well-being. It also isn't a lack of mercy to set the record straight with the truth, especially when doing so may protect innocent people. Jesus spoke out against the Pharisees, not to retaliate against them for attacking Him personally, but to protect innocent people from being deceived by them. At the same time, Jesus demonstrated incredible mercy to the very same Pharisees by verbally saying, "Father forgive them," while they were demanding His crucifixion. He also extended mercy in Luke 5:17 when He made healing power specifically available to them.

Like Jesus, show mercy to those who hurt you and know that one day you may need a harvest of mercy to be available for you.

Prayer

Father, teach me how to be merciful toward people, especially those who have hurt me. I make a commitment not to be vengeful, and I thank You that I receive a harvest of mercy in my life. Amen.

Your Countenance Refreshed

"The Spirit says, let not the heaviness from the stress and demands of life cause your face to become weathered and beaten down. Keep your focus of servitude upon Me, and I shall ease your burden and refresh your countenance."

Prophetic Scripture

A merry heart maketh a cheerful countenance... (Proverbs 15:13).

A person's face says a lot about them. What is expressed on the face is a clear reflection of what goes on in the heart. Without even realizing it, we can allow the everyday demands of life to start putting pressure on our minds and hearts. Sometimes it comes from a busy schedule or just from trying to sort out multiple problems all at once. If we aren't careful, eventually this internal stress starts reflecting on our faces. If this heaviness continues long enough, it creates permanent changes in people's appearance.

The Lord has a provision that helps us overcome the stresses that weigh our countenance down. Jesus gave us the ability to come to Him with our heavy burdens. He said, "Take my yoke upon you...for my yoke is easy and my burden is light" (Matt. 11:29-30). The yoke spoken of here was the "burden" of servitude to Christ. In other words, being under the burden or yoke of service to Him actually liberates you. Instead of spending so much time "serving" the demands of this life, refocus your service back to Jesus. It is the key to easing the burdens that weigh down your countenance. Focus your heartfelt service back on Him today and let Him refresh your countenance.

Prayer

Lord Jesus, I bring You every heavy burden today. I refocus my heart-felt service and commitment to You. I give You my time and energy and I thank You for liberating me and refreshing my countenance. In Jesus' Name, amen.

A Secure Journey

"Know that everywhere you go, in whatever method you travel, I shall watch over all your goings, and angels shall secure every vehicle you journey in. So declare this day that blessing is upon you as you go, says the Lord."

Prophetic Scripture

Blessed shalt thou be when thou comest in, and blessed shalt thou be when thou goest out (Deuteronomy 28:6).

The world is getting smaller and more and more people are on the go these days. People travel the world as part of their occupations or for pleasure. City streets and highways are filled with traffic as people work to get to their intended destinations. We need the protection and security of God to cover our travel every day. The Bible has promised that those of us who are part of His covenant are blessed wherever we go. God made travel security part of the plan, and we should always expect to arrive at every destination safely. Of all the travels the apostle Paul made during his ministry journeys, the enemy could not take him out via any accident or attack on his travel. While the devil tried a few times, the end result was always a powerful testimony that promoted the power of the Gospel. This isn't to assume we shouldn't use wisdom or ignore the law when it requires things such as wearing a seatbelt. We need to use proper safety guidelines as expected by travel instructions or authorities. However, what we can trust is that God is seeing to it that our travel is being overseen by angelic powers.

Thank God today for your covenant promise of travel safety in whatever method you travel, even if on foot! See the angels that are covering you and declare today that blessing is upon you wherever you go!

Prayer

Father, I thank You that angels cover all methods of my travel. I shall arrive at every destination safely and securely. I rest in Your promise to always have a secure journey. In Jesus Name, amen.

The Dominion of the Living God

"So take dominion now and keep your righteous stand against the darkness of this world. For though the spirit of antichrist would attempt to intimidate you, I am the Living God of dominion and I shall rescue you."

Prophetic Scripture

...For he is the living God, and steadfast for ever, and his kingdom that which shall not be destroyed, and his dominion shall be even unto the end. He delivereth and rescueth, and he worketh signs and wonders in heaven and in earth, who hath delivered Daniel from the power of the lions (Daniel 6:26-27).

God created man to be a ruler. In Genesis 1:28, God told Adam to have dominion over everything. Dominion means to take the authoritative position, to tread down and dominate. Adam and Eve fell prey to the devil by giving up their dominant position. They forgot that God was backing them. They could have stood up to the devil and he would have had to back down. Instead, they became intimidated and took a submissive position to the devil. When Daniel was thrown in the lions' den, he could have easily been intimidated and squelched his stand for God. During his years in Babylon, Daniel always took his position of dominion by openly serving God. He wasn't afraid to pray publicly, knowing a law was written against it. It looked for a short time like Daniel was doomed to the lions for taking that kind of dominion. However, his refusal to be intimidated caused God's dominion to be released and it delivered Daniel from the lions.

Take dominion for righteousness today even though the darkness of the world may try and intimidate you. When you do, surely the dominion of the Living God will always rescue you!

Prayer

Lord, I thank You that I have been given a position of righteous dominion. I choose to take dominion today with a bold stand for righteousness. I declare that darkness will not intimidate me and my God will rescue me. Amen.

JUNE 14

Time for Special Miracles

"Begin to look for the manifestation of special miracles to occur. For those who have been bound by certain conditions for many years shall suddenly be healed, and it will be reported that this type of unusual miracle has never been seen before, says the Lord."

Prophetic Scripture

And God wrought special miracles… (Acts 19:11).

When Paul went about territories preaching the Gospel, God did many miracles through his hands. However, on one particular occasion, it says God wrought special miracles by the hands of Paul. The Amplified Bible says they were unusual miracles. In other words, they were the kind of manifestations of miracles that went beyond normal miracles. That is hard to fathom, because any miracle is miraculous and can't be explained in human reason. However, these special miracles were not only unexplainable but so extraordinary that they were less common and in many cases never seen before. While the Bible doesn't describe all the kinds of unusual miracles seen, one was that a number of handkerchiefs were filled with supernatural power to heal. What we do know is that even though the apostles performed many miracles, this particular occasion notes a time for special miracles beyond the level of what had been seen thus far. Jesus also had similar types of unusual miracles in His ministry that had never been seen (see Mark 2:12).

We need to expect these times for special and unusual miracles to be upon us. God wants to do things that have never been seen before, so let's call for times of special and unusual miracles that will touch everyone who needs them.

Prayer

Heavenly Father, I believe that You want to do unusual miracles in the lives of those who need them. I ask that the time for special miracles would manifest in this season. Help us to create the environment for them so that You will be glorified. In Jesus' Name, amen.

Floods of the Spirit

"Know that the flood of My Spirit is even upon you and your family. For it is a life-giving Spirit that is now watering all your dry places even to your next generation. For this day, see My flood upon you and your children, says the Lord."

Prophetic Scripture

For I will pour water upon him that is thirsty, and floods upon the dry ground: I will pour my spirit upon thy seed, and my blessing upon thine offspring: and they shall spring up as among the grass, as willows by the water courses (Isaiah 44:3-4).

When you think of floods, you don't think of a small trickle of water. Floods speak of overflow. They don't paint the picture of "barely enough." When God said that He will flood your dry ground, it means there will be more than enough supply to fulfill you and anyone near you. In the verse above, God's blessing was also upon their offspring, which tells you that your nearest family is sure to get wet if the flood hits you! When the water is in flood stage, more than one person will get swept up by the tide. Don't worry about your children or family members today, because when you get drenched by His Spirit, be assured that the overflow will run upon your children and closest relatives. Use your faith that the floods of the Spirit from your life will wash over them and their dry ground will receive a drink. Then instead of living in disappointment, both they and you will spring up with the blessing and power of God!

Prayer

Dear Lord, cause me to experience a fresh flood of the Holy Spirit upon my life. Let that overflow of Your Spirit bless my family and my children right now! I declare today that Your Spirit washes over all that concerns me. In the mighty Name of Jesus, amen!

Breath of Fresh Air

"I have breathed life into you, says the Spirit. Breathe deeply now and say...The Spirit of Life is upon me. I shall not be short of breath, nor short of any provision, for the Holy Spirit gives me life and a breath of fresh air!"

Prophetic Scripture

...He giveth to all life, and breath, and all things (Acts 17:25).

When God made Adam, he didn't come to life until God breathed into him (see Gen. 2:7). Breath gives life, both spiritually and physically. Health experts say that there are certain health benefits to clear and proper breathing. In addition to other important lifestyle changes, some reports have said that deep and proper breathing techniques can reduce high blood pressure by increasing oxygen in the blood. Many who have suffered from things such as allergies, asthma, and similar conditions that affect the ability to take clear and deep breaths know how a lack of good breathing can reduce the quality of life. When God breathed into Adam, it gave him physical life. Then later, Jesus breathed on His disciples to receive the Holy Spirit which gave them spiritual life (see John 20:22). Acts 17:25 says that God gives both life and breath and provision for all things.

Take a deep breath today and let the life of God fill your lungs and your soul. Even if your breathing has been hindered by a physical condition, do so by faith and declare that because God is the author of life you can breathe deeply. Let each deep breath cause you to see yourself drinking in the life of God, spiritually, emotionally, and physically. Receive a Holy Spirit breath of fresh air!

Prayer

Father, I know all life and breath comes from You. I take a deep breath now and say that the Holy Spirit of Life is upon me and I shall not be short of breath, either physically or spiritually, and all things are provided for me! In Jesus' Name, amen.

JUNE 17

No More Shame

"Know that there is no shame or condemnation upon you, says the Lord. For as your heart is set upon Me, see that I shall restore your future as though the mistakes and sins of your youth never were."

Prophetic Scripture

...For thou shalt forget the shame of thy youth... (Isaiah 54:4).

Everyone has done what is considered to be some foolish mistakes or perhaps even regrettable sins. For some, it was before the salvation experience, but for others it was while they backslid away from God. Some live in the shame of sinful mistakes they made as teen or young adult, and it haunts them into adulthood. Others' errors were later in life. Regardless of the scenario, God does not leave us in the guilt and shame of the past if we are truly repentant.

David, as the King of Israel, was delivered from the shame of adultery and murder. While he couldn't prevent the consequential death of the child born from the adulterous affair with Bathsheba, God later removed David's shame by giving him Solomon, which means "peace." Through Solomon's birth, David received peace knowing that God wasn't leaving him in a state of shame. Jesus demonstrated the same thing when He told Mary Magdalene that her sins were forgiven and to go home in peace (see Luke 7:48-50). Like David, her repentance caused her to receive the peace of knowing that God wasn't condemning her and that she had a future to look forward to that was free from her shame.

If you have made some thoughtless or youthful mistakes for which you are truly sorry, God is more than able to give you peace today and take away the shame of your youth, as though it never happened.

Prayer

Father, I thank You that You have not left me in shame. I know every part of my future shall be bright as I serve You, and every past mistake shall be as though it never happened. In Jesus' Name, amen.

Eat This Bread and Live

"The Spirit says, let not the vain philosophies of the day form your ideals or principles. For some in My Kingdom are turned aside to these things. But I call you to continually eat the bread of My Word and know that you shall avoid deception and surely you shall live."

Prophetic Scripture

...He that eateth of this bread shall live for ever (John 6:58).

Jesus reiterated many times that the only way to finish our Christian race is to continually feed on the bread of His Word. Our society has many distractions that could easily pull us away from this necessary, daily meal from God's table. The practice of the communion meal helps make this a constant reminder. When Jesus broke the bread, He said, "This is my body" (Matt. 26:26). Jesus also said He was the bread that came down from Heaven (see John 6:57-58). Then John 1:1 further says that Jesus was the Word of God. Combining the truths from these verses together, we learn that as we eat of the communion bread and drink of the cup, we are showing that we are one with Christ and we are committed to constantly "feed" on Him. We literally live that out by feeding on His Word every day. Matthew 4:4 says we cannot survive on physical bread alone. We need a continual meal from God's Word to survive. That is because without the constant life that comes from God's Word, we will eventually feed upon the wrong things that come from this world, which produce deception and death.

Make a point today and every day to feed upon His Word and know that they will cause you to rise above this world and live!

Prayer

Father, I feed upon Your Word today. Let it stay fresh in my mind and come to my remembrance with everything I encounter. I thank You that Your Word is causing me to rise above the deceptions of this world and I shall live. Amen.

Confusion Shall Depart!

*"Even now all confusion shall depart from your heart and mind so that you are no longer perplexed by what to do. For the chaos that has come by way of human reasoning shall come to rest. And written over your head this day is the word **stability**."*

Prophetic Scripture

For God is not the author of confusion, but of peace... (1 Corinthians 14:33).

The word *confusion* in the New Testament means instability. It speaks of being in a state of disorder, where the natural ability to act according to sound judgment is compromised or rendered inoperative. Typically, we see a state of confusion settle in when human reasoning takes a front seat ahead of God's wisdom. One example is conflict resolution between two people. The human psyche is very complex. Volumes have been written to teach human psychology, and while this is helpful it has limits. We can only delve so far into the intricacies of the human mind and heart. Because we are created in God's image, we are complex beings. I often wondered why the Bible doesn't spend more time teaching us the psychology behind human behavior to help us better work through our differences with each other. I believe it's because God's knows that the depths of the human heart and mind can never be fully figured out. That method can only solve some things and when focused upon too much it creates confusion. Instead, we can override confusion by simply obeying God even when it seems ineffective to do so. For example, sometimes it means keeping quiet when it feels more reasonable to make your point.

Remember, God is not the author of confusion, and when we keep Him involved things will stabilize and all confusion will depart!

Prayer

Heavenly Father, I thank You that every form of confusion must come to rest and depart from my life. I declare that I live in stability and peace, and that You are solving every situation with supernatural wisdom. Amen.

Helpers Have Come

"I am sending you those who will help ease the workload and carry the burden, says the Lord. I will not give you more than you can bear, and know that I shall send you people here and there who shall lift up your arms and strengthen you."

Prophetic Scripture

...And they were among the mighty men, helpers of the war (1 Chronicles 12:1).

Not everyone is able to hire help for all the many tasks they have to accomplish every day. People from all walks of life can feel overwhelmed by their task list at times. Whether it's the businessperson who needs new employees, the pastor who needs committed helpers in his church, or perhaps the single parent who is juggling the needs of a family, the reality is that we all need help. When God sent David men at Ziklag, He sent people whose jobs were specifically to be helpers of the war. In other words, they were the people who did odd jobs that helped the warriors be more effective at battle. Their tasks probably weren't what many would think deserved major recognition. Yet they alleviated the burden enough to help David's men wage war more effectively. By sending David these helpers, God was also reminding David that He wasn't going to leave him without ample people to get the job done.

Undoubtedly, if God could send these types of people to David, He will send them to us at various times. We use faith for many things, but we need to pray and ask the Lord to send us helpers. Whether long-term or for one short task, ask the Lord to send you key helpers who will ease your workload today.

Prayer

Father, I ask You to bring people across my path who will be a help to me. Send people who will help alleviate the burden of what I have to accomplish. I trust You and thank You for it. In Jesus' Name, amen.

Healing for All

"The Spirit says, know that I have extended My healing hand to everyone and no one is left out. Let anyone who would call upon Me for healing come, for I have brought healing to all!"

Prophetic Scripture

...And great multitudes followed him, and he healed them all (Matthew 12:15).

One of the major truths all through the four Gospels is that Jesus never rejected any sick person who needed healing. The only ones the Bible mentions that weren't healed through Jesus' ministry were those who deliberately resisted Him (see Mark 6:1-6). In fact, multiple verses indicate that He healed everyone with all manner of disease presented to Him. Matthew 12:15 says, "and he healed them all." Everywhere multitudes came, He healed them in mass numbers (see Matt. 4:23-25; 19:2). The only indirect example of someone who it seems was not directly healed while Jesus traveled the region may have been the lame man in Acts 3. Since he was sitting at the Gate Beautiful since birth, it seems highly likely that Jesus passed that way many times, but for whatever reason the man wasn't healed then. However, Jesus did heal him eventually through the ministry of Peter and John, so he still was healed in the power of Jesus' Name.

The truth is that nearly every biblical account on healing indicates that people received healing rather than not. Everyone who came to Jesus was included, so why would we want to assume Jesus isn't including everyone today? Jesus' track record is one of healing for all. So see yourself healed today, simply because you know that Jesus healed them all!

Prayer

Lord Jesus, Your biblical track record shows that You heal all those who come to You for healing. I call upon You for divine health in every part of my body today and also for _____ who also needs to be healed today. I thank You today that healing is available for all who need it! Amen!

Decree for the Prophets

"The Spirit says, pray for the prophets worldwide. Decree that their words shall shoot out across the earth and be honored. For I am establishing new prophetic sounds and raising up those who have My pulse, so decree this day for blessing to be upon My prophets."

Prophetic Scripture

Finally, brethren, pray for us, that the word of the Lord may have free course, and be glorifed, even as it is with you (2 Thessalonians 3:1).

Delivering the word of the Lord, whether as preaching or prophecy, is often met with persecution or resistance. Of all the ministry gifts and expressions, God's prophets are often among the most misunderstood and targeted. While prophets or those with a prophetic edge all come in different packages, they each have a key role in presenting the word of the Lord. Some prophets prophesy directly to the masses and speak to entire nations, while others speak more to the Body of Christ or churches. Others are more apt to prophesy to individuals. Some stand in the office of the prophet while others simply prophesy. Some don't prophesy in the traditional sense, but simply are gifted to get the pulse of Heaven. Regardless of their unique packages, prophets help the Body of Christ be on track with what Heaven is doing. Paul asked people to pray that the word of the Lord, in whatever method it's delivered, would succeed.

Pray and decree for the success of the prophets and prophetic ministries. Command the word of the Lord to grow and be received and pray that the prophets would be strengthened. There is a blessing that these ministries and individuals carry for us, so let's make a decree today for the prophets!

Prayer

Lord, I decree that Your prophets and the prophetic word will have success. Open the minds and ears of the hearers. Strengthen the prophetic vessels worldwide, and I declare that they shall not be hindered! In Jesus' Name, amen!

Complimented by God

"Let Me tell you what I love about you, says the Lord. For I have come with a kind word and to give compliments to you so that your confidence will be strengthened this day."

Prophetic Scripture

By faith Enoch was translated...for before his translation he had this testimony, that he pleased God (Hebrews 11:5).

As we listen to the Lord speak to us, we commonly listen for directional things. These are things such as which job to take, who to witness to, or how to walk through a problem or trial. We also spend a great deal of time listening for admonitions or even warnings from the Lord either via the Scripture or within our own hearts. All of these are very important, and God is regularly speaking to us along these lines. Warnings and admonitions from the Lord are necessary as much of the New Testament is a book of warning. This is because the Holy Spirit is aware of the potential dangers everywhere that could deceive us in one way or another. On the other hand, we often forget that God is our loving Father, and just like any dad He has things that He loves about each of us uniquely. Throughout Scripture, we find God complimenting people such as Abraham for being a godly parent (see Gen. 18:19). He complimented David for being a man after His heart (see 1 Sam. 13:14) and then also Enoch was noted to have pleased God.

Listen for the Lord to tell you what He loves about you specifically. Don't be fearful that you are taking on a higher view of yourself than you deserve. God loves many things about you and wants to compliment you today.

Prayer

Father, cause me to hear the complimentary things that You have to say about me. I know You love me and love many things about me. I also ask You to help me grow in the areas I need to, so I will become more like You. Amen.

Oil of Gladness

"I have poured forth an anointing of gladness upon you even when some expect you to be sad. For it shall wash over you like oil causing you to experience relief from every trial, and many will say of you, how can you smile this way?"

Prophetic Scripture

Thou hast loved righteousness, and hated iniquity; therefore God, even thy God, hath anointed thee with the oil of gladness above thy fellows (Hebrews 1:9).

One of the earmarks of the Christian life is the ability to experience joy in the midst of adversity. Part of that ability comes from choosing to keep our eyes on the Lord over tough circumstances. This is definitely an important part to experiencing gladness in the Lord. However, we find God referring to Jesus in Hebrews 1:9 by saying that because of His Son's commitment to righteousness, there was a special anointing poured forth upon Him. It's called the oil of gladness. When something is anointed by God, it means His tangible power steps in. When God anointed Jesus with the oil of gladness, it was a surge of divine power that enabled Him to be filled with gladness amidst negative circumstances. It wasn't something that had to be mustered up by digging deep into the strength of human fortitude. Instead, the oil of gladness bursts forth from within supernaturally.

When the oil of gladness washes over you, you feel a sense of unexplainable relief that makes you smile. Others cannot understand how you can be glad when times are so tough. So just rest today and believe for the oil of gladness to pour forth upon you!

Prayer

Lord, I receive the oil of gladness right now. I have faith for it to bubble up from within me supernaturally. Let it pour forth upon me and cause me to smile and experience relief and victory! In the Name of Jesus, amen.

In Control and in Charge

"Know that power for leadership lies in self-control. For even as Joseph was able to govern himself against temptation, so shall I teach you how to be in charge of your own vessel, and you shall be elevated to be a leader in your generation, says the Lord."

Prophetic Scripture

That every one of you should know how to possess his vessel in sanctification and honor (1 Thessalonians 4:4).

When you read about the life of Joseph, it isn't hard to see that his ability to live in self-control elevated him to prominence. When Potiphar's wife tried countless times to get Joseph to sleep with her, Joseph emphatically refused. One day when she grabbed him and he ran from her, she made up a lie and told her husband that Joseph tried to rape her. Her husband was angry and threw Joseph in prison. However, immediately after it happened, Genesis 39:21 says, "But the Lord was with Joseph." The Lord saw Joseph's self-control and defended him. Eventually, Joseph was elevated to second-in-command in Egypt. His ability to govern himself caused him to go from the prison to a position of leadership. The result was that he played a key role in saving countless lives from famine, including that of his own family.

Every believer should ask the Lord to show them where they need to exhibit more self-control so that temptation doesn't eventually get the better of them and cut short their potential for destiny. Ask the Holy Spirit to help you be in charge of your own vessel today, because God wants you to be a key player in bringing salvation to your generation.

Prayer

Lord, show me the areas where I need to make adjustments and learn better self-control. Reveal to me any area that might be a pitfall, and I ask You to help me govern myself in righteousness so that I will be an example to my generation. Amen.

God's Work Will Stand

"In this hour you will see My true work stand out from the false and counterfeit. That which I have endorsed shall carry on, and My work through your life will remain steadfast as a beacon of light in this season!"

Prophetic Scripture

...For if this counsel or this work be of men, it will come to nought: but if it be of God, ye cannot overthrow it; lest haply ye be found even to fight against God (Acts 5:38-39).

It can be difficult at times to discern what is from God and what is not. When the early apostles were persecuted for presenting a new and unheard message, a Pharisee named Gamaliel reminded everyone that if what they were preaching was genuine it would survive long-term. While there are many ways to discern the genuine things of God, one way is that God's work can't be overthrown. One major modern example is regarding the baptism of the Holy Spirit. Many groups have persecuted it; however, the Pentecostal or Charismatic movement has continued as the most rapidly growing movement worldwide since the Azuza Street Revival in 1906. Groups and denominations everywhere are constantly experiencing some form of Holy Spirit renewal. If this movement was not of God, it would have dwindled long ago, but instead has lasted over 100 years and keeps spreading.

When God endorses something, His work will stand. If God has given you a call or mandate to work for Him, you don't need to worry about whether or not it will survive. If something is truly from God, it will prosper long-term despite setbacks. Have the assurance today that God's work in your life will always stand!

Prayer

Father, help me discern the genuine work of Your spirit for my life, and I take authority over every hindrance against it. I declare that Your work all across the earth shall stand strong and every counterfeit shall be cut off! In Jesus' Name, amen.

A Counted Member

"I have nominated and counted you as a necessary member of My Body. Therefore, never count yourself as unimportant, for the other members rely upon you and your involvement supplies a breath of life to countless souls."

Prophetic Scripture

For we are members of his body, of his flesh, and of his bones (Ephesians 5:30).

Each part of the human body is important. While we don't sit around pondering each part's function, you definitely notice when one part isn't working! Ephesians 4:16 says that the Body of Christ is held together by that which each individual body part supplies. We may think some parts are less significant than others, but First Corinthians 12:15-24 says that each part is significant. You may not think about your pinky toe that much. Yet, if you've ever gotten up at night to get a glass of water and stubbed your little toe on a piece of furniture, that little toe becomes very noticeable! With your toe throbbing in pain, your entire ability to walk is compromised, and you realize how much you are affected even when something as small as your pinky toe is out of the game.

The Body of Christ is no different, and when we don't supply our part because we think it to be insignificant, the other members feel it and are hindered overall. Others can work harder to make up for it, but how much easier it would be if every part was functioning peacefully together as they were meant to do. The Lord has counted you a key member today, so don't believe for one moment that you are not needed! Many souls truly are depending on you.

Prayer

Lord Jesus, I see myself as an important member of Your Body, and I commit to stay involved and supply my part. I give of my time, finances, and talents to serve in whatever capacity becomes available, and I thank You for counting on me. Amen.

War Against Cancer!

> *"The Spirit says, know that I am grieved by the evil spirit behind cancer and its onslaught angers Me. So use your authority this day and command cancer to leave those you know and even those in My Church, for the Lord of Hosts wars against cancer!"*

Prophetic Scripture

> *...And gave them power and authority over all devils, and to cure diseases* (Luke 9:1).

Jesus spent a great deal of time teaching His disciples how to preach the Kingdom, heal the sick, and cast out demons. Countless times Jesus expected them to heal people with all manner of debilitating illnesses (see Matt. 10:1; 17:16-20; Mark 9:17-20; Luke 10:17-20). Luke 9:1 says Jesus gave them power and authority. The word power is the Greek word *dunamis*, which means miraculous ability. The word authority is *exousia*, which means a delegated right. Jesus gave them the delegated right to act with miraculous ability. Jesus enabled them to literally declare war against disease. Then after Jesus ascended back into Heaven, it became their job to continue demonstrating healing. When the Holy Spirit came at Pentecost, the Church received *dunamis* power (see Acts 1:8). That healing responsibility hasn't ended, and we the Church are to war against disease with healing authority the same way Jesus taught His disciples.

Among such diseases that Jesus taught His disciples to cure was leprosy. It was a dreaded disease of its day, similar to how many people today see modern-day cancer. We need to war against cancer! There are too many people suffering from it, and we need to use our power and authority to cast it out! The Lord hates disease, so let's stand up together and war against the demon of cancer!

Prayer

> *Lord, I use my authority today against evil spirit of disease. I command _____ to be healed from cancer and I say that cancers everywhere must dry up and leave the people of God! In the Mighty Name of Jesus, amen!*

Worship and Bow Down

"Know that there is great power released when you bow down to Me, says the Lord. For as you do, you are surrendering all things into My hands, and I shall take up your cause and handle all your situations according to My unlimited divine power."

Prophetic Scripture

O come, let us worship and bow down: let us kneel before the Lord our maker (Psalms 95:6).

When the devil tempted Jesus in Matthew 4:9, he wanted Jesus to kneel before him. Satan knew that the physical act of kneeling or bowing before someone is the ultimate expression of total surrender. It tells the one you are bowing to that you acknowledge that their power and position is higher than yours and you admit dependence on them. For example, when a citizen bows in honor to a king, they are acknowledging surrender and dependence. When we bow down to the Lord, we are admitting total surrender and that we cannot survive without His divine provision. We are saying that we cannot do things on our own because He is our maker and is higher than we are. The physical act of kneeling can have a profound effect on your heart. It reminds you that you need the Lord. The best part is that when we bow before Him and acknowledge our total dependence, He then rises up and becomes our total provider. That is who the Lord wants to be for us, because He made us and knows everything we need. Therefore, by kneeling on a regular basis, we continually position ourselves to recognize that. Kneel before your Lord today. It will keep your heart dependent on Him, and He will step in to provide all you need.

Prayer

Heavenly Father, I kneel and bow down before You today. You are my Maker, and I acknowledge total dependence upon You. I surrender everything to You and seek You for total provision. In Jesus' Name, amen.

Your Decisions Are Reliable

"I am the Lord who always helps you make reliable decisions so that you will never be in a dilemma about what to do. So set your face in a confident direction today and see that I will not let you fall!"

Prophetic Scripture

For the Lord God will help me; therefore shall I not be confounded: therefore have I set my face like a flint, and I know that I shall not be ashamed (Isaiah 50:7).

Not everyone feels proficient at making the right decisions, especially when the different choices in front of them can all present both beneficial and detrimental outcomes. However, God is there to help us make reliable decisions even when we aren't so sure. To begin with, we need to put into place all the principles we have learned about hearing from God, coupled with following the commandment of Scripture. These two things will help us make good decisions. However, once we have put the right principles into place, we need to have confidence that after we step out on a decision God will be there to fine-tune and course-correct us as needed. That means sometimes we just need to set our face like a flint and make a decision that is set in stone and then trust that God will be there to keep us from falling. Doing this is an expression of faith. It says that you know God will always be there, guiding your decisions even when you don't see it. Feel confident to step out today and realize that even though you may second-guess your decision-making skills, the Lord won't let you fall!

Prayer

Lord, You are faithful and always there to help me make the right decisions. As I step out in faith and make decisions today in the area of _____, I will not be in a dilemma about what to do and You will never let me fall! In Jesus' Name, amen.

Escape from Error

"Take heed, says the Spirit. For evil spirits are unleashed to teach numerous forms of subtle error, and many people will flock to those who will only tell them what they want to hear. So be watchful in this hour and cleave with vigilance to the whole truth of My Word that you may escape."

Prophetic Scripture

For the time will come when people will not put up with sound doctrine. Instead, to suit their own desires, they will gather around them a great number of teachers to say what their itching ears want to hear (2 Timothy 4:3 NIV).

An increasing populace doesn't want to live with any accountability or rules. Unfortunately, the "live and let live" mentality is slowly filtering into the Church in subtle ways that are often undetected. People increasingly want to hear all things positive that make them feel good. Of course, we need positive and encouraging teaching, but some of it these days borders on leaving out the all-important side of Scripture that warns and admonishes.

One of the predominant ways the kingdom of darkness is infiltrating the Church is by offering doctrines and teachings that suit the wants of the people. If it makes people feel good it sells, but if it convicts or commands accountability it is labeled legalistic. I believe the Spirit is imploring us to be watchful and also be open to both the encouraging and the admonishing sides of Scripture. Someone who receives personal correction from the Scripture usually has a better footing to discern error than the one who doesn't. Ask the Holy Spirit today to help you know how to cleave to the whole truth of God's Word so you can avoid the error being unleashed in our time.

Prayer

Holy Spirit, I open my heart to all sides of the Word of God and allow it to both encourage and correct me. Help me always cleave to sound doctrine and escape every form of erroneous teaching. In Jesus' Name, amen.

Investments Recovered

"I always have a recovery plan for every investment lost. For I will never leave My people lacking and I will always restore increase back to them many times over if they will trust in My instructional plan and closely follow after Me."

Prophetic Scripture

...For thou shalt surely overtake them, and without fail recover all (1 Samuel 30:8).

When David was attacked by the Amalekites at Ziklag, the things he had invested in were suddenly snatched away. His family members were kidnapped and the city was burned, destroying people's possessions. Some people wanted to stone David. Yet because he served the Lord, God had already set a plan in motion for David to recover his investments. The Lord told him to pursue after the Amalekites and that he would recover all. Not only was David able to get all his family members back, God also restored the people's material possessions (see 1 Sam. 30:18-19). However, his success was because he first reaffirmed his faith in the Lord (see 1 Sam. 30:6). He could have sat around wondering why it happened in the first place, but he didn't do that. Instead, he unquestionably believed the Lord's faithfulness, and when God told him the next step David went after it fully confident that God would ensure success.

Perhaps you have lost some investments, a job, or a business that has caused financial strain. Like David, begin the recovery process by reminding yourself that God always has a recovery plan waiting in the wings. While it may seem that everything is gone today, stay with the Lord and know that He will eventually bring it all back and more.

Prayer

Lord, I trust You unquestionably, and while I don't have all the answers regarding every loss experienced in my life, I do know that You always have a recovery plan in place. Show me the next step for following You in that plan, and I know that I shall definitely recover all! In Jesus' Name, amen.

His Blood Is upon You

*"Surely, innocent blood was once upon your hands to condemn you, **but now** the blood of Christ is upon your whole being to save, heal, deliver, and protect you. So rejoice this day and say, surely His blood is upon me and upon my family!"*

Prophetic Scripture

...His blood be on us, and on our children (Matthew 27:25).

When God created man, the penalty for sin was eternal death. God knew man would sin, so He determined that someone sinless would have to pay man's death sentence. Having found no one, God Himself came in human form as Jesus, offering innocent blood to pay the penalty. Just prior to Jesus' death, those who wanted Him crucified shouted "Let his blood be on us and on our children." They thought Jesus deserved death, so they believed they could safely assume responsibility for condemning Him. However, they didn't realize that it was innocent and not guilty blood they were calling for. Once shed, that placed it upon the hands of every sinful human being. However, since Jesus gave it freely (see Rom. 6:23), demanding no repayment, we can remove His blood from our hands by accepting it as His gift and then allowing Jesus to forever govern our lives. We go from having innocent blood on our hands to the blood of the all-powerful Christ covering us completely. It covers us with all Jesus is, which is salvation, healing, deliverance, and protection. So when the people shouted for His blood to be upon them, not only was it showing humankind guilty for causing Jesus' death, but it later revealed that when we accept the free gift of His blood, it then covers our entire lives with the power of Christ. So declare today, surely His blood is upon me and my family!

Prayer

Jesus, thank You for freely giving Your innocent blood for me. I accept it as a free gift and declare today that it is upon me and my family! Amen.

The Young Have Come!

"I have always had a generation of the young people to uphold the nations. For though the powers of evil would desire to use the youth to promote rebellion, so shall a righteous revolution of the young come to bring the Gospel to the nations of the world. So pray this day for the youth!"

Prophetic Scripture

...I write unto you, young men, because ye have overcome the wicked one... (1 John 2:13).

There is something powerful about youth. While they lack the wisdom gained from years of experience, they have a determination to make their voice and opinions known. Right or wrong, they are often unafraid to stand up to commonly accepted ideals. In Second Chronicles 26, we read about young King Uzziah who reigned in Judah at just sixteen years old. His youthful zeal enabled him to accomplish incredible things. He built Eloth, a strong shipping port by the Red Sea. He also overcame their formidable enemy, the Philistines. As he sought the Lord, God prospered him. Young Uzziah was so powerful that he eventually became prideful and his legacy fell short of its full potential. That is the risk with the young generation, but if our youth will stay humble and close to the Lord, God can use their youthful energy and zeal to accomplish great things for the Kingdom. Let's pray for the youth of our nations and ask the Lord to raise up young people who are free of pride and self-exaltation, but who aren't afraid to confront the evils of the day and who will create a Gospel revolution worldwide. The young have come to help us and we need to pray for them today!

Prayer

Father, I pray for the godly youth of the nations today. I ask You to keep them from evil and help them to keep a submitted heart to You. Cause them to rise up with a holy fervor to help overcome evil and promote the Gospel worldwide. In Jesus' Name, amen.

Your Backbone Stands Straight

"I am placing an anointing of strength upon you to give you a backbone that can stand up straight. For you shall have a new confidence to stand in your place and not be bowed down by anything that would try to weaken or intimidate you."

Prophetic Scripture

Then he touched her, and instantly she could stand straight... (Luke 13:13 NLT).

When Jesus met the woman whose back was bent over from a spirit of infirmity, it was representative of both a natural and spiritual condition affecting many people. Of course, people have varying forms of physical back problems, and this story demonstrates that the Lord wants them healed of these conditions. We can also see from this how the devil wants God's people to be "bent over" and rendered ineffective because their spiritual backbone has been weakened. In Luke 13:16, Jesus defended His healing of this woman against the Pharisees, saying that as a daughter of Abraham she had the right to be free of her condition.

Many Christians for varying reasons have lost the backbone to stand up for God. Perhaps they feel intimidated by the onslaught of the antichrist agenda in the world or others simply feel unqualified to take a bold stand for the causes surrounding the Gospel. Like this woman, they need their backbone strengthened so they feel able to stand up. I believe God wants to touch you so you are able to stand strong with a new kind of backbone today. The early apostles asked God for this type of bold backbone (see Acts 4:29). Whether your condition is spiritual, physical, or both, or even if you just want increased boldness for God, ask the Lord to touch your backbone so you can stand confidently upright today!

Prayer

Father, through Jesus You demonstrated that You want back conditions healed. I declare that my backbone, both physically and spiritually, is strong, and I am confident to stand up straight in all situations! In Jesus' Name, amen.

Gifted for This Hour

"It is not by accident that you were born in this time. For you have been graced for it, says God. Focus upon your gifts and abilities and let Me enrich them one by one, for I have gifted you especially for this hour!"

Prophetic Scripture

I thank my God always on your behalf, for the grace of God which is given you by Jesus Christ; that in every thing ye are enriched by him, in all utterance, and in all knowledge; even as the testimony of Christ was confirmed in you: so that ye come behind in no gift; waiting for the coming of our Lord Jesus Christ (1 Corinthians 1:4-7).

The reason many people don't live to their fullest potential is because they focus too much on their inadequacies and don't believe in themselves the way God does. God has personally graced you. You weren't born by accident or at the wrong time. You were born during the perfect time to do something wonderful on earth. The key is to break past all the obstacles that have obstructed you from seeing your own gifts and unique capabilities. You can begin to see more clearly how God has gifted you by putting into practice these four things: 1) Believe you are gifted by God; 2) See your talents bigger than your inabilities; 3) Never complain about what doesn't seem to work out right; and 4) Refuse to see yourself as a failure even when circumstances make you feel like one. If you begin here with a positive attitude, then God can open the way for your gifts to be developed and enriched by His Spirit. See that God has anointed you powerfully today!

Prayer

Father, I thank You that I am gifted to do great things during this time in history. I believe today that I am not going to fall short in any talent You have given me, and You shall help me grow in each one of them. Amen.

Clean and Free

"Know that you are clean now through the word that I have spoken to you. I have cleansed you and set you free from all that would make you feel dishonored or degraded. Yes, I have freed you and placed the banner of purity over your head."

Prophetic Scripture

Purge me with hyssop, and I shall be clean: wash me, and I shall be whiter than snow (Psalms 51:7).

Israel used hyssop not only as a physical cleansing agent, but it represented spiritual cleansing. The night before Israel was delivered from Egypt, God instructed Moses to take a bunch of hyssop and dip it in lamb's blood and wipe it over the doorframes of their houses (see Exod. 12:22). The hyssop that wiped blood over their homes was a sign of complete cleansing, and it placed a banner of purity over their lives. Later on when David asked God to cleanse him with hyssop, he would have remembered Israel's deliverance from Egypt. He was asking for a complete cleansing from all the effects of sin and for a banner of purity to be placed over his life.

Spiritually speaking, the blood of Jesus has been applied over the doorframe of your life with spiritual hyssop. The hyssop is the Word of God. In John 15:3, Jesus told His disciples that they were clean through the word He spoke to them. When the powerful truth of God regarding Jesus' blood enters your heart, you become clean and free from the degradation that sin once placed upon you and the banner of purity is written over your life. Have peace that you are completely clean and free today!

Prayer

Lord, I thank You that I am clean and free because of the blood of Jesus. I receive the Word of God concerning the cleansing power of the blood, and I know that my whole being is pure from all the effects of sin! Amen.

God Comes in the Night Watches

"There is unique revelation found when you seek Me in the night hour, says the Spirit. For I am the God who never sleeps, so listen for Me in the night watch and I will fill you with dreams and My secrets there!"

Prophetic Scripture

My soul shall be satisfied as with marrow and fatness; and my mouth shall praise thee with joyful lips: when I remember thee upon my bed, and meditate on thee in the night watches (Psalms 63:5-6).

There is something about seeking God during the night hours that just can't be reproduced during the day. It creates a sense of aloneness, just you and God. The world is quiet, the phone doesn't ring, and appointments aren't waiting. You aren't focusing as intently on all the things that need to be checked off your task list. In fact, most people are usually less goal-oriented at night and tend to reflect more on life, their lifestyles, and their relationship with God. Night is a personal time. I believe this is why God fills us uniquely at night, because we are more open and receptive to Him. We seem more willing to take a good look at ourselves, too. In the verse above, David writes that he is uniquely fulfilled when he seeks the Lord during the night watches. These are special periods in which to wake, watch, and seek the Lord and then sleep again. Sometimes those nights when you just can't sleep are the perfect opportunities for a night watch with the Lord. Jesus sought God at night (see Mark 1:35). Sometimes He continued in prayer all night (see Luke 6:12). Before you sleep tonight, be open to the Lord and ask Him to fill you during the night watches.

Prayer

Lord, I long for You in the night hour. Fill me and open my eyes to Your secrets, and I thank You that I shall find new fulfillment during the night watches. In Jesus' Name, amen.

JULY 9

Guarded from Behind

"Fear not any unseen foe that lurks behind you this day, says the Lord. I will not allow you to be caught off guard, so rest assured that I am guarding you from what you cannot see. Think not on it, for I have already caught your enemy from behind."

Prophetic Scripture

...For the Lord will go before you; and the God of Israel will be your rereward (Isaiah 52:12).

More people get caught up in the fear of what could happen rather than what has happened. The word *rereward* above simply means God is your rearguard. In other words, He's got your back. God and His angelic forces are working around you like warriors protecting a secret agent in some great sting operation. They are making sure that as you go and obey God nothing is going to catch you unprepared. The reason that many of us are caught unprepared is because we fear the unexpected and thus open a door for the devil. We need to renew a daily confidence that God is warding off the devil, and we need to not spend time worrying about things. Undoubtedly, we couldn't count how many times God protected us, kept us, or sustained us from something we didn't even know was there. Often the power and blessings of God are found in what we didn't see, rather than what we actually experienced. We may never know, until we get to Heaven someday, the things God kept us from! Take a hold of this word from the Lord today and know that you don't have to worry because God has already covered your back!

Prayer

Lord, I stand confident today that You are my rearguard and You are watching my back. I reject any thoughts of fear or worry about some unexpected tragedy or circumstance. Thank You, Lord, for guarding me on every side today. In Jesus' Name, amen.

Occupational Promotion and Expansion Comes

"Ask me for promotion, says the Lord. For I can set up things that you could not do on your own. Even as you fulfill your work-related duties, I shall empower you beyond your natural ability that will cause others to take notice to set you up for occupational promotion and expansion in all your business."

Prophetic Scripture

For promotion cometh neither from the east, nor from the west, nor from the south. But God is the judge: he putteth down one, and setteth up another (Psalms 75:6-7).

As we all work in our different occupations, we have to remember that the Lord is the one behind success. While hard work is expected, our success isn't based on our efforts alone. Success comes from the Lord. No matter what you are called to do, it is not human beings who hinder or make the way for you. Sure God uses people, but we can't put the expectation upon them to ensure success. When we serve God and are faithful with those things He puts in our hand, no one but God or ourselves can alter our outcome. You may think that you have a boss, leader, or even business partner who is preventing you from getting ahead. However, God always has a unique way of promoting you regardless of who is on the playing field. The key is to know that God promotes diligent workers who are faithful to Him. He can take your efforts and multiply them so that no matter what seems to hinder you today, it will move aside and promotion and occupational expansion will be yours.

Prayer

Lord, I know that promotion only comes from You and no one can either make it happen or stop it. I trust You that in the long run You will promote me in my work. Help me to be diligent and faithful, and I place my occupational future in Your hands. Amen.

Fully Persuaded for a Miracle

"Know that the presence of miracles rests over you. Don't look to the left or the right and wonder if it will ever come to pass, for the Spirit says it's time to look beyond logical circumstances and be fully persuaded for a miracle!"

Prophetic Scripture

And being fully persuaded that, what he had promised, he was able also to perform (Romans 4:21).

Abraham had within him the ability to believe in the miraculous without analyzing it. When God introduced Himself to Abraham in Genesis 12, He told him to move without even telling him exactly where to go, and Abraham packed his things without question. When God told him he would have a child, he believed what God said even when he and his wife were past childbearing. Then when Abraham finally gave birth to Isaac, his son, God told him to sacrifice Isaac upon an altar. Abraham didn't question; he immediately took steps to obey until God interrupted him. He did so because God already promised that Isaac would be the seed to produce many sons (see Gen. 21:12; Heb. 11:13). Abraham so believed God's words that he expected God to even raise Isaac from the dead if necessary (see Heb. 11:19)! Abraham had no proof other than a verbal promise. He remained fully persuaded even though it took 25 years from the time God first mentioned it until Isaac was born (see Gen. 12:2-4; 21:5).

As you look for the miraculous things of God to occur, begin by believing God based on His verbal promises from Scripture. Keep rehearsing those promises in your heart. As you practice this just the way Abraham did, surely you will become fully persuaded for a miracle!

Prayer

Father, I thank You that Your promises are reliable. I receive a miracle regarding _____. I declare that I shall not be persuaded by circumstances but on Your biblical promises alone. I am fully persuaded for a miracle today! In Jesus' Name, amen.

Relaxed and Stress Free

"Let Me calm the storms of life this day, says the Lord. For though there are things that would add excess pressure, know that there is a place in My throne room where tensions melt away and you shall feel relaxed and stress-free."

Prophetic Scripture

He maketh the storm a calm, so that the waves thereof are still (Psalms 107:29).

Sometimes life is a roller coaster of things to either complete or solve. Without realizing it, we can live under excess stress as we try to manage everything. The devil wants God's people to unknowingly get caught up in the stress cycle. In John 16:33, Jesus said there will be tribulation. However, God's people can have peace in the midst of it because Jesus is more powerful than this world. In other words, even in a stressful environment we can experience a supernatural calm from the Lord. It requires us to turn off our busy agenda sometimes and discipline ourselves to focus our minds only on the Lord. Without that, we will never experience reprieve from all the things that put pressure on us. The world practices all sorts of relaxation techniques, some good and others not so good. Yet their missing element is the supernatural element of the Holy Spirit that only comes from times of focusing only upon Him. So make sure today and every day that you are taking time with the Lord that isn't all about asking for help or trying to figure everything out. Have times where you do nothing but sit back, take a deep breath, and reflect on how wonderful He is. God will surely meet you there, and all your tension will be forced to melt away!

Prayer

Father, I place my thoughts on You today. I choose to set aside all my needs, circumstances, and the questions that add emotional stress to my mind. I thank You that You are calming every storm today. In Jesus' Name, amen.

Anointed with Fresh Oil

"The Spirit says, for I am giving you a fresh anointing in the areas where it seems you are going nowhere and stuck in an empty routine. For fresh oil has come to give you renewed direction so you can make supernatural progress in this season."

Prophetic Scripture

...I shall be anointed with fresh oil (Psalms 92:10).

I don't know much about cars, other than they need fuel and fresh oil to keep running. While a car can run out of gas and still be okay, to run it out of oil is detrimental. It freezes up the engine and the damage is usually irreparable. We all have brief moments when we "run out of fuel," but when we get to a place where the oil of anointing has run dry, real problems arise. Here are a few signs: 1) You aren't receiving or pressing in for fresh revelation from God very often, if at all; 2) Your time with God is sporadic or has become a routine that rarely feels alive; 3) You are satisfied with a church or ministry experience that doesn't challenge you; and, 4) You have lost a degree of enthusiasm or interest regarding spiritual things.

In Psalms 92:10, David apparently recognized he needed a fresh anointing, and we need one from time to time as well. It's what keeps our relationship with God fresh, where it isn't just a routine or religious duty. When the anointing is fresh upon your life, you anticipate every step with the Holy Spirit, and you experience continual spiritual growth and real progress in your life. It's time to be anointed with fresh oil, so ask the Holy Spirit for it today.

Prayer

Holy Spirit, I ask You for a fresh anointing today. Let the oil of Your Spirit wash down over every part of my life, causing me to experience renewed spiritual growth and progress in my life. I thank You for it. In Jesus' Name, amen.

Your Tenth-Hour Visitation

"As the disciples did abide with Jesus at the tenth hour of the day, so I call you to abide with Me in your tenth hour. For when it seems the day is winding down, keep abiding and you will surely see breakthrough in your tenth hour, even when a heavenly visitation seems far overdue."

Prophetic Scripture

... They came and saw where he dwelt, and abode with him that day: for it was about the tenth hour (John 1:39).

In John 1, when the disciples asked Jesus where He lived, He took them to His house. This occurred at the tenth hour of the day, which was between 3 and 4 o'clock in the afternoon according to the time-telling method back then. The tenth hour is that transitional period we traditionally see as a time when we aren't expecting too many more appointments or events. It represents an hour of winding down the business day to begin preparing for evening. For Jesus' disciples, it was too late for any travel, so they stayed with Jesus for the night.

Spiritually speaking, a tenth hour can be when we give up expecting anything divine to happen because it seems the needed miracle is overdue. Yet it is often the very moment when we are positioned for a heavenly visitation. That's when we need to abide close to the Lord and refuse to think it's just too "late in the day" for God to come through. If you feel you are in a tenth-hour situation, abide even closer to the Lord and hold fast to His promises. Then remind yourself that you are right in position for a tenth-hour visitation.

Prayer

Father, I thank You that You are never late. I abide in You and will not give up on Your promises, even when it seems to be a tenth-hour moment. I know You will always come through with a divine visitation. In Jesus' Name, amen.

Shake Out the Darkness!

"Once again I shall shake out the darkness to give My people the purity they have cried out for in their lives, homes, cities, churches, and nations. Run with me now, says the Lord, and together let's create a fresh stream of holiness in the earth!"

Prophetic Scripture

Whose voice then shook the earth: but now he hath promised, saying, Yet once more I shake not the earth only, but also heaven. And this word, Yet once more, signifieth the removing of those things that are shaken, as of things that are made, that those things which cannot be shaken may remain... (Hebrews 12:26-27).

It is always a good thing when God begins to shake things up. I think of it as similar to when you shake an area rug and all the dust comes flying out! Afterward, it looks so much better. When God removes areas of sin and darkness from our lives, it is always with love and mercy, even though a good shaking doesn't always feel pleasing. Yet it's better for God to do the shaking rather than the devil after he has gained access through uncontrolled darkness. Remember, when God shakes the darkness from our lives it is not with harm and shame, but with mercy. He begins with a word. It's important at that point to respond and make changes in whatever He tells you. When we respond and work with God to get the impurities out of our own lives, we enable Him to build with all the good things that remain. Then God can work together with us to remove the darkness that exists in our schools, cities, and nations so that His love and glory can fill the earth!

Prayer

Father, I ask You to help me shake out impurities from my life. I ask You to use me as a vessel of light to create a standard of holiness all over the world. In Jesus' Name, amen.

JULY 16

Season of Many Streams

"It is the season upon the earth when many streams of My Spirit shall flow. Not just one expression here or there, but it will be many expressions of the Body of Christ coming together, and there shall be depths of glory so great that none shall stop it."

Prophetic Scripture

...And it was a river that I could not pass over: for the waters were risen, waters to swim in, a river that could not be passed over (Ezekiel 47:5).

In Scripture, God appeared to people in many different ways. Once as a burning bush, another time as a warrior, and even as a wheel within a wheel. It shows us that there are many different expressions or "streams" to God's Spirit. Just because we have not seen something does not mean that God is not in it. In our limited lifespan, it is impossible to experience all the expressions of God's Spirit. That is why, when the disciples of Jesus wanted to stop a man who wasn't part of their group from casting out a demon in Luke 9:49-50, Jesus interrupted them by saying, "Listen, if He is for me, then leave him alone." His expression and style might not have been just like theirs, but the Lord defended it. We can easily get hung up in one or two familiar expressions, but God is bigger than these limitations. He is a God of many streams and expressions. As we see the many streams of God come together in this season, it will create a river of God's glory so rich and deep that it cannot be stopped. Let's get ready for something incredible, for it truly is the season of many streams!

Prayer

Lord, help me recognize the fresh streams of Your Spirit. Let the expressions of Your Spirit be manifest in my life right now, and I receive the fresh rivers of Your glory today! In the Name of Jesus, amen!

It's Raining!

"Watch as I begin to appear as the gentle rain, says the Lord. For even in times of drought shall I appear to you in the soft scent of the rain. And it shall be a sign unto you that I am with you even as you experience days of light and gentle rains."

Prophetic Scripture

Then shall we know, if we follow on to know the Lord: his going forth is prepared as the morning; and he shall come unto us as the rain, as the latter and former rain unto the earth (Hosea 6:3).

There is something we all love about a gentle rain. It isn't pouring and flooding everything, it's just that light rain that begins to sprinkle down while the outside temperature is cool, but perfectly comfortable. It makes you want to run outside and look up into the sky and let it fall on your face. It has a sweet scent that feels clean and refreshing. Nothing can explain that feeling when there hasn't been a great amount of rain, then suddenly it begins to sprinkle. It feels so clean and new! Think of those moments when you have experienced this kind of gentle rain, and then remember that God appears to His people this way. Right when you feel a little tired and worn, something soft and gentle unexpectedly touches your life. It's like a moment of divine revelation that washes over you and changes your entire outlook on life.

Begin to look for God to manifest to you as the rain, and then next time you look out your window and see a gentle rain begin to fall, remember that God is manifesting among you!

Prayer

Father, I see You today as a gentle rain. I ask that the gentle rain of the Holy Spirit would begin to fall upon my life and give me revelation and divine experiences with You. In Jesus' Name, amen.

Be Strong! Yes, Be Strong!

"The Spirit says, for I am decreeing strength over you today that you shall be able to walk in all the things I have called you to do. Every impartation that I bring you will come with My strength, and you shall be able to hear Me speak deep and intimate things you haven't heard before. So be strong now, I say to you, be strong!"

Prophetic Scripture

...Fear not: peace be unto thee; be strong, yea, be strong. And when he had spoken unto me, I was strengthened, and said, Let my lord speak; for thou hast strengthened me (Daniel 10:19).

God doesn't expect us to serve Him in our own strength. We simply cannot serve and interact with God in our own power. God's power is so great that we are entirely dependent on His grace to walk in it. When the Lord appeared to Daniel in Daniel 10, the vision he received zapped him of all his own physical strength. That was until God provided him with supernatural strength so that Daniel was able to receive what God wanted to give him. That strength came into Daniel in a five-word phrase. It was, "Be strong, yea, be strong!" Daniel 10:19 says that at that moment, he was physically strengthened with the ability to follow God into the deeper things the Lord wanted to give him.

Perhaps you have felt that you don't possess the ability to follow God into all the things He has for you. However, God is prophesying to you in the spirit today and telling you to "be strong," so no matter what He has given you to walk in, you are being miraculously strengthened for it today!

Prayer

Lord, I receive the supernatural ability to be strong today. Enable me to take in all Your Spirit has to give me and help me hear it as You intend. I declare that I am strengthened today! In Jesus' Name, amen.

You Can't Miss It

"I have planned and ordered every chapter of your life so that even when it seems that you have lost your way, I will always cause you to course-correct and stay on track as you determine to walk in step with Me."

Prophetic Scripture

The steps of a good man are ordered by the Lord: and he delighteth in his way (Psalms 37:23).

When we hear God say that our steps are ordered, we need to take those words at face value. God is literally saying that He has the entire course of our lives mapped out, and by serving Him we can embrace that course. Sure, there are times when we make mistakes and wonder how we will ever recover, but God isn't taken off guard. Our mistakes or simple oversights may create detours, but they don't take us out of God's plan as long as we continue to serve Him. God gets us right back where we need to be even when we feel like we have totally blown it. And even when we haven't blown it and are just trying to walk out our future, we need to rest assured that God has it all prepared.

So rest in the fact that you are not going miss your breakthrough or end up out of His will somehow. Even if you feel that you don't know what to do today or what the outcome of the future looks like, God is ordering your steps for a prosperous and fruitful outcome. You will enjoy His plan of blessings and your life will stay on course. You can't miss it!

Prayer

Lord, I know that You have every part of my life mapped out. I will never get out of Your plan and I shall walk in all the miracles, blessings, and wonderful things you have in store for me. In Jesus' Name, amen.

Your Family Unified

"I have a plan to unify your family. So ask Me to create communication and bring understanding so that each member of your family shall surround you with a unified heart and mind. Have faith that I can do this in many divine ways, says the Lord of Hosts!"

Prophetic Scripture

Thy wife shall be as a fruitful vine by the sides of thine house: thy children like olive plants round about thy table (Psalms 128:3).

The scene of the family table is something that is under attack in our modern culture. Families are dispersed by ever-changing work schedules, school activities, hobbies, and more. You don't see the family dinner table in the same way it used to be in years gone by. The dinner table once represented family communion and unity. It was a time when the family came away from their daily activities, sat facing one another, and shared their challenges, insights, and stories from the day. When the Book of Psalms describes the family sitting round the table, it is depicting a picture of unity and communion among the family members.

Whether your children are still young or grown, the Lord wants you to experience family unity. Perhaps your children have taken a path opposite your values and ideals and it has created a separation. If you are married, maybe there is a division between you and your spouse, or as a single person you have lost touch with your parents and siblings. Whatever the case might be, ask God to keep putting a spirit of unity between you and your family members and know that He can cause each member to surround the "family table" with a new perspective that creates communication, unity, and peace.

Prayer

Lord, I ask You to bring my family together in unity. Help there to be communication and understanding in the difficult areas, and I ask that You would open all of us to the truth of the Holy Spirit. Amen.

Ready to Prophesy

"I have placed a spirit of prophecy upon My people. Some shall be known to prophesy while others will experience moments of prophecy, but know this, that prophecy shall continue to rest upon the Church. So be open and ready for Me to prophesy through you at any hour."

Prophetic Scripture

Having then gifts differing according to the grace that is given to us, whether prophecy, let us prophesy according to the proportion of faith (Romans 12:6).

Not everyone in the Bible who prophesied, even those who spoke some of the most amazing words from the Lord, were prophets. Many of them were everyday people God used to deliver a divine message. Some examples were Ananias who gave the word of the Lord to Saul (see Acts 9:17-18). Philip also had four daughters who prophesied (see Acts 21:9), and even King Saul prophesied when he got around a prophetic atmosphere, but he wasn't a prophet (see 1 Sam. 10:11). God is still using prophets today more than ever. Just like these in the Bible who God used to prophesy a key word at an unexpected time, we need to remain open to the Holy Spirit who can use us at any moment to speak the word of the Lord.

If you want God to use you in prophesy, keep a humble heart and stay close to Him. Remain submitted in a local church where your character and ethics can be held accountable and be molded and developed. Lastly, don't feel you have to force anything, but also don't shy away from it. Let God set it up in a divine way and open the door for you. The key is be ready and willing at any time to prophesy!

Prayer

Heavenly Father, I open my heart to be ready to prophesy. Teach me how to be more effective and accurate in prophecy and strengthen my ability to deliver the word of the Lord with taste and grace. Amen.

One Voice Crying!

"The Spirit says, I shall raise up voices in this hour who shall begin to echo a resounding sound. They shall come together as one voice crying and give My church advance notice on what I am doing in the earth. So listen for their message that you may be better equipped for the current time."

Prophetic Scripture

The voice of one crying in the wilderness, Prepare ye the way of the Lord, make his paths straight (Mark 1:3).

When John the Baptist was raised up, it was to prepare the world for the coming of Jesus. He came in advance to get hearts ready and open to the Gospel message. Whenever God gets ready to do anything in the earth, He always sends messengers to prepare His people. God never wants us to be unprepared, because He wants us to participate in the things He is doing. He works in partnership with His people to accomplish a divine purpose. Begin to listen for a common message coming from the ministries and vessels that the Lord has given a platform to speak. Look for a common subject matter in the things being preached and even prophesied that will help define God's direction for the upcoming season. You may also find that some of these things will be right in line with things you are hearing from God in prayer and study as well. Then ask the Holy Spirit to help you know your part to play in the key things He wants to accomplish in the earth. We are here to prepare the way for the Lord's return, so let's tune our ear more readily than ever to hear the Holy Spirit crying with one voice!

Prayer

Holy Spirit, help me to hear the key resounding messages that You are speaking worldwide. I pray for the leaders You have raised up who speak for You and ask that You would help me do my part to help Your purposes be accomplished. Amen.

Your Health Springs Forth

"See this day that I am the God who creates good health. Therefore, set aside special times to fast and seek Me and you shall see infirmities and nagging ailments decline, for I shall cause your health to spring forth that you may live a full and enriched life."

Prophetic Scripture

Then shall thy light break forth as the morning, and thine health shall spring forth speedily... (Isaiah 58:8).

The Bible reveals several methods for promoting good health. We know Jesus paid for our healing and revealed that it is God's will for us to be well (see Isa. 53:4-5). Then we learn that faith in God's healing power brings supernatural healing into manifestation (see Matt. 9:22,28). Also, living a righteous lifestyle reduces the power of disease and promotes healing (see Exod. 23:25). Additionally, there are many biblical examples of natural foods shown to have countless health benefits. So a proper diet plays a key role as well. However, we read in Isaiah 58 that a regular practice of fasting acts as its own unique healing agent. This chapter talks about how fasting causes us to live a life that is liberated from the power of sin and free from nagging illness and heavy burdens. Even when Jesus taught His disciples principles for casting out demons, He showed them that prayer and fasting has the ability to break the power of certain strongholds (see Matt. 17:20-21). That is because sometimes it takes the dedication and cleansing of fasting to build certain faith levels and it also helps us listen to God more effectively.

God wants you healthy, so if you need some areas of infirmity broken, set aside some dedicated times of prayer and fasting, and surely your health shall spring forth speedily!

Prayer

Heavenly Father, I know You want me well. Help me implement the things necessary for a healthy lifestyle, and even as I choose times of fasting and prayer with You, cause healing power to work in me. In Jesus' Name, amen.

Warriors on Your Side

"Know that I have set an army around you to prevent the principalities from their attempts to make you afraid. I shall open your eyes and mind to see that the army of warriors on your side is far greater than those on the side of evil!"

Prophetic Scripture

And Elisha prayed, and said, Lord, I pray thee open his eyes, that he may see. And the Lord opened the eyes of the young man; and he saw: and, behold, the mountain was full of horses and chariots of fire round about Elisha (2 Kings 6:17).

When Elisha and his servant were under attack by the Syrians, in the servant's eyes it looked like certain doom. Enemy chariots circled the city and the servant cried to Elisha saying, "Master! What shall we do?" Then Elisha asked God to open the eyes of the servant so he could see into the spirit realm. Suddenly Elisha's servant saw the entire mountain nearby completely filled with heavenly chariots of fire. At the command of Elisha, the heavenly warriors struck the opposing army with blindness and set them before the King of Israel, who sent them home. The whole event ended all future attacks of Syria upon Israel.

The powers of darkness use any number of things to try to inflict the people of God with fear and make them believe that they will experience some form of devastation. Yet, if we could see into the spirit realm we would quickly realize that God has far more fighting for us than the devil has fighting against us. Ask the Lord to help you see today that you have heavenly warriors on your side!

Prayer

Father, I ask You to help me receive a revelation of how many heavenly warriors are fighting for me in the spirit realm. I commission these warriors to defend me against the powers of darkness and I will not be afraid! In Jesus' Name, amen.

A New Song

"Because you hold the mystery of Christ within you, there is always a new song with new words to sing. For even as you sing about the marvelous works of the Lord this day, your song shall go forth as a victory cry, and you shall experience victory in a new way, says the Lord."

Prophetic Scripture

O sing unto the Lord a new song; for he hath done marvelous things: his right hand, and his holy arm, hath gotten him the victory (Psalms 98:1).

When Psalm 98:1 talks about the right hand of the Lord, it is a prophetic picture of Jesus who won the victory for us and is now seated at God's right hand. The reason Jesus is seated at God's right hand is because the right hand speaks of favor and complete victory. Because of Jesus, we are also seated on God's right hand of favor where there is continual revelation flowing about all the marvelous things He has done for us (see Eph. 2:6). The mystery of Christ in our lives is so expansive that there is always something new to rejoice about. Continually rehearsing it increases your sense of victory. However, the Psalmist doesn't tell us to just talk about it—he tells us to sing. Singing does something that talking cannot. When song is attached, it opens you to a realm of flowing revelation that bypasses your logical mind. It adds an emotional dimension that causes an overwhelming victory to arise in your heart as you realize how big God is and that there is always something new to sing about regarding Him! Sing about God's wonderful works in your life today, and watch it bring you into a new victorious experience!

Prayer

Lord, I sing today about all Your marvelous works because of what Jesus gave me. I am seated at Your right hand of favor with Christ, and as I sing today about it, victory shall arise all around me! Amen.

Entertaining Angels Unaware

"Know that because there is increased angelic activity in this hour, many shall encounter angels like never before. So always be ready, says the Spirit, and do good to those I bring across your path, for surely angels are walking among you."

Prophetic Scripture

Do not neglect to show hospitality to strangers, for by this some have entertained angels without knowing it (Hebrews 13:2 NASB).

In our busy lives, we can get so caught up getting to the next appointment or event that we run right past people who God may want us to encounter for a divine purpose. The Bible shows us that some such people could be angels and we do not even know it! That is why, in our busy society, it is important not to get in such a rush that we forget to pause and show hospitality or minister kindness to people who cross our path. You never know if it's that person in the grocery store, new customer, visitor at church, or person you encounter at a busy mall or airport. Because God has many angels working among us, we never know how many times we are actually encountering them. Countless believers have stories of meeting or crossing paths with someone they suspected was an angel. It's very possible that it has happened in your life even more than once! Ask the Holy Spirit to show you how to express hospitality when the right opportunity comes along. The key is knowing that angels are here and carrying out heavenly business all around us. Let's be ready to interact with them whenever God orchestrates it!

Prayer

Heavenly Father, I thank You that angels are all around. Help me be sensitive to their presence and remember to be hospitable to those who cross my path so that I will not miss a divine opportunity to entertain angels unaware! Amen.

JULY 27

It's Your God Moment!

"Get ready, says the Lord, for surprise and sudden moments when I shall step in and change your course. Even when it seems a certain path is taking shape, so shall Jehovah interrupt it and undo what is in motion and you will surely say, "This has been my God moment!"

Prophetic Scripture

...And suddenly there shined round about him a light from heaven (Acts 9:3).

Before the apostle Paul was converted, he was doing everything he could to come against God's church. He was on a determined path, at least until God interrupted him. We know the story in Acts 9 about how God met him on the road to Damascus. He had a "God moment" when a heavenly light suddenly appeared out of Heaven. That one encounter with God changed his entire life from that point forward, and the current path he was on was no longer relevant. Many people in the Bible had similar God moments that changed their entire course. Jacob experienced a God moment when he encountered the ladder descending from Heaven (see Gen. 28:12-16). Peter had a God moment when he saw the great sheet come out of Heaven (see Acts 10:9-17).

A God moment is a sudden encounter with God that changes everything before you. It may come as a sudden revelation, a vision, dream, a prophecy received, or even as a sudden miracle. The key is when God steps in this way, you know that everything has changed for the better. Begin to decree that you shall experience God moments when the Lord will step in and interrupt you, and it will undo things the devil has set in motion against you. Say, "Today is my God moment!"

Prayer

Heavenly Father, I ask You to cause me to experience a sudden interruption of Your Spirit in the area of _____. I ask for a super-natural encounter with You that shall radically change my course for the better. I believe it and receive it right now! In Jesus' Name, amen.

Your Assets Are Protected

"The Spirit says, even as I gave the garden to Adam, I have also placed things under your care that you have been granted responsibility to watch over. Know that I have given you full authority over all your assets to push back every enemy so that they have no authority to interfere with you."

Prophetic Scripture

And the Lord God took the man; and put him into the garden of Eden to dress it and to keep it (Genesis 2:15).

When God put Adam in the Garden of Eden, with the exception of one tree Adam was given full authority over the garden. He was told to take dominion over it (see Gen. 1:28). We find in Genesis 2:15 that man was there to dress and keep the garden. The word *dress* here simply means to work. Adam was to make an occupation of working around the garden and keeping it in proper condition. Secondly, the word *keep* basically means to hedge, guard, and protect. God was already preparing Adam that an enemy was lurking and it was Adam's job to drive the enemy out of what belonged to him.

We have been given authority over evil spirits and attacks, to drive them away from what God has entrusted into our care. They have no right to what belongs to us! Every asset God has given you receives total protection under the power of Jesus' Name. You can command it to leave your stuff! Look at the enemy coming against your assets today and tell them that they have to back down right now and get out of your garden in the mighty Name of Jesus! Rejoice today, because your assets are protected!

Prayer

Heavenly Father, I thank You that I have authority over the things You have put in my hands. I tell every demon to take its hands off my job, family, home, and all my possessions. My assets are protected right now! In Jesus' Name, amen.

Awakened to Light

"It's not the hour to become weary and tired or be lulled to sleep. For it's the time now to rise up in those areas that you have become lethargic and be awakened to the light once again. For even now a new beam of heavenly light shines upon you."

Prophetic Scripture

Wherefore he saith, Awake thou that sleepest, and arise from the dead, and Christ shall give thee light (Ephesians 5:14).

Sometimes we let the truths that we know as part of our spiritual root system grow dim. It happens when we get sidetracked, too busy, and sometimes tired of fighting many battles. Sometimes we get lethargic simply because we are too lazy in our walk with God. Signs of spiritual lethargy are loss of interest in Bible reading, prayer, and church attendance. It also manifests as an overall lacking excitement for spiritual things that once used to get you excited. Perhaps you aren't as excited about evangelism as you once were, or maybe you aren't as committed to build your faith on God's Word for divine healing.

Waking up in the spirit is like waking up in the natural. It means you have to decide to rise up when you don't feel like it sometimes, but once you do your metabolism gets going, and before you know it you are out facing the day with renewed zeal. Make a decision to shake off all subtle forms of spiritual lethargy if you see it creeping in. Before long, you will find yourself back in the light of Christ getting fresh revelation and impartation from Heaven!

Prayer

Heavenly Father, I make a choice to wake up in the spirit today. I shake off all signs of spiritual lethargy, and I awake once again to renewed zeal. I ask that the light of Christ would shine afresh over all areas in my life that have grown dim. In the Name of Jesus, amen.

Rest for the Churches

"See that I shall create seasons in which My Church shall experience rest and refreshing and they shall be comforted from the battles against them all around. Watch for these times of refreshing and expect My churches and My people to grow and multiply in exponential ways."

Prophetic Scripture

Then had the churches rest throughout all Judea and Galilee and Samaria, and were edified; and walking in the fear of the Lord, and in the comfort of the Holy Ghost, were multiplied (Acts 9:31).

When Saul was persecuting the Church relentlessly, it put a great deal of pressure on the Christians. However, after he was saved, it created rest for the churches. It gave them the opportunity to experience relief from the battles at hand so they could focus on growth. The Bible says it caused them to experience comfort and allowed them to multiply. The Lord knows that for His Church to multiply and be edified, there must be seasons of rest and refreshing. Yes, the devil still roams about doing everything he can to come against the Lord's Church. So it doesn't mean that we just take a spiritual vacation and take our eyes off of the enemy. A season of rest allows the people of God the ability not to spend so much time fighting battles, so they are able to experience growth. This included both local church growth and personal, spiritual growth as individuals. We need to take advantage of these seasons. They are the times to build our faith in God's Word, examine how we are living, and refresh ourselves in the Lord. I believe God wants to pour these seasons of refreshing upon you, so be looking for them and ask God to help you grow in amazing ways during these times.

Prayer

Heavenly Father, I pray for Your Church worldwide. Cause churches, people, and leaders everywhere to experience seasons of refreshing so they can grow and be comforted. In Jesus' Name, amen.

Set on Fire

"I ignite you afresh and I have set you ablaze with new zeal and I have called you My servant of fire. For now, every place you go people shall see your light and power burning among them, says the Spirit of the Lord."

Prophetic Scripture

Out of Zion, the perfection of beauty, God hath shined. Our God shall come, and shall not keep silence: a fire shall devour before him... (Psalms 50:2-3).

It is through our lives that the power of God shines. Yet we all have times when we might feel like our light resembles a dwindling ember. It's then that God sends His wind to blow on our fire and rekindle it again if we are hungry to receive it. When the fire of the Lord comes, it manifests itself though us. That is why in Acts 2:1-4, when the Holy Spirit came and rested upon the people, it came like a fire. Jesus is the one who came to baptize us with the Holy Ghost and with fire (see Luke 3:16). Our God is a fire, and He has come to set you and me on fire too! When your life has been set ablaze by the Holy Spirit, that anointing will devour obstacles and open up a path through resistance and it cannot remain hidden from others. Once a powerful fire has come in contact with something, it will never be the same. This is what God wants for you! God will set you on fire to be seen so that His power will not only deliver you, but minister the same anointing to someone else. Let the Holy Spirit set you on fire afresh today!

Prayer

Lord, set me ablaze with a new anointing to minister and change the things that need to be changed. I stir up the embers of my life today and ask You, Holy Spirit, to blow upon me and increase my fiery zeal! In Jesus' Name, amen.

AUGUST 1

A Day of Comforting

"Let me comfort you this day, says the Lord. For know that I love you deeply and have come this day to strengthen your mind and your heart in all that concerns you."

Prophetic Scripture

Now our Lord Jesus Christ himself, and God, even our Father, which hath loved us, and hath given us everlasting consolation and good hope through grace, comfort your hearts, and stablish you in every good word and work (2 Thessalonians 2:16-17).

Never forget God is a loving Father and He knows there are those times when we need a good hug! He understands the things we deal with and is there to walk us through all of it. He understands our feelings, knows our strengths and weaknesses. He will walk us through everything we deal with if we take the time with Him. He is the God of all comfort and is there to help your faith. In Mark 9, when the father of a demon-possessed boy came to Jesus for help, Jesus encouraged him to believe. The man's response through tears was, "Lord, I believe; help my unbelief" (see Mark 9:24). Jesus didn't disqualify him, but quickly cast the demons from the boy and he was completed healed.

The Lord knows what you are facing today, and while you need to build faith to walk through it, God is there to comfort you in times that are particularly tough just like He did with this young boy's father. Take some time over the next several days and allow the Lord to comfort you. The Holy Spirit is called our Comforter (see John 14:26). So it's perfectly okay to call upon Him for some comfort. He loves you and knows that you need it. So enjoy the comfort of the Holy Spirit today!

Prayer

Holy Spirit, I ask You to comfort me in all things today. Let me experience a comforting presence all around me. I know You love me and are there for me in everything. I love You! In Jesus' Name, amen.

Praise to the Great God!

"Give praise to the greatness of your God this day. For there are things that you have yet to learn about Me, but even as you offer praise to the Great God, so shall you see into the depth of My riches for you and your challenges shall become very small."

Prophetic Scripture

Great is the Lord, and greatly to be praised; and his greatness is unsearchable (Psalms 145:3).

God is so great that our limited human understanding cannot fully figure it out. That is what the Bible means when it says His ways are unsearchable. In other words, there is so much to Him that there are not enough words to give Him the full praise He deserves. Romans 11:33 says that the depth of His riches, wisdom, and knowledge are past finding out. That is because there is simply too much to grasp! Yet, the reason we praise is because the more we do, the more God's unsearchable greatness is revealed in our hearts. Little by little, we begin to see Him bigger than our problems and impossible situations. The more you praise, the more your problems shrink in your own mind because you suddenly realize deep down that these problems don't hold a candle to the Lord. It is important to know that *praise* is a verbal word. You can't just "think" praise. Yes, while you can think on God's greatness, it doesn't have the same effect as actual verbal praise. Verbal praise makes the greatness of God real. Make a practice of verbalizing praise to the Lord, and soon you will begin see the depth of who He is while your problems melt before Him!

Prayer

Lord, You truly are the Great God! I praise You for who You are today, and as I do, I ask that You reveal to me how great You are. Let me enter into the depth of Your wisdom, knowledge, and riches. In Jesus' Name, amen.

AUGUST 3

Relief from the Midday Heat

"Pause in the middle of today and call upon Me. Take a moment to pray and worship, says the Lord, and I will reveal a new dimension of Myself that will bless the remainder of your day. Let Me give you relief this day from the midday heat."

Prophetic Scripture

...Jesus therefore, being wearied with his journey, sat thus on the well: and it was about the sixth hour (John 4:6).

Many years ago before I was in ministry, I used to love going out to my car or to a park during my lunch hour to spend some time with the Lord and read my Bible. It was an enjoyable retreat from my workload, but also an opportunity to get away from the sometimes ungodly lifestyles of my coworkers. It was a much-appreciated midday break. When Jesus went to visit the woman at the well in John 4, it was at the sixth hour of the day, which for us would be about noon. It is that middle part of the day when people are looking for a break from everything the day has handed them thus far. It is no accident Jesus visited this woman at that hour. Her entire life was in the middle of midday heat so to speak. She had been married five times and was now on her sixth relationship. Not only does six represent the hottest part of the day, it is also the number of man, which speaks of man-made efforts. This woman found Jesus when her life was the most heated and she was feeling exhausted and also when she was at the end of her own man-made efforts.

Whether it's just a reprieve on your lunch break or from a time in your life when you feel like you have found yourself struggling in your own efforts, Jesus is there to meet you. Take some time in the middle of today and talk to the Lord. He is here to bring you relief from the midday heat!

Prayer

Lord Jesus, I know You have come to meet me in the middle of my busy schedule and even in the middle of every challenge that I encounter during the day. Remind me to take a moment during the midday to worship and acknowledge You as my source for comfort and relief! Amen.

AUGUST 4

Preserved and Alive

"Give to those in need this day, says the Lord. For in so doing, I have created a plan to preserve you and keep you alive in all situations, and no form of sickness shall be able to overcome you!"

Prophetic Scripture

Blessed is he that considereth the poor: the Lord will deliver him in time of trouble. The Lord will preserve him, and keep him alive; and he shall be blessed upon the earth... (Psalms 41:1-2).

The Bible is filled with Scriptures that talk about how to have long life. Some of the common ones are Psalms 91:16 and Exodus 23:26. However, it's important that we don't forget that there are some verses where the Bible gives specifics about certain practices that promote longevity. One of them is giving to those in need. In other words, you shouldn't close your compassionate heart to those who need help. I believe this includes those who are literally poor financially-speaking, and also those who are spiritually poor and need ministry. Predominantly, however, this verse is speaking about the literal poor individual. We should give to the poor through organizations that help the poor. We can also do so by helping those we come in contact with as the Holy Spirit prompts us. The key is not to leave the poor out of your heart, because keeping them in consideration is one of the promoters of long life. Psalms 41:3 says it is also a deterrent to disease. Ask the Lord to show you today how you can improve your consideration of those in need and let it impart long life into you today!

Prayer

Father, help me become more sensitive to the poor or those in need. Show me those I am to minister to as people come across my path. I thank You that as I consider the poor today, You are breathing long life and health into me! In Jesus' Name, amen!

AUGUST 5

You Can Rise Above It!

*"Yes, the Spirit says, you **can** rise above it. Don't think for one moment that you are not able, for I am in you and with you and know that I am pushing you on to victory, so rise up! Yes, rise above it!"*

Prophetic Scripture

Ye are of God, little children, and have overcome them: because greater is he that is in you, than he that in the world (1 John 4:4).

Many of us are very familiar with this verse of Scripture in First John 4:4. Yet, sadly, we don't always talk and live like it's true. This is one of those Bible verses that makes you think you can overcome and rise above anything. Did you know you *can* rise above anything? That is not because you or I are anything spectacular. We are well aware of our weaknesses. But thank God we don't have to remain limited to these shortcomings. What we need is confidence in knowing that God is pushing us through to complete victory. Because the Lord is our propeller, so to speak, we need to see ourselves with the ability to stomp out any problem, but it first begins with the belief in our heart. We have to see ourselves rising above it! If we see ourselves failing, then we are literally saying that we don't think God is helping us push through. Sure, sometimes when the pressure gets hot and heavy, you think, *Where did you go, Lord?* However, that's when God just wants us to trust Him. He will push you through! So be confident today and know that no matter what, because of God you *can* rise above it!

Prayer

*Father, I know that You are causing me to rise above every challenge today. I will not see myself in **any** form of defeat. I cast down every thought of failure and refuse to say anything contrary. I say today that I **can** rise above it! In Jesus' Name, amen.*

Your Father Is God

"See this day that I am your God, but also your Father. I care for you as a Father and want you to bring every need to Me. When you do, know that as your God, I will use My unlimited power to meet all of those needs!"

Prophetic Scripture

...My Father's God, and I will exalt him (Exodus 15:2).

When Moses and Israel began to sing after the chariots of Pharaoh were drowned in the sea, they sang, "my Father's God." There is a key revelation in this phrase that will reassure you every time you repeat it. It is kind of like when children on the playground brag about who has the toughest, richest, and most cool dad. This phrase is a form of bragging rights against the devil. But more than that, it reveals a two-fold side to the Lord. It gives us the revelation that we have a Father. He is Dad and we can go to Him about anything that is on our hearts. We can literally spill our guts with Papa! Yet, the other side of the Lord is that He also happens to be *God!* This is the side of Him that tells armies to get out of the way. The mountains melt like wax before Him and nothing can stand up against Him. To us He is our Father who loves us dearly, but our Father is also Jehovah God who holds all power in His hands. God your Father cares about your needs today, and He is also God who makes His power available to meet those needs. So keep declaring or singing today, "My Father's God!"

Prayer

Father, I know that You are Daddy and Papa to me. I give You all my needs. My most prominent needs are _____. I lay them at Your feet and know that as my God, You shall make great power available to meet every one of them! In the Name of Jesus, amen.

Entitled to Sonship

"Never forget that I have given you the rights of sonship, says the Lord. Know that I have accepted you freely and have taken upon Myself all the parental responsibilities, and you are entitled to all the privileges and inheritances of a son. You are now part of My family."

Prophetic Scripture

…But ye have received the Spirit of adoption, whereby we cry, Abba, Father (Romans 8:15).

A paralegal friend of mine once shared with me some wording about how adoption proceedings take place in court. During the hearing, the judge will say to the adopting parent something like: "Now, do you understand and accept freely that you are now becoming the legally responsible parent of this child and that they are now entitled to all rights, privileges, and inheritances that you would give to a natural-born child?"

Then the adopting parent says, "Yes."

Then the judge turns to the child being adopted, if they are old enough to understand, and says, "Do you now understand that you are becoming part of this family and accepting this person as your parent and that you are entitled to all rights, privileges, and inheritances as if you were a natural-born child?"

Then the child being adopted says, "Yes."

Through this proceeding, all the parties involved understand their role. The parent takes full responsibility to care for the child, while the child understands that he must accept the parental role to govern them, but also that they are entitled to the full rights of sonship. Know that you are entirely adopted. God accepts you freely today, and you are entitled to sonship with the heavenly family!

Prayer

Father, I accept You as my heavenly parent. You have the right to govern over My life, and I know that You will always take care of me. I also know that I have the confidence as Your child to live in all the blessings of the heavenly family! Amen.

Evangelists Released

"Know that I am releasing a fresh move of evangelism, says the Spirit. For the simple Gospel must be preached once again, and I shall release a new wave of evangelists across the world who shall preach the power of the cross with fervor and new anointing."

Prophetic Scripture

...Do the work of an evangelist... (2 Timothy 4:5).

An *evangelist* simply means a preacher of the Gospel or good news. Ephesians 4:11 says that God raises up full-time evangelists in the earth to preach the Gospel. These preachers present the power of the cross and resurrection with a special anointing. However, we should all be evangelistic in nature. Paul told Timothy to do the work of an evangelist. What was he saying? He was telling him to make sure he was always sensitive to present the Gospel to those who need it. In that effort, we need to pray for God to raise up a fresh wave of evangelists who preach the Gospel with fervor so that the masses will be saved. The Bible says in Romans 10:14, "How shall they hear without a preacher?" The Holy Spirit is releasing evangelists in this hour, and we can be prepared to work with and welcome them in two keys ways: 1) Pray for them to be raised up and released and that their message would fall upon open ears; and 2) We need to do the work of evangelism by sharing the Gospel with people God places in our path.

It's time for a fresh era of evangelism to be released across the globe, so let's stand in faith and call it into manifestation today!

Prayer

Lord, I pray for a new wave of evangelism to manifest on earth. I ask that You would raise up key evangelists who are anointed to present the Gospel to the lost. Help me do my part by sharing the Gospel with those You place in my path. In Jesus' Name, amen.

You Have a Future!

"Always declare that you have a future, says the Spirit. Never say anything to the contrary. For you shall live out your future because I have detailed plans for you and they shall not be aborted!"

Prophetic Scripture

"For I know the plans I have for you," declares the Lord, "plans to prosper you and not to harm you, plans to give you hope and a future" (Jeremiah 29:11 NIV).

The devil cannot take you out early if you see yourself in your future. One of the biggest lies of the devil is to make people think they either don't have a good future or that they may not have one at all. Whatever your hopes and dreams might be, you need to see yourself fulfilling them. God has already detailed a good outcome for you, but you need to come into agreement with it. We will never realize a good future if we complain and say things like, "I am just not sure how or when it will work out," or, "Am I ever going to make anything good of myself?" If we see our good future aborted, then that is what we will live out. Proverbs 23:7 says of the wicked man, "As he thinketh in his heart, so is he." Well, if a wicked man lives according to what he thinks, so can we. Whatever you see your outcome to be, chances are you will talk about it and adjust your life according to it. The things we dwell on shape our future.

Know that God has a good future for you! Therefore, never say or do anything contrary to it. God's plans can't be aborted by anyone but ourselves, so just say today, "I have a good future!"

Prayer

Father, I know that I have a good future that You have planned for me and it shall never be aborted. My outcome shall be wonderful, and I see myself fulfilling everything You have planned. In Jesus' Name, amen.

Children of Truth

"The Lord says, remember that there is always liberty in a lifestyle of truthfulness. Even in times when it seems difficult to stand on the side of truth, always know that it makes Me rejoice when My children walk in truth, for prosperity will follow them."

Prophetic Scripture

I have no greater joy than to hear that my children walk in truth (3 John 4).

Third John is a short letter written by John to Gaius. John expresses in the letter his love for his friend, but also his appreciation that Gaius lived a life of truthfulness. Then John goes on to say that he rejoices when his children walk in truth. Living in truth is presented in three main ways. First, by choosing to speak the truth. That means we should not deceive, cheat or participate in behaviors that go along with lying. Second, it comes by choosing to stand for the truth. Sometimes we get caught in situations where we are fearful to stand up for what's right out of fear of persecution or controversy. Third, it comes by holding fast to biblical truth. Much of the Christian world is compromising biblical truth today.

We need to make every effort to live a life of truth. It isn't always as easy as we think to walk in truth since we often experience interference by our own fears, religious ideals, sinful habits, or similar things. However, it may propel you to walk in truth more confidently to know that it pleases God, just as much as John said it pleased him. Ask the Holy Spirit to help you walk in truth today. He will help you and you will live with the freedom of knowing that you are one of God's children of truth!

Prayer

Lord, I make a commitment to a lifestyle of truthfulness. Forgive me for any areas of untruthfulness or even times when I was fearful to stand up for the truth. Cause my life to be known for walking in truth. Amen.

AUGUST 11

The Lord Is Listening

"Each time You speak of Me I am listening, says the Lord. I listen and record all the discussions and thoughts you bring up about Me. And know that in days of trial, I remember those words and separate you from calamity."

Prophetic Scripture

Then they that feared the Lord spake often to one another: and the Lord hearkened, and heard it, and a book of remembrance was written before him for them that feared the Lord, and that thought upon his name (Malachi 3:16).

We all love to get personal notes and cards from people we love. Many people cherish the kind words written in them and read them again in the future. People also love to hear when someone talks fondly of them. As people, it builds our confidence and makes us feel loved. According to Malachi 3:16, we see that the Lord is not much different in that regard. Each time people discussed Him amongst themselves, the Lord was listening. Not only was He listening, but He created a memory book! As you read further along in Malachi 3, you find that God promised that those who make Him part of their conversations will be spared from harm and separated from those who leave the Lord out of their lives.

So make it a priority to talk about God with your friends and family. Make Him part of the conversation and include Him in what is happening. Just like it means a lot to you, it means a lot to the Lord because He loves to fellowship with you. Remember, in everything you discuss, the Lord is listening!

Prayer

Lord, I love You and want to make You a part of the conversations I have with others. Thank You for remembering the things I say. Forgive me for times I didn't include You when I should have, and remind me that You are always listening. I love You, Lord. Amen.

His Word Never Fails!

*"My Word unto you **never** fails, says the Lord. If I promised it, I shall make it good. So let this be your only thought today, and any time thoughts come to mind that oppose My Word, reject them. Know for certain that My Word never falls short of its intended purpose."*

Prophetic Scripture

So shall my word be that goeth forth out of my mouth: it shall not return unto me void, but it shall accomplish that which I please, and it shall prosper in the thing whereto I sent it (Isaiah 55:11).

When God's speaks, it's the final authority. We have to take hold of that like we really mean it because circumstances will constantly try to be in opposition to God's Word. Sickness will try to arise when God's Word promises healing. Poverty and lack will try to settle in when God promises abundance. Rejection and fear will try to overtake God's promises of acceptance and faith. Often, negative circumstance will try to speak to your mind and can be unrelenting! Therefore, we need to keep God's Word fresh in our hearts. Instead of just quoting a Scripture you have memorized, open your Bible and get that word deep into your heart afresh. Read it to yourself and read it aloud. Say it over and over and "chew on it" in your mind. Think about what it means to you and thank God that it's true. If you keep staying with it, eventually that Word will drop into your heart in the form of faith and it will overtake your circumstances. His Word will never fail and will accomplish what He sent it to do!

Prayer

Father, I thank You for Your Word today. I know that the promises in Your Word are sure and I see them coming to pass in my life. I cast out every thought contrary to that and say that Your Word never fails! In Jesus' Name, amen.

Zion Is Calling

"Even as there is a natural place called Zion, so is there a spiritual Zion experience. There you shall know My covenant is always with you and shall never be broken. For there you shall find liberty and My tangible presence. Know that Zion is calling you this day, says the Lord."

Prophetic Scripture

They shall ask the way to Zion with their faces thitherward, saying, Come, and let us join ourselves to the Lord in a perpetual covenant that shall not be forgotten (Jeremiah 50:5).

Jeremiah 50:5 speaks of a company of people from Israel and Judah who were hungry to find Zion. They knew Zion to be the place where they would encounter the Lord. Zion became a synonymous term with Jerusalem, the place of God's throne. While this passage represents a natural experience, the Bible also points to a spiritual Zion under the New Covenant. The people of spiritual Zion are a group of believers hungry to know their God, who has given them an everlasting covenant of promise. They want a spiritual experience with the Lord that gives them the confidence to rely on that covenant in every part of their life. These people look for churches that emulate Zion where there is a charged spiritual atmosphere and the preaching of God's Word is rich and alive. Those hungry for Zion look for a worship experience that is full of God's high praise and is joyful and free. It's a place where you know God intimately and He knows you and His tangible presence is there.

Ask the Lord to show you the way to continually experience Zion and let the call to Zion-Christianity fill your heart today.

Prayer

Lord, I ask that You would continually show me the way to find Zion in my walk with You. I am hungry to be in the tangible place of Your presence before Your throne. I worship You, Lord, King of Zion! Amen.

Witchcraft Be Bound!

"So take authority over witchcraft this day, says the Spirit. Command every curse that the powers of darkness have used against you to leave your family and bloodline. For you have the authority over them!"

Prophetic Scripture

...Paul, being grieved, turned and said to the spirit, I command thee in the name of Jesus Christ to come out of her. And he came out the same hour (Acts 16:18).

In Acts 16:16-18, we find the woman with the spirit of divination, which is the demon behind witchcraft, following Paul and his ministry group around. Verse 17 says she was following them and crying out to everyone that Paul's group had the message of salvation. She wasn't trying to compliment them, but rather mock them. After this went on for many days, Paul finally had enough and cast the spirit out of her. Sometimes we put up with these little attacks and demons before we finally realize that there is a demon operating. Quite often, the onslaught comes from actual witchcraft which is very real today. It is common knowledge that witches send curses to attack believers. However, we have authority to bind up these attacks and curses in the Name of Jesus so they have no effect over us. Paul knew he had authority over this spirit and cast it out.

If you have been facing a particularly heavy onslaught of attacks, tell every spirit driven by witchcraft against you to be bound. Witchcraft is no match for the power of the blood of Jesus and His Name. It has to stop every attack against you and leave today!

Prayer

Father, I thank You that I have authority over every witchcraft curse in the name of Jesus. I command every curse to leave my family, bloodline, life, and ministry in Jesus' Name, and I say to witchcraft that none of your efforts shall prosper against me, in the Name of Jesus! Amen.

No Thought, No Worries!

"Command your thoughts to come in order, says the Lord. For there is no need to live fretting over what could happen and seems eminent. Know that everything is subject to change and adjustment under the hand of My might and power. Therefore, don't worry or fret!"

Prophetic Scripture

Therefore I say unto you, Take no thought for your life, what ye shall eat, or what ye shall drink; nor yet for your body, what ye shall put on... (Matthew 6:25).

When things in life don't go just right, it can be tempting to give into fret and worry. We can start mulling thoughts over and over in our mind, wondering what could happen. When we get caught up in that cycle, we start to conjure all sorts of negative scenarios in our minds that are excessive and inflated. Jesus told us to take control of our thoughts and not allow our minds to dwell on "what ifs." We need to make a practice of living above this tempting habit. In Matthew 6, Jesus tells us repeatedly not to take on worrisome thoughts about our lives and futures. It must be a common problem with people or Jesus wouldn't have had to mention it so much.

The best way to take authority over fretful thoughts is to speak to them. Command all fearful thoughts to leave you. Keep doing it over and over if necessary, but the key is to discipline your mind not to go there! Just dwell on God's promises and tell yourself—no thoughts and no worries!

Prayer

Father, I make a decision to cast down every worrisome and fearful thought today. I bind all forms of fear and command my mind to come into divine order right now! I take up no negative thoughts and I am worry free! In Jesus' Name, amen.

AUGUST 16

Backsliders Welcomed Back

"I am the God who welcomes every backslider who repents. My Spirit is whispering now to the backslider. For I accept them freely and will heal them with open arms, says the Lord. So call for the backslider to come back to Me this day"

Prophetic Scripture

I will heal their backsliding, I will love them freely: for mine anger is turned away from him (Hosea 14:4).

When God is speaking about backsliders, He isn't talking about the world. He is talking about Christians who got off track or fell into sin. When Israel backslid, God welcomed them back and loved them freely. He offered a clean slate and a do-over. When backsliders repent, God will heal them, and the junk that came upon their life during their season of backsliding, God will restore. He won't hold anything over them. Just like the father of the prodigal son did by giving his son the fatted calf, God will abundantly give the returning backslider all the blessings available from His hand. He will not withhold healing, deliverance, material provision, love, acceptance, or peace.

If you have any areas for which you feel backslidden, go to God and repent. Then know that He loves you freely and welcomes you with open arms. If you know someone who is in a backslidden condition, pray for them and ask the Holy Spirit to reveal His love to them afresh. In our churches, we need to show love and acceptance when the backsliders return and let them know that God will fully restore them. Our loving God is welcoming the backslider back into His arms today!

Prayer

Father, I pray for backsliders today. I call out the names of _____. Reveal Your love to them in a fresh way today and let them know that You are present to heal and deliver them and that You love them freely. Forgive all areas of backsliding in my own heart as well. In Jesus' Name, amen.

The Lord Is Good to All!

"I have depths of goodness to give you. You are My handiwork and My mercies hover over you in everything. Watch Me show you this day that I am good to you, says your God."

Prophetic Scripture

The Lord is good to all: and his tender mercies are over all his works (Psalms 145:9).

For various reasons, the idea gets put into the heads of people that God is cranky and angry and always ready to strike. The last thing the devil wants us to feel confident about is the goodness of God. The Bible has far more to say about the good and merciful side of God than His judgment. And we find that whenever the judgment of God fell, it was upon those who deliberately defied and rejected Him. When an entire generation in Israel was overthrown in the wilderness, it was because they tempted God. To tempt God literally means to say, "God, are you with us or not?" (see Exod. 17:7) They hatefully assumed that God brought them into the wilderness to kill them. They simply refused to believe, even after all God did to deliver them from Egypt, that the Lord was good. Sure, they experienced some situations that looked bleak, but instead of referring back to how God helped through similar situations in the past, they shook their fist against God and Moses.

As believers, we need to take an immovable approach to everything in life by always saying, "The Lord is good to all." His mercy hovers over His people. He wants to bless and help you in ways that you couldn't even come up with in your own mind. So just lay your head upon Him and rest in the fact that He is good to you today!

Prayer

Father, I know You are always good. Your mercy hovers over me today. I will not doubt Your goodness and that You will always take care of me. In Jesus' Name, amen.

Revival Is Here

"I am sending a corporate outpouring upon My people now. For where it has seemed that churches and people are just going through the motions, I am sending angels and opening the heavens to create revivals in certain places and to revive hearts and minds. Know that revival is here once again!"

Prophetic Scripture

Wilt thou not revive us again: that thy people may rejoice in thee? Shew us thy mercy, O Lord, and grant us thy salvation (Psalms 85:6-7).

God has always ordained outpouring and revival events to refresh His people. As we study church history, it was always seasons of sovereign outpourings that fell upon the people of God that resulted in waves of God's power. We have seen revivals of certain biblical truths, healing revivals, salvation revivals, deliverance revivals, and revivals pertaining to the ministry of angels. The list is extensive, but what we need to know is God will always have a remnant of people or a person to begin a revival event. Some revivals last weeks and others for years or decades. Many revivals have created entire denominations and sovereign moves of the Holy Spirit. The key is that revival will have lasting impact, usually on a large number of people. However, there are smaller revivals that affect certain local churches or groups of people and even private revivals in the hearts of individuals. So just because we don't hear about it on Christian media doesn't mean the revival wasn't genuine. The key is when revival falls, it changes everything and uplifts everyone who is part of it.

Let's pray for revival to be poured out and know today that God is always going to have an outpouring. It's time, for revival is here!

Prayer

Lord, I ask You for a fresh outpouring of revival upon Your people. Let there be fresh waves of Your Spirit in nations, cities, churches, and in the hearts of individuals. I call for revival to fall upon us right now! In Jesus' Name, amen.

AUGUST 19

Prepared by Holy Oil

"I have prepared you with a holy oil, says the Lord. You have been set apart for a holy purpose that is being carefully watched over by My hand, and people will say of you, who is this one who walks in such grace? For My holy anointing is visible upon you."

Prophetic Scripture

And thou shalt make it an oil of holy ointment, an ointment compound after the art of the apothecary: it shall be an holy anointing oil (Exodus 30:25).

The holy anointing oil was a mixture of spices used to represent the presence of the Holy Spirit. It was made of four costly spices added to olive oil. Each spice represents a characteristic of the Spirit upon us. The spices were: 1) Myrrh, which means submission. It was given to Jesus by the magi to signify His submission in death. As the predominant spice in the oil, it signifies our primary necessity is total submission to God. 2) Cinnamon represents holiness. It means "erect or upright," which signifies integrity. We need integrity in the anointing. 3) Calamus is a tube-like reed or branch. It shows us being the branches upon the vine (see John 15), and that without Jesus we can do nothing. 4) Cassia means to be bowed down in a prayer posture. We cannot have a strong anointing without prayer. So in short, it takes submission, holiness, dependence on the Lord, and a life of prayer for us to walk in the anointing. These ingredients are combined with the oil of the Holy Spirit who brings them together and creates a beautiful ointment to be poured forth upon the lives of others.

The Lord is preparing you with a holy oil of His Spirit today. Offer your ingredients to Him and know that many will see His visible anointing upon you!

Prayer

Lord, I offer myself that You may create a powerful anointing upon me. Create something amazing from my life that shall be visible and poured forth to minister to many people. In Jesus' Name, amen.

Strength for God's People

"See a season now when the onslaughts against the people of God shall diminish, and as they face the giants of the land, so shall I give strength to their minds and shall envelop them with peace. It is even yours this day, says the Lord."

Prophetic Scripture

The Lord will give strength unto his people; the Lord will bless his people with peace (Psalms 29:11).

If you have ever been standing in faith for a breakthrough, there are those times when you feel emotional pressure to quit. Of course, we cannot give up and we do need to keep standing. Ephesians 6:13 says, "…having done all, to stand." However, the Lord knows when our minds and bodies feel weakened. It reminds us again that we are entirely dependent upon Him. While we need to build faith for breakthrough, it isn't only about our faith-building abilities. It's also about our simple trust that the Lord is there to help strengthen us so we can keep standing. In Psalms, David talked about many days in his life when things didn't look so good, but his faith always came back to the fact that God was there keeping him strong. On those difficult days when you want to fall apart, the Lord helps make up for your weak moments. Psalms 29:11 says He *gives* strength to His people and will bless them with peace. When you don't feel you have any strength, God Himself provides the strength and envelopes you in peace.

Many of God's people have been under severe attack, but know that God is giving us the strength and peace to have total victory. Have faith for it in your life right now!

Prayer

Lord, I ask You for an impartation of Your strength today. Envelop me with peace that all shall be well and cause me to rest in You and know that every attack shall end in victory. In Jesus' Name, amen.

Your Next Step Revealed

"Expect Me to reveal your next steps now, says God. For where you feel unsure about what to do regarding this or that, I shall cause you to see the path and best course to take and it shall be easy for you."

Prophetic Scripture

...Cause me to know the way wherein I should walk... (Psalms 143:8).

The phrase "cause me to know" used in Psalm 143:8 from the King James is translated in some other Bible versions as "show me the way" or "teach me the way." David is asking God to reveal his next steps on what to do and how to live his life. Sometimes we think we have to figure everything out, and it's good to use our good senses and logical minds to make wise choices. However, all the wise choices in the world aren't enough for following God into our destiny. That is simply because we can't always figure out the future. However, God can supernaturally cause or teach us the way. He can guide us and give us ideas and things we didn't previously consider.

If you are feeling today like you are unsure of your next step in life or perhaps you have some difficult decisions to make today, ask the Lord to teach you the way. Of course, that doesn't mean an angel with a scroll in hand will show up, and you may not have an open vision of Jesus. Although any of those things certainly could happen, the key is realizing that God will cause it to happen even in unnoticeable ways or even in what seems to be the last minute. Ask God to show you and then walk out today with confidence that He will make it easy for you!

Prayer

Father, I ask You to reveal my next steps in the area of _____. Cause me to know Your will in each area, and I trust that it shall be easy for me. In Jesus' Name, amen.

Compassion Is Yours

*"Know that because You have pursued My ways and My Word, I have compassion upon you because of your sacrifice. I see every effort made and the many things you have laid down to follow me, and now **My** compassion shall feed you with blessing."*

Prophetic Scripture

I have compassion on the multitude... (Mark 8:2).

When Jesus fed the multitudes in Mark 8, He took careful notice of how sacrificially the people were following Him and coming to hear Him preach. They followed him for three full days to the point that they had run out of food. That is pretty impressive, since most of us believers can't make it through much more than a one hour and thirty minute church service without our stomachs growling for that Sunday buffet line! Yet these people listened to God's Word for three days. There were entire families present. To be honest, I don't know how they did it, especially with small children in tow. Nevertheless, Jesus saw their sacrifice and made a powerful statement. He said, "I have compassion on the multitude because they have been with Me three days and don't have any food." He recognized their sacrifice and extended His compassion upon them. He saw that they laid down their own schedules to be with Him. Because of it, they received compassion from the Lord in return.

Realize that the Lord sees every sacrificial effort you have made to follow Him and obey His Word. Even if people don't see it, God does. You can feel good today knowing that God will extend compassion and "feed you" in your times of need, and He will always bless you in return.

Prayer

Father, I know that You see every sacrifice I have made for You. I thank You that You have extended compassion to me in every situation of need, and I commit to give everything in my life to You. Amen.

AUGUST 23

Leaders Are Born

"There are coming born leaders sent of Me who will stand up in the midst of controversy and be a voice. They shall be a new breed who are born to bring the most abused souls out of a worldly culture to Me. Pray for them and support them in this season, says the Lord."

Prophetic Scripture

Speak up for those who cannot speak for themselves; ensure justice for those being crushed. Yes, speak up for the poor and helpless, and see that they get justice (Proverbs 31:8-9 NLT).

There are leaders, and then there is a certain type of leader born with a quality that isn't afraid of controversy in order to stand up for something or someone. The apostle Peter was a born leader who preached a controversial sermon on the Day of Pentecost and stood up to the leaders of his time to reach the world with the Gospel. Peter, who was once afraid to stand up for the Lord and once denied Him, ultimately had a born leadership quality that made him one of the most prominent apostles of the Bible. In modern-day terms, these kinds of leaders are those who will stand in the midst of a secular culture and speak up for fellow Christians, stand for Gospel issues, and also be a voice to the most hurting and hopelessly lost people of the world.

Prepare for the Lord to raise up such leaders. They will appear in politics, sports, major corporations, various organizations, ministries, or on television programs. We need to recognize these natural-born leaders, pray for them, and support them as they become a voice that will stand up for all of us.

Prayer

Father, I pray for the leaders You are raising up to be a voice in the secular culture. Help them become a voice for Your Church who will stand for Kingdom issues. Strengthen them and show me how to support them. Amen.

It Shall Be Done!

> *"Come in agreement in prayer, says the Spirit. For many in My Church do not yet understand the full power of agreement and that heaven waits to hear two or more unified on the same request. So agree and it shall be done!"*

Prophetic Scripture

> *Again I say unto you, That if two of you shall agree on earth as touching any thing that they shall ask, it shall be done for them of my Father which is in heaven* (Matthew 18:19).

We all have powerful times of prayer alone, but something happens when you pray with others. The prayer goes to another level. You feel the faith and power of your fellow believers as requests are being offered up to God. If you are struggling in prayer or need a boost, get someone to pray with you. While a prayer partner may not always be available, it helps to have one especially in more challenging situations. Find someone who will take your prayer need seriously and help push you into a victorious answer. The agreement is really powerful when your prayer partner wants to see the answer just as much as you do, when they aren't giving up until it happens. Another way to experience agreement in prayer is by attending prayer meetings with other believers who are all unified on the same mission in prayer. Things happen in that environment. When the early church was being persecuted, they got together and lifted their voice in prayer until power was released (see Acts 4:29-31).

According to Jesus, when two people get together in agreement they get answers from Heaven. Make a point to pray with someone today, even if it's your spouse and family members. As you agree, it shall be done!

Prayer

> *Father, I thank You for the power of agreement. I make a commitment to pray with my fellow believers and help them pray for their needs. I know every time we pray together, it shall be done! In Jesus' Name, amen.*

Cry Out!

"Never hesitate to cry out to Me, says the Lord. Even in times when you have done wrong, don't run away from Me, run to Me! And at the moment when you cry out, so shall I surely come to save you."

Prophetic Scripture

...I cried by reason of mine affliction unto the Lord, and he heard me... (Jonah 2:2).

When Jonah got out of God's will and ended up in the belly of the great whale, he realized that he had taken a wrong turn in running away from God. I am sure it was no pleasure ride inside the fish's smelly stomach. In fact, Jonah referred to it as "hell." Yet, when Jonah cried out to God in the midst of his situation, the Lord heard Jonah. Of course, we know the end of the story—how the fish spit Jonah out on dry ground and Jonah obeyed God's call for him.

Sometimes we think that because we disobeyed God or took a wrong turn somewhere that God stops listening to us when we cry out to Him. On the contrary, that is exactly what God wants us to do. The Lord was waiting for Jonah's cry just so He could rescue him from his situation. God is waiting for you to cry out to Him today. Your calling out to Him has nothing to do with your own righteousness or lack thereof. He answers because of His mercy. So, no matter where you are, what has happened, or what you have done right or wrong, always run to the Lord and cry out!

Prayer

Father, I know that You are always listening for my cry. You don't answer based on my own right or wrong. You hear my cry because of Your mercy. I will always run to You in my time of need and never run away. In Jesus' Name, amen.

AUGUST 26

Fiery Darts Extinguished!

"Raise up your faith shield this day and know that your enemy, the devil, fears your stand against him. Even when he tries to shoot arrows all around your dwelling, every fiery dart shall be extinguished by your faith."

Prophetic Scripture

Above all, taking the shield of faith, wherewith ye shall be able to quench all the fiery darts of the wicked (Ephesians 6:16).

According to Ephesians 6:16, the best way to stand up against the fiery darts of the devil is by putting up a shield. A shield is bigger than a dart and its job is to make arrows bounce off so that you don't even feel them. The way the shield of faith works against the devil's arrows is to render them completely ineffective. It's as if they aren't even in your vicinity! The Bible describes Satan's arrows as fiery, that they come at us looking like a serious threat. Yet the shield of faith makes it so that they have no effect on you.

Look at whatever flaming arrows seem to be coming against your life today. Take a moment to sit back and picture yourself holding a great big body-sized shield. See the devil's arrows shooting at it while you sit safely behind the shield unharmed and untouched. Often, the reason the darts of the enemy get through to us is because we see them getting through. Remember, faith is being assured and convinced (see Heb. 11:1). Tell yourself today that you are assured by faith in God's protection and the devil's fiery darts are all being extinguished!

Prayer

Father, I have faith that You are protecting me from every fiery dart of the enemy. I lift the shield of faith today and expect every arrow to be extinguished and none of them shall have any effect on me. In Jesus' Name, amen.

A Positive Spirit

"The Lord says, resist the temptation to lean in the direction of the negative approach. For the world responds with negativity and fear, but you have been given a positive and joyful spirit from Me."

Prophetic Scripture

Then said Thomas, which is called Didymus, unto his fellowdisciples, Let us also go, that we may die with him (John 11:16).

Many years ago, a relative of mine responded to a negative doctor report about a loved one in an amazing way. Their loved one was fighting for their life, and the doctor said that they had a 50/50 chance of living. The doctor gave his assessment with a very serious look on his face as if to say, "I am saying 50/50, but it's unlikely the patient will improve." My relative responded to the report by saying, "Well doctor, I am going to lean on the positive side of the 50/50 then. Since you are saying they could go either way, I say they will go the direction of living!" Do you know what happened? Their loved one lived!

Often our outcome is largely determined by our outlook. It's common knowledge, even in the medical industry, that when patients are facing debilitating medical conditions, it's the ones with the positive outlook who overcome their challenges. We who are of God should always have a positive and joyful outlook because we know what the Bible promises us. Not only does it promise the ability to overcome in this life, it promises us the blessing of eternal life. We can't lose! So look at your life and circumstances today with a new outlook because the Lord is on your side!

Prayer

Father, I thank You that I can have a positive outlook today because I am Your child. I repent of all negativity and ask that You would help me approach life positively and according to Your Word. In Jesus Name, amen.

Move Forward!

"Though the enemy would pursue you this day, keep moving forward, says the Lord. Don't look at yesterday or analyze what the enemy did or even might do; just raise your rod of authority and move forward. And yes, you will come out on the other side!"

Prophetic Scripture

The Lord shall fight for you, and ye shall hold your peace. And the Lord said unto Moses, Wherefore criest thou unto me? Speak unto the children of Israel, that they go forward: but lift thou up thy rod, and stretch out thine hand over the sea, and divide it: and the children of Israel shall go on dry ground through the midst of the sea (Exodus 14:14-16).

Many years ago, there was a point in our lives that it seemed like there was one storm after another. I am sure every believer can say "ditto" to that! We felt like we were in a tornado with only moments of relief. Our pastor back then gave us some simple but incredible wisdom. He said, "Though there are many storms, there is only one devil." That really took the magnitude out of our problems. The devil was behind all of it and we needed to use our authority and keep pressing forward. Sometimes, our tendency is to retreat or beg God. In the Scripture above, the Lord told Moses, "Why are you crying to Me? Use your rod, Moses, and go forward!" God knew He had put authority in Moses' rod! We have been given our rod of authority through Jesus' Name. Ephesians 2:6 says we are seated with Christ in heavenly places, far above all evil powers and might. So don't retreat from the devil today, just raise your rod of authority and move forward!

Prayer

Lord, I thank You that I have the authority to move forward today because of Jesus. I take my rod of authority right now and command the way of my deliverance to be opened and every storm to cease. In Jesus' Name, amen.

AUGUST 29

In the Quiet

"Spend time in quiet moments, for it is in times of quiet that you will hear Me speak to you. Even as you pray, wait for Me in times of silence and surely you will sense My presence and see salvation as you never have before."

Prophetic Scripture

It is good that a man should both hope and quietly wait for the salvation of the Lord (Lamentations 3:26).

In Lamentations 3:26, the Hebrew word for *wait* means to be in silence. Often when we come to prayer, the conversations we have with the Lord are one-sided. We do all the talking as we rattle off our list to God. Sometimes we need to become better listeners! This verse teaches us that it is beneficial for us to spend time in silence as we wait and listen for the Lord. Sometimes during extended times of prayer and fasting, I spend time praying and then afterward just lie down on the couch or bed and quiet down. Sometimes I fall asleep or I just lay there in twilight sleep. While it doesn't happen every single time, it's most often the time I hear the Lord speak. Those times of quiet, when you shut off your mind and just focus on the Lord, are when you position yourself to hear God. Make it a practice to have times of silence when you pray.

If we want God to give us direction and show Himself strong, we need times of silence where all we do is tell the Lord we are just there to listen, nothing else. It helps us experience His presence and see His salvation working in our lives. Spend some time in the quiet today!

Prayer

Lord, I just want to spend a few moments in silence before You today. Speak to me, let me hear Your voice, and show me Your salvation. Teach me how to hear You, for I am listening. Amen.

You Are Forgiven

"Know that when you have brought your sins to Me and confessed them, they are gone. I do not remember them, says God, and I will not deal with you after them, so I call you to forget them this day."

Prophetic Scripture

If we confess our sins, he is faithful and just to forgive us our sins, and to cleanse us from all unrighteousness (1 John 1:9).

Although many Christians know for a fact that they have forgiveness through the blood of Jesus, they still think somehow that God will only bless them once they get certain sin habits or shortcomings dealt with. Of course, we need to eliminate sin and bad habits from our lives. First, because our lifestyle needs to reflect the freedom in Christ we have been freely given, we avoid sin because we love God and His ways. Second, sowing constant sinful behavior results in reaping the harvest sin brings. Simply said, wrongdoing has bad results. However, God isn't determining whether or not to bless you according to your ability to do the right thing all the time. He knows you cannot. He forgives us because of the blood of Jesus. It's not based on how good we can be; it's based on the blood of Jesus. God does not want us to conceal wrongdoing from Him, and He wants us to live a repentant lifestyle that is open and honest before Him. He allows us to freely bring to Him our wrongdoing and lay it at the cross where we are cleansed from all unrighteousness. So forget your sins; God does, and you are forgiven today!

Prayer

Lord, I thank You that I have total forgiveness by the blood of Jesus. I am washed pure of all sin, and because You have forgotten my sins I choose to forget them too and know that You will bless me. In Jesus' Name, amen.

Come Up Higher

"I call you to come even closer to Me, says the Spirit. For there is always a higher place for you to ascend, a place where you can experience greater things in the supernatural and greater revelation directly from My throne. So never stop pressing to come up higher."

Prophetic Scripture

...Come up hither, and I will shew thee things which must be hereafter (Revelation 4:1).

No matter how much we grow in the things of the Spirit, there is always more to learn. It's astounding to think that even after the apostle John had encountered Jesus so powerfully in the first chapter of Revelation, there was more to come. The Spirit told him to come up to yet another level. There is always another place, another dimension with the Holy Spirit. I am certainly not saying that every Christian is expected to have an "apostle John experience." However, I do know that there are always supernatural realms with God that we have yet to know. We need to press in for these realms. While we don't want to get unbiblical and goofy in our quest, we also don't want to get complacent as though there is nothing left to encounter. Sometimes we have become too familiar with it, as if it is somehow old news.

As we pray and press into God, we need to ask Him to show us how to go deeper in supernatural things. Honestly, until we have the results we saw in the ministry of Jesus and the early apostles, we still have a long way to go! So make it a quest today to press in for God's power and choose to come up higher!

Prayer

Lord, teach me how to continually grow in my experiences with You in the things of the Spirit. Help me not to become complacent with Your power and always press in for more. Lord, I am coming up higher today! In Jesus' Name, amen.

Have Confidence

"Immerse yourself in the promises of My Word, says the Lord. For they will build your knowledge and settle your faith. Then you shall have confidence that I always answer when you make requests."

Prophetic Scripture

And this is the confidence that we have in him, that, if we ask anything according to his will, he heareth us: and if we know that he hear us, whatsoever we ask, we know that we have the petitions that we desired of him (1 John 5:14-15).

God's Word is His sovereign promise to you, and everything He says in His Word is what He will do. His Word will build confidence in you. However, if you don't spend time in God's Word, you simply will not have confidence in how God will respond to you, especially in difficult situations. You may have a mental understanding, but that isn't confidence. Confidence is the absolute belief that comes because you have spent devoted time in His Word. You become assured and confident at what you spend time doing, so by spending time in the Bible you become confident of the promises written inside. Many Christians simply don't spend enough time delving deeply into God's Word. They read a few verses in the morning before work, but that's about it. They don't make a constant focus on God's Word to the point where it builds confidence in them that God will do what is written. Immerse yourself in God's Word and let it build a confidence of faith in you so that when you pray, you *know* the Lord has heard you and you will receive the answer!

Prayer

Lord, I commit to spend more time in Your Word. I know that everything You have said in Your Word is what You will do. I believe it and thank You that Your Word will cause me to have confidence today! Amen.

Repaid from Heaven

"Remember that I repay and give back all you have given to the poor. For your gifts are in your heavenly account and ready to be withdrawn through prayer in your time of need."

Prophetic Scripture

He that hath pity on the poor lendeth unto the Lord; and that which he hath given will he pay him again (Proverbs 19:17).

God has many different attributes, but many Scriptures describe God in the business banking sense. Jesus said to lay up for yourselves treasures in Heaven (see Matt. 6:19-20). In other words, He was saying to make deposits in Heaven. In this context, He was talking about giving money into heavenly things, including giving to the poor. He was saying that God keeps a record of what we have deposited. Then Paul, talking to the Philippians about giving offerings into his ministry, said that he wanted them to do so not just so he could receive a gift, but also so that fruit would abound to their account (see Phil. 4:17). What account was he speaking of? Their heavenly account of deposit! Proverbs 19:17 shows us that not only can we deposit into a heavenly bank account, but we can expect to withdraw from one, particularly when we give to the poor. Paul emphasized this truth to the church at Macedonia in Second Corinthians 9:6, again regarding offerings for his ministry, when he tells them "he which soweth sparingly shall reap also sparingly." In modern terms he was saying, "He who deposits a little will only be able to withdraw a little."

Know today that the Lord will repay every gift given and in your own time of need you will have a full heavenly account to draw from!

Prayer

Father, I thank You that as I give to the poor and into Your Kingdom work in various places, I am filling my heavenly account. Lord, show me where to sow a seed today and I thank You that You will repay again! In Jesus' Name, amen.

Strength for the Weakened Hands

"Now I am providing you with assistance in areas where your hands have felt weakened and unable to hold on, and you shall be strengthened to finish tasks and do things you have felt unable to before."

Prophetic Scripture

And all they that were about them strengthened their hands... (Ezra 1:6).

When the leaders rose up to rebuild the temple in the Book of Ezra, the surrounding people banded together to help them. The Bible says that their efforts strengthened the hands of the workers. In other words, they assisted them so that they were able to accomplish the work. Just like arthritis of the hands makes people feel as though they cannot hold onto things, some Christians are experiencing "weakened hands" and it seems they will not finish certain tasks they have set out to do. They need help to strengthen their hands. In the days of the temple rebuilding, God saw to it that the needed help was provided so they could keep hold of the task before them.

In your case today, no matter what task you are trying to keep hold of, know that the Lord is providing you help. It may seem like the thing you are trying to hold onto is going to fall, but know that the Lord gives strength for the weakened hands. Even if you are facing literal arthritis, trust that God is going to give you relief and enable you to do things you have been unable to before because strength has come for weakened hands.

Prayer

Father, I thank You that You have strengthened my hands to complete every task before me. You bring relief to my hands and all my efforts. Everything I take hold of shall be maintained in my grasp and nothing shall be left incomplete. In Jesus' Name, amen.

The Lion Prevails!

"Yes, the Lion of Judah does triumph in all things and shall prevail over nations, cities, and local municipalities and shall even govern the political elections of this time. For what it seems cannot be done at the hand of man, the Lion shall roar and His purposes shall prevail!

Prophetic Scripture

…Behold, the Lion of the tribe of Judah, the Root of David, hath prevailed to open the book, and to loose the seven seals thereof (Revelation 5:5).

When most of us look at modern-day governments and politics we all sit back and say, "What is the world coming to?" We wonder where the world will be by the time our children and grandchildren grow up. The world landscape appears rather daunting. Yet what we need to remind ourselves of is that even when certain elections don't seem to go the way we thought they should, God has everything arranged to work for His prophetic timetable. Of course, that doesn't remotely mean we should just fold our hands and not be involved in political things or make our voice be heard. We need to do that, but what we have to remember is that no matter the outcome, God will always prevail. He will still accomplish what man cannot and is in complete power over the global picture. In Revelation 5:5, when there was no one available to open the book, the Lion of Judah was found able! It says He has prevailed. Pray for world events, governments, and elections today and know that in every situation, the Lion prevails!

Prayer

Lord Jesus, You are the Lion of the Tribe of Judah and You prevail over everything today! You are able to do what man cannot, so I pray for world events today, even those concerning _____. I pray for the governments and elections in _____. Let Your purposes be established in these things. Amen!

Everything Submits

*"Know this day that every word and illegal activity the enemy has used to threaten you must **now** assume the submissive position. For you have been seated with Christ and every power and authority bows down to Him!"*

Prophetic Scripture

Who is gone into heaven, and is on the right hand of God; angels and authorities and powers being made subject unto him (1 Peter 3:22).

If there is any revelation we need to get down inside of our spirit, it is the revelation of who we are in Christ. Often the reason we allow our minds to get overwhelmed by life is because we forget where we have been seated. Ephesians 2:6 says, "And hath raised us up together, and made us sit together in heavenly places in Christ Jesus." You have been seated with Christ! The enemy tries to throw all sorts of threatening thoughts and attacks against us. Yet, it's much harder for any of those efforts to succeed when you know who you are seated next to! Not only are you seated next to Jesus, but that location places you above the enemy's attempts. That is because according to First Peter 3:22, *all powers* have been made subject unto Him! *Nothing* can stand up to Jesus!

So get bold and take every problem you are facing today and see it submitting to you. You may even consider writing those problems on paper, then putting it on the floor and standing on it just to remind yourself that these things are submitted under your feet. Not only are these problems subject to Jesus, but they are subject to you because you are seated with Him. Everything the devil has tried to do submits to you today!

Prayer

Lord, I know that I am seated with Christ today. I declare every demonic attack is under my feet and must submit to me because they must submit to Jesus. All powers are subject to Christ and I have overcome them! In Jesus' name, amen.

Retaliate by Love

"Look this day for ways to retaliate against evil by showing compassion. For even as you do shall signs and wonders be your portion, says the Lord."

Prophetic Scripture

And Jesus went forth, and saw a great multitude, and was moved with compassion toward them, and he healed their sick (Matthew 14:14).

When John the Baptist was beheaded, it was a painful moment for Jesus. John was not only Jesus' cousin, but he was the divine messenger from Heaven who prepared the way for His ministry. He was the one who baptized Jesus and said, "Behold the Lamb of God" (John 1:29). John was extremely dear to the Lord, so when John died, Matthew 14:13 says that after Jesus heard about it He went to a desert place to be alone. Most people at that moment would have shut the world out for a while so they would have time to get through the grief. Of course, Jesus knew John was beheaded through the influence of demonic power, so Jesus' response to the whole event truly became an amazing retaliation against the devil. When He tried to get time alone, people followed Him. Instead of asking them to give Him some space, He responded with compassion by healing their diseases! First, He retaliated by allowing compassion to rise up in Him, and second, healing them became a retaliation against the demons of infirmity. What a blow to the devil!

We can retaliate against the powers of darkness coming against us by showing compassion to people in the middle of our own challenges. Just like Jesus, the outcome will result in miracles. Retaliate with love today!

Prayer

Father, I make a decision today to show compassion to those who need ministry as a retaliation against every demonic power. Show me where to express Your love, and I thank You it will result in miracles. In Jesus' name, amen.

Transformed by the Holy Ghost

"This day My Spirit within you is stirring once again. For even when the Spirit came upon you and filled you with power, it was a pivotal event. Therefore, know now that you cannot go backward because everything in you has been transformed by the Holy Ghost."

Prophetic Scripture

But ye shall receive power, after that the Holy Ghost is come upon you... (Acts 1:8).

Pentecost was a pivotal event that changed history. It was what transformed Jesus' disciples from a group of timid individuals who fled His crucifixion into a group of ministry machines who stood up to controversy and performed signs and wonders. Pentecost was the event that caused everyday people to walk in the miraculous, pray in the spirit, and enabled them to cast out formidable demons. It caused the shadow of Peter to pass over people and heal them (see Acts 5:15). Every person in the New Testament who encountered the power of Pentecost was transformed. Jesus prepared His disciples for the historical moment that would change people's lives forever by saying, "You shall receive power after the Holy Ghost is come upon you." He was letting them know, "Listen guys—after the Spirit fills you, your life will never be the same!" I don't know about you today, but my life radically changed once I was filled with the Holy Spirit. My Christianity took on a new, exciting direction. I have never once wanted to return to the way it used to be. That's because when the Holy Ghost hits you everything is transformed. Don't take the Spirit within for granted today because He is stirring in you again. He won't leave you alone, because you have been transformed by the Holy Ghost!

Prayer

Holy Spirit, thank You for filling me with power. Cause me to move out in that power that is stirring within me. My life has been transformed by the baptism of the Holy Ghost and I will never be the same. Amen.

No Comparison

"Know that there are many resources for information to investigate that can offer solutions and knowledge, but there are no resources that can match up to what I have promised you. So let nothing distract you, for there is no comparison."

Prophetic Scripture

To whom then will ye liken God? or what likeness will ye compare unto him? (Isaiah 40:18)

We live in an information age. You can click on the Internet for just about anything that you want to research, and with the click of a finger find countless facts and opinions on any subject. While this and other resources can be helpful, we have to be careful that we are not letting all the information out there interfere with our reliance on God. Even as dedicated Christians, our human nature side sometimes wants a human resource. In other words, we want to hear what another person has to say. For example, sometimes we want to hear what public opinion is on health issues rather than trust God's healing promises. We want to look at all the factual ways to fix our family lives, but we sometimes ignore that it's prayer and Bible time as family that keeps us united. Again, while not all information out there is bad, we need to make what God has to say our first priority. We need to determine that His promises outweigh even what good advice and natural solutions have to offer. When it comes right down to it, there is nothing out there that can match up to the God who put the stars in the sky and formed the universe. If He can do all those things, what He can do for you is unlimited. There is no comparison!

Prayer

Father, I thank You that there is nothing this world can offer as an answer or solution that can match what You can do. I keep my eyes on You today and trust Your promises as my final authority. There is no comparison! Amen.

The Sick Raised Up

"I am spreading an anointing upon the land, says the Spirit, to raise up those on death beds and those who have no hope. Even those with long-term, nagging ailments from which it seems they will never find relief—I am raising them up. So neglect not to pray in faith, anoint with oil, and attend healing gatherings, because it is time for the sick to be raised up!"

Prophetic Scripture

Is any sick among you? let him call for the elders of the church; and let them pray over him, anointing him with oil in the name of the Lord: and the prayer of faith shall save the sick, and the Lord shall raise him up; and if he have committed sins, they shall be forgiven him (James 5:14-15).

If there was ever a time for a healing revival, the time is now! There are too many sick believers and too many unsaved sick people who need a healing miracle. It's time for healing revival to sweep the land and for the sick to be raised up! We can start cultivating the seeds of a healing revival in three ways. First, pray and ask God to raise it up. Second, look to God's leaders. While all of us can pray for the sick, there is a key piece that is carried by the "elders" that God needs. James says "call for the elders." So expect God to establish healing meetings with those anointed specifically for this task, and don't neglect its importance. Third, anytime you have opportunity, pray for the sick in faith.

It's time once again for those with no hope to experience the healing power of God in ways that man cannot explain. It's time for the sick to be raised up!

Prayer

Lord, I ask You to raise up a healing revival. Raise up leaders and those anointed for this task, and I will do my part to support them and pray for the sick whenever the opportunity presents itself. In Jesus' Name, amen.

Make a List

"Keep a journal now of the things I do for you in the months to come, both great and small. For You will see greater supernatural acts than you have known thus far, but keep a list of them. Then surely you will find from your list that through Me there is nothing impossible, says the Lord."

Prophetic Scripture

Praise ye the Lord. O give thanks unto the Lord; for he is good: for his mercy endureth forever. Who can utter the might acts of the Lord? who can shew forth all his praise? (Psalms 106:1-2)

One of the best ways to give thanks to the Lord and show forth His praise as seen in Psalms 106:1-2 is to make a thankfulness list. Each time God does something amazing in your life, take the time to write it down, no matter how small it seems. Every answer to prayer should be recorded! Israel's biggest mistake with God was they forgot to rehearse all the incredible things He did to deliver them, so when new challenges arose they didn't expect God to intervene with a miracle. It's hard to imagine how they could forget the parting of the Red Sea, but they did. If they could forget something of that magnitude in their time of trial, we could easily forget also. Sure, we all say, "God is good," but you have to get specific. When Moses and Israel sang right after they were delivered from Egypt, they rehearsed a specific list of what God did (see Exod. 15). David rehearsed it for them again all through Psalm 106.

Begin making a list today and record everything God does for you over the next year. Watch what happens to your faith! You will find nothing is impossible with your God!

Prayer

Lord, even today I begin my list of thankfulness. I thank You for _____. Help me remember each wonderful thing that You have done and are doing for me right now. Thank You, Lord! Amen.

Looking for His Coming

"Never lose sight that I am coming again. Keep looking upward, says the Spirit, for your redemption draws nigh. So even be encouraged this day by these words."

Prophetic Scripture

Nevertheless we, according to his promise, look for new heavens and a new earth, wherein dwelleth righteousness (2 Peter 3:13).

A few decades ago, you heard countless sermons that had something in them about the Lord's return. These days, while we still have some strong end-time prophecy teachers around, it seems less and less preaching refers to the Lord's second coming in any context. We hear very little about it in a way that sobers us and reminds us to be ready for Him or references His coming in a way that encourages us about the wonderful things we have to look forward to. Second Peter 3 talks throughout the chapter about a time when people will begin to promote the idea that Jesus isn't returning any time soon, if at all, by saying "What happened to the promise that Jesus is coming again? ...Everything has remained the same since the world was first created" (2 Pet. 3:4 NLT). We see this discussion throughout the chapter that reminds us not to get our eyes off Jesus' return. We are supposed to be expecting Him every day! Keeping His return in our focus is meant to encourage us and remind us that the things we face here on earth will only last a short time and that we will forever be with the Lord. Take a moment today to meditate on the Lord's return and allow it to strengthen you again.

Prayer

Lord Jesus, I look for Your coming and I wait for the day when I will experience the new Heaven and earth the Bible talks about. As I meditate on it today let it encourage my heart, and I say come quickly, Lord Jesus! Amen.

SEPTEMBER 12

Irrefutable Proof

"Let Me show you things that you cannot see with the natural eye. See them through the eye of faith so that you already have the proof of them before they happen. Then when the enemies of life press in hard, you will have unshakeable and irrefutable proof that the things I have shown you will come to pass, says the Lord."

Prophetic Scripture

NOW FAITH is the assurance (the confirmation, the title deed) of the things [we] hope for, being the proof of the things [we] do not see and the conviction of their reality [faith perceiving as real fact what is not revealed to the senses] (Hebrews 11:1 AMP).

One of the main foundations to our Christianity is believing in what we cannot see with our physical eyes. That begins with believing in Jesus even while we cannot see Him physically. However, that shouldn't be our only experience with faith. We need to have faith in all of God's promises this way. We believe them without question until they manifest in our lives. Hebrews 11:1 says faith becomes all the proof we need. It's the title deed that the answer exists and belongs to us. We can build that kind of faith by reading God's Word and getting it into our hearts (see Rom. 10:17). When you read and meditate regularly on the written promises of God, they begin to become just as real to you as if you were seeing them with your natural eye. When we build that kind of faith in us, eventually we live out what we believe internally. This is the kind of faith we need when the enemy is putting pressure on us. Let faith become your irrefutable proof today!

Prayer

Lord, I thank You that I have Your written promises in the Bible. Even when I can't see them, I know they are true by faith. Teach me how to live by faith and let it become my irrefutable proof of Your blessings today! Amen.

No Injuries!

"Never forget that you have authority over all demons so that none can cause accident or injury in your life. Declare this day that you are accident-free because angels are with you and no injuries are allowed in your jurisdiction!"

Prophetic Scripture

Look, I have given you authority over all the power of the enemy, and you can walk among snakes and scorpions and crush them. Nothing will injure you (Luke 10:19 NLT).

When our children were going through those difficult months of learning to walk, we consoled many bumps and scrapes! A few times, some of those injuries became serious enough that it occurred to me I needed to pray against that. God's angels cover our kids when they are learning to walk! (See Psalms 91:11.) Don't think for a moment that the devil doesn't want to get in the middle of everyday life and cause unnecessary injury. We began to pray over our kids and declared that they would not experience injury at the hand of the devil. Our kids, now nearly grown, have never once gone to the hospital for a first-aid related injury. I believe it's because we can take authority over evil spirits that want to cause injury, not just to our kids but in general. While we won't avoid little scrapes here and there, we don't have to tolerate serious and continual injury. When Jesus said we have authority over the enemy, accident, injury, and trauma are included.

If you have suffered or are seeing a continual number of injuries, break the power of them in Jesus' Name. Even if you haven't had any, still command protection and know that nothing can harm or injure you!

Prayer

Lord, I thank You that I am protected from trauma and injury according to Your Word. I break the power of accident and injury over me and my family in the Name of Jesus, and I declare no injuries! Amen!

SEPTEMBER 14

Great Things Are Happening!

"No, it is not a time to retreat or a time to fear. Even as you see certain fearful events take place across the world, know that I will use these things to create open doors and divine appointments for My people to display the anointing. Look and see that by My hand great things are happening in the earth, says the Spirit of the Lord!"

Prophetic Scripture

Fear not, O land; be glad and rejoice: for the Lord will do great things (Joel 2:21).

Whenever the greatest challenges are before us, we also know that is when the anointing and power of God is ready to be displayed. As the church, when we see earthquakes, natural disasters, and nations in conflict, we cannot sit back and shake our heads or let fear cause us to run from the battle. We are the voice to the suffering world before us and these events should serve to remind us that we need to ready ourselves in the anointing and be prepared to preach the Gospel and display the power of God. We can't become a group of people who sit around wringing our hands in fear, wondering if we should dig a bomb shelter or hide in the hills somewhere. No! God is on the move and we are His vessels of light. We need to expect that during worldwide disaster and turmoil God will open doors and give us opportunities to share the good news and minister by His power. It's a great time to rejoice and be alive because the Lord will always do great things in the earth!

Prayer

Lord, even as I see catastrophes happening around the world, I know that You are on the move. Help me be prepared in the anointing to minister by Your power, for I know You are doing great things! Amen!

Your Love Gives Joy

"Let your love act as a foundation of encouragement for someone else. For know that there are those who are relying on your touch and even words of encouragement this day, so let your love give them joy, says the Lord."

Prophetic Scripture

Your love has given me great joy and encouragement... (Philemon 1:7 NIV).

When Paul wrote his letter to his dear friend, Philemon, he complimented him on many things. One of the main things was that Philemon was a person who encouraged people by his love. Paul first mentions the great love Philemon expressed toward all the saints (see Philem. 1:5), showing this was a normal characteristic of this man. However, Paul says something about him we all have needed to feel from time to time. He showed Paul expressions of love. Philemon, because of his love, was a great encouragement and source of joy for Paul. Paul's ministry was filled with many trials, but Philemon refreshed Paul in the middle of it. It was his love that lifted Paul's spirits while he was in prison.

Expressions of love mean a lot to people. Often we don't have any idea the things people are dealing with every day, whether externally or internally. Sometimes it's that unexpected card, gift, email, or text message that reminds someone that they are not alone and that someone cares. If the great apostle Paul needed people to show love and give him joy, then we do too! Let your love give joy to someone today.

Prayer

Father, teach me how to show more love to the people around me and to those who are important in my life. Let my expressions of love bring them joy and encouragement. Amen!

I Will Do It for You!

"Don't stop asking and petitioning me, says the Lord. For there are things you need to unashamedly ask and know once again that I will do it for you."

Prophetic Scripture

If ye shall ask any thing in my name, I will do it (John 14:14).

There are so many Bible verses that encourage us to ask the Lord for things. While prayer isn't all about going to God with your list like He is some kind of Santa Claus, God is the one who keeps telling us to ask Him. Prayer has many expressions and dimensions, but one of the major ones associated with prayer is asking. Matthew 7:7 says, "Ask and it shall be given you." Then verse 8 says, "For every one that asketh receiveth…." John 15:7 says if God's Word abides in you, you can ask what you will and it will be done for you by the Father. Jesus emphasized that we should ask the Father for what we need in His name. John 16:23-24 says ask and it will be given that your joy would be made full. Jesus teaches it again to the disciples in Matthew 21:22 by saying that all things you ask in prayer, believing, you will receive. So we can conclude that it's God who wants us to make a regular practice of asking Him to meet our needs. It isn't because He thinks we are treating Him like Santa Claus, but it's because the Lord wants to be our Source for everything we need in life. He wants to be involved no matter how large or small. So go to Him today, ask, and know that He will do it for you!

Prayer

Father, I ask You for _____ today. I know You will do it because You promised to take care of me and will give me all I need. I believe what You have promised and I know that You will do it! In Jesus' Name, amen.

Ruler over Many Things

"I am looking for people now who will govern all they own with excellence and be faithful in every place of service. For I have a place of rule for all My people, but I need reliable workers in this hour, says the Lord. And know that I look this day to even make you a ruler of many things."

Prophetic Scripture

Well done, thou good and faithful servant: thou hast been faithful over a few things, I will make thee ruler over many things: enter thou into the joy of thy lord (Matthew 25:21).

In First Timothy 1:12 Paul says, "He counted me faithful, putting me into the ministry." Paul recognized that one of the reasons he was able to govern a major ministry is because he proved to be faithful and reliable. Jesus taught it so well in the parable of the talents by saying that it is through faithfulness that we gain the ability to lead (see Matt. 25). We all have to admit that we have some areas to fix. It's not that we have to be perfect; God knows that no saint has everything together! What we do need to address are those areas where we need to quit going around the same old things that are out of order. Personal faithfulness will enable faithfulness and reliability in other areas such as on the job, with school work, or in church involvement.

God has a position for everyone somewhere, but we need to be on a quest for faithfulness so we will handle the things God has given us with excellence. Ask the Lord to reveal and help you with areas you need to improve. Then know that faithfulness will make you the ruler of many things.

Prayer

Father, teach me how to be faithful and reliable and how to bring the areas I need to change into divine order. Show me the areas You have for me to rule and help me walk in them. In Jesus' Name, amen.

Fiercely Pressed In

"Even like the Syrophenician woman pressed in for a miracle, press in at this hour. Be among those who are fiercely pressed in for the things of My Kingdom. Don't let them pass you by, for they are already yours."

Prophetic Scripture

The law and the prophets were until John: since that time the kingdom of God is preached, and every man presseth into it (Luke 16:16).

Luke 16:16 was written regarding the many Gentiles who would press themselves into the Kingdom of God after hearing the Gospel preached. The word *presseth* in this verse means to force your way in. A great example of this was with the Syrophenician woman in Mark 7:27. She came to Jesus for the deliverance of her daughter who was possessed of a devil. Jesus told her that it wasn't right to take the children's bread and give it to dogs. He said that because she wasn't a daughter of Abraham, the healing covenant didn't belong to her. Do you think that caused her to give up? No way! She responded to Jesus by saying, "Lord, even dogs get the crumbs that fall from the children's table." Instead of walking away, she pressed in even harder to get what she came for.

As believers who have heard the Gospel, we are already pressed into the Kingdom of God through salvation, so now the covenant of God belongs to us. We aren't dogs; we are children! We have a right to God's Kingdom, so let's not take it for granted. Let's be fiercely pressed in and not allow one blessing to pass us by!

Prayer

Father, I thank You that I am a child of God and all the blessings of the Kingdom are mine. I press into the Kingdom today and will not allow any blessings to pass me by. In Jesus' Name, amen.

Season of Favor

"I have released My people into favor, says the Lord, and I will cause many to see favor upon them in this time. So expect new doors to open and resources to be placed in your hands, because My season of favor is surely upon you!"

Prophetic Scripture

Thou shalt arise, and have mercy upon Zion: for the time to favor her, yea, the set time, is come (Psalms 102:13).

We are in a prophetic season right now when we should expect the favor of God to be upon us. It is going to open amazing doors for the Church and cause many people who have hardened their hearts in the past to turn to the Lord. In the Bible, when God placed His favor upon His people it caused nations to tremble and prosperity was always attached to it. We need to live every day expecting favor! Expect people to give things to you. When God gives you favor with people it is so we can tell them about the Lord and further God's Kingdom in the earth. Begin to talk about favor every day. Rather than expect rejection all the time, begin to believe that people will accept you and receive you when you present the Gospel to them. Begin to expect favor in business dealings during this season. Expect finances to grow and increase. See many coming to the Lord and filling our churches. When we expect favor, we will step into what the Lord has ordained for this season of time. If we expect nothing, we may miss some of the greatest blessings the Lord has prophetically ordained. Yes, this is your set time to stand in the favor of the Lord!

Prayer

O Lord, I receive Your favor right now! I expect it in my workplace, at home, and in every place I go. I receive the increase of favor and commit myself to look for it every day. I believe new doors are opening, and I thank You for favor today! In Jesus' Name, amen.

No Problem Too Difficult

*"The Spirit says, look at My Word once again and see what I can do! For what has ever left Me perplexed? I surely say to you this day **nothing** is too difficult for Me! For I made everything and surely I shall take care of you."*

Prophetic Scripture

Ah Lord God! behold, thou hast made the heaven and the earth by thy great power and stretched out arm, and there is nothing too hard for thee (Jeremiah 32:17).

One time while flying in a plane coming in for landing in a particular city, I looked out the window and saw all the buildings and highways. I remember thinking how the cars along the freeway looked liked little toys. It seemed from the plane that I could reach down and just pick one up or move a building around any way I wanted. Once on the ground, those things seem so much bigger than they do from the air. We think the things of this life can be so big, but God looks at them from a different perspective. To Him they are so much smaller than He is, and His power and wisdom are above it all. Everything is under His control and no problem on this planet leaves Him puzzled. He made everything! We need times when we just reflect on how big our God is and try for a moment to get His perspective on the world and even regarding our own lives. We need to imagine in our minds how God sees the problems we face and realize that to Him they are so small and not hard at all for Him to fix. Just rest in the Lord today and realize that no problem is ever too difficult for God!

Prayer

Lord God, I see how big You are today. You created everything that my eyes can see right now and there is nothing You cannot solve. Give me Your perspective, and I know no problem is too difficult for You. Amen.

A Light Given unto You

"See this day that the light of God has been provided you and is in you. Know this day that the light shall separate you from the world, and no harmful or evil thing can come near you!"

Prophetic Scripture

And the angel of God, which went before the camp of Israel, removed and went behind them; and the pillar of the cloud went from before their face, and stood behind them: and it came between the camp of the Egyptians and the camp of Israel; and it was a cloud and darkness to them, but it gave light by night to these: so that the one came not near the other all the night (Exodus 14:19-20).

I remember one particular year when it was raining heavily in our area and some of our neighbors' homes were experiencing flooding. Of course, we prayed over our house, and one day I said to my husband, "We won't have any floods in our house because it is always light in Goshen!" Of course, I was referring to the plague of darkness that fell on Egypt while it remained light in Israel and how God always separated His people from destruction (see Exod. 10:22-23). When Israel was finally delivered from Egypt and then, shortly thereafter, pursued by the chariots of Pharaoh, God once again sent an angel to stand between Israel and Egypt and the two were separated. In Exodus 14:19-20, the angel brought the pillar that was light to Israel and darkness to the Egyptians.

Never forget that the light of God stands between you and the world today and separates you. When darkness is upon the world, the light of deliverance will always be given unto you!

Prayer

Lord, I thank You that a light has been given unto me that separates me from the world. When evil comes upon the earth, I know that it shall not befall my dwelling. In Jesus' Name, amen.

Confirming Signs Are with You

"Keep being bold to declare My Word, for as you speak the Word everywhere you go and to those you meet, signs shall be with you and confirm to them that what you say is truth."

Prophetic Scripture

And they went forth, and preached every where, the Lord working with them, and confirming the word with signs following (Mark 16:20).

J esus didn't send us out into the world without His power. When Jesus came to the earth preaching the Kingdom, signs and wonders followed Him to confirm for those who heard Him that He was anointed and sent from God. Matthew 4:23 says, "And Jesus went about…preaching the gospel of the kingdom, and healing all manner of sickness and all manner of disease among the people." When He preached the Word, signs followed Him. Then when He sent forth His apostles to preach in Matthew 10:1, He gave them power to cast out demons and heal sickness. After Pentecost, the early apostles continued to preach, and signs and wonders followed the preaching of the Word. That same mandate has not ended, and we need signs to follow the preaching of the Word more than ever.

We need to expect signs and wonders to follow our lives as we share the Gospel with people we meet. God does not expect us to present a powerless Gospel that doesn't promise any tangible results. We all meet people on a regular basis who need real miracles. We need to feel confident to tell them that God heals and delivers and can do the miraculous in their life. Know that confirming signs are with you today!

Prayer

Father, I thank You that as I declare and speak Your Word, signs follow and confirm it. Teach me how to minister the Gospel with a tangible anointing that helps people receive real miracles and real results. In Jesus' Name, amen.

You Can Remember!

"Never say that you cannot remember things or that you are short of memory. For My Spirit causes you to have a sharp memory and to recall the things I have put in your heart, says the Lord. So say this day that Your memory will always operate at full capacity."

Prophetic Scripture

But the comforter, which is the Holy Ghost, whom the Father will send in my name, he shall teach you all things and bring all things to your remembrance, whatsoever I have said unto you (John 14:26).

With all the concern over diseases like Alzheimer's and dementia, we need to reverse that concern by declaring that our minds and memories are blessed by the Holy Spirit. Sometimes people joke about being forgetful and say things in jest like, "I think I am losing it," or, "Am I crazy?" Sometimes we joke about it being our age. While people mean it in good fun, we don't want to be forming a mind-set because of our constant jest in this area. Even serious talk of memory loss can form a mind-set in your heart that you are a forgetful individual. That is because you begin to believe what you say about yourself. In some cases, people are dealing with real memory loss issues and they need God to heal them. John 14:26 teaches us that the Holy Spirit will cause our memory to remember what Jesus has told us in His Word. If He can recall the Scripture to our memory, then we can expect the Holy Spirit to speak to our memory in other areas.

Call your memory blessed today and declare over your life that your memory will always operate at full capacity.

Prayer

Holy Spirit, I thank You that You are bringing to my memory everything Jesus has said. Cause me to recall the Word of God that is in my heart and I declare that my memory will always operate at full capacity. In Jesus' Name, amen.

His Name Is Therapy

"Let My Name wash over you this day, says the Lord. For even as You say My Name it shall be as therapeutic ointment that shall calm your heart and bring peace and quiet to your mind."

Prophetic Scripture

...Thy name is as ointment poured forth... (Song of Solomon 1:3).

We definitely know there is power in the Name of Jesus. His Name causes demons to flee. Everything must bow down to the sound of His Name. Yet there is a special, intimate side to His Name that we need to make a part of our lives. The Song of Solomon is the detailed account of a love story. While written as between a man and wife, it is truly the love story between the Lord and His people. Song of Solomon 1:3, in reference to the name of his true love, says, "Thy name is as ointment poured forth." He was indicating that every time he heard or spoke the name of his one true love, the sound of it washed over him like a soothing ointment on dry, irritated skin. The sound of it alone brought relief. We can all think of someone special in our lives who whenever you hear their name spoken it moves you in a way that other names do not. Even people with the same names of those we love, when the name is spoken it reminds us of our loved ones and can make our heart leap.

When you experience times when your heart feels heavy or your mind is agitated or tempted to worry about something, let the Name of Jesus become a therapy to your soul. Just repeat His Name aloud and let the sound of it wash over your mind and calm you. His Name alone is your therapy.

Prayer

Today, Lord, I just say the Name of Jesus. There is no other Name that can satisfy my thirsty soul and bring relief to my heart and mind. The sound of Your name washes over me...Jesus.

The Lord Is Your Portion

"Know that I have given Myself fully to you, says the Lord. I am in you and you are in Me. I want to commune with you and be everything to you. You are Mine and I am yours and nothing can separate us from each other."

Prophetic Scripture

Thou art my portion, O Lord: I have said that I would keep thy words (Psalms 119:57).

When the Psalmist says, "thou art my portion," he was saying, "Lord, you are mine" (Ps. 119:57 NLT). He could say that because he had given everything to the Lord and from that realized that God had given everything to him, which made them inseparable. God has given Himself and all that He is to you through Jesus, and when you give yourself to Him nothing can come between you. We, ourselves, can allow other things to come between us and God, but none of these things has the independent power to do that. In Romans 8, Paul says that through adoption we have literally been given *God!* (See Romans 8:15.) His DNA is interwoven into your being. From that truth he says, "Who shall separate us from the love of Christ?" Then he lists all the absurd possibilities to make the point that there are no contenders. So he says he is persuaded that neither death, nor life, nor angels, nor demons, and nothing within the dimensions of the universe can separate us from God! (See Romans 8:35-39.)

There is nothing on this planet that can take God away from you except yourself. The Lord is yours and you are His, and nothing has the ability to come between you. The Lord is your portion today!

Prayer

Lord, I thank You that You are mine today and I am Yours. I give everything to You and have confidence that all You are is also mine. I depend on You and know that nothing can separate us! Amen.

SEPTEMBER 26

You Are Curse Free

"The Spirit says, don't allow the curse to have any place in your life. Do not talk about it, remember it, or discuss it with friends or family. Let it not have any space in your mind and don't give it your attention, for you are curse free!"

Prophetic Scripture

Christ hath redeemed us from the curse of the law, being made a curse for us: for it is written, Cursed is every one that hangeth on a tree (Galatians 3:13).

Have you ever noticed how when friends or family get together they like to compare notes? Some talk about the oddities in their family tree and how they have noticed themselves having some of those odd traits. Others discuss their medications and medical experiences. Women especially love to compare notes with other women on childbirth stories. While some of this activity can be useful and uplifting, we have to be so very careful we don't glorify the negatives or give acceptance to the curses. We don't want our conversations to give power to the very attacks and bondages we are fighting against. Deuteronomy 28 lists both the blessings and the curses of the law. The list of curses is far more descriptive than that of the blessings. Why? Because I believe it reveals how much Jesus set us free from. Galatians 3:13 says that Christ has paid for us to be free from these curses. If you are free from the curse, then you certainly don't want to keep giving it your time and attention. Don't give credibility to the curse in your conversations. If you are facing a trial, pray. Feel free to get others praying, but don't give it undue attention because you are curse free!

Prayer

Lord, I thank You that because of Jesus I am set free from the curse and I will not give it undue attention. Put a watch over my words and conversations so that I will not give power to the curse. I am curse free! In Jesus' Name, amen.

Father to the Fatherless

"Many have a tainted view of a true and caring father, caused by that which lacked with their own early fathers. For even good earthly fathers can only provide limited understanding. So watch Me reveal to you the true meaning of fathering, for even am I a Father to the fatherless."

Prophetic Scripture

A father of the fatherless, and a judge of the widows, is God in his holy habitation (Psalms 68:5).

It is getting more common for people to grow up without a proper father. Some have been abused or had a father who deserted them. Many grow up without basic life skills that make them well-rounded and capable adults. Even those with good and godly fathers still lack certain qualities that can only be imparted from God the Father. Truthfully, all of us need a new perception of fathering in some way or another. Our heavenly Father is so vast that we can't fully correlate a natural father to Him.

In Matthew 7:11, Jesus teaches by asking, "If ye then, being evil, know how to give good gifts unto your children, how much more shall your Father which is in Heaven give good things to them that ask him?" The key is in the phrase, "how much more." In other words, no matter what your earthly experience was with a father, God is more. He imparts to those areas where we are "fatherless" or lacking the correct fatherly perspective. So, whether you had a good father, an abusive one, or didn't have a father, Father God is everything your earthly father fell short of. If your earthly father gave you good things, God will give you more. If your earthly father neglected you, God will care for you. Surely, your God is a Father to the fatherless!

Prayer

Dear heavenly Father, I receive You today as my Father. I ask You to impart to me the true meaning of a father and to amend any areas where I am lacking in my perspective. You are my Father! In Jesus' Name, amen.

You Shall Endure

"Know that I am forming within you the fortitude to stand up to all manner of testing, says the Lord. For when you shall see the world in upheaval, so shall you stand strong and not retreat. I even call you this day a soldier that shall endure!"

Prophetic Scripture

Thou therefore endure hardness, as a good soldier of Jesus Christ (2 Timothy 2:3).

As much as living the Christian life is about loving God and enjoying the peace He gives, we have to remember that Christianity drafts us into an army called the army of God. Whether we want to face it or not, we are in spiritual war. The entire Bible is filled with combative discussion about the power of God defeating evil. In Matthew 10:34 Jesus said, "…I came not to send peace, but a sword." Jesus isn't saying He doesn't offer peace; He is saying that when the Kingdom of God enters an atmosphere where there is darkness, conflict arises. Everywhere Jesus went He created a stir. The early apostles encountered ongoing and vehement opposition. We shouldn't think that we will encounter less if we are truly in the Kingdom.

The Lord needs us to willingly enter the battlefield as a soldier, not just as peace-loving believers who don't want to make waves. So even in the trials you face in your own life, you need to approach them as a soldier. While that won't be the only angle with which you address these trials, it does need to be one of them. In everything you face, God is developing your skills specifically as a soldier, so you can withstand anything. So declare today that you shall endure!

Prayer

Lord, I willingly offer myself to the heavenly spiritual battlefield. Teach me how to war against spiritual opposition and endure hardness as a good soldier of Jesus Christ. I declare that I shall endure! In Jesus' Name, amen.

Create a Pattern

"Know that with each individual decision you make to do what is right, you are creating a pattern that someone else will eventually follow, even in ways you may never realize. So go ahead and set the course for good and know that your efforts have great reward, says the Lord."

Prophetic Scripture

In all things shewing thyself a pattern of good works... (Titus 2:7).

The Book of Titus is largely about setting the example for someone else. Paul spent a majority of his discussion teaching Titus how to be an example and teach others the same. Whether we know it or not, our lives have influence on someone else. Every human being alive will have an impact on another human being, either good or bad. In his teaching, Paul tells Titus to create a pattern of good works. In other words, it wasn't to be an inconsistent thing. A pattern of good works is something consistent and reliable for someone else to follow. Of course, you may already be thinking that you have areas that you are inconsistent with and wonder if you will ever measure up. Be reassured that we all have those areas, but the good news is that patterns are not created overnight. Patterns are cut through repeated effort. If you think of the way a river cuts a pattern through the rocks, you know that doesn't happen in one day! It comes by hitting the same area again and again. Focus your consistencies on one individual decision at a time. Then know that each time you do someone is benefiting from it, and little by little you are setting the right course for someone else. There is no reward better than that!

Prayer

Lord, help me create a pattern of good works for someone else to follow. Speak to me about the key decisions I make and always help me choose what is right. I thank You for it. In Jesus' Name, amen.

Get Up and Run!

"The Spirit says, I call you to run! Run for the prize, run for your deliverance, run for your healing and for your crown of glory! Do what you already know to do and make a run for it. See the answer and make a run until it comes to pass!"

Prophetic Scripture

Do you not know that those who run in a race all run, but only one receives the prize? Run in such a way that you may win (1 Corinthians 9:24 NASB).

No one gets results at anything with half-hearted effort. You can't get a good job without effort. You can't cook a meal, enjoy a nice home, or raise kids without effort. One of the cardinal rules of life is that if you work at something, you will experience results. In First Corinthians 9:24-25, Paul says that it takes discipline and determination to get results in your Christian walk. Like a runner, you have to do it like you want to win. Some good Christians rarely get results because they are indifferent with the things of the spirit. Some have become unenthusiastic about the anointing, so they don't pray. If you want to see more results, you have to run like you want it. If you need divine healing, run for it. If it's deliverance, run for it. The prize to run for is not just getting to Heaven one day. Run for the things you want to see come to pass in your life right now! In fact, as a prophetic act of faith that you are going to run harder than ever before for the things you want to see take place, jump up and run right now if you can! It's time to get up and run!

Prayer

Lord, I make a determination today to run for the things I want to see come to pass. I make a fresh commitment to Your Word and the things of the Spirit and I make a run for it right now! In Jesus' Name, amen.

Peace to Your Descendants

"I have given you the position and the authority to help form the future of your descendants. For even as Mordecai the Jew paved the way for his descendants to live in peace, you are given the ability to do so."

Prophetic Scripture

For Mordecai the Jew was next unto king Ahasuerus, and great among the Jews, and accepted of the multitude of his brethren, seeking the wealth of his people, and speaking peace to all his seed (Esther 10:3).

When the Lord gave Mordecai a position as second-in-command over the providences of King Ahasuerus (Xerxes), Mordecai made a point to see to the welfare of the Jews and his own personal descendants. One key way he did that was by giving them a peace declaration. In Esther 10:3, the King James says "speaking peace to all his seed." The Amplified says it similarly. Some other translations say he spoke up for their welfare. I believe both angles apply. Mordecai had the position to not only give voice to the people's needs, but he also spoke over them in such a way that it set their course in peace.

As God's people, we have been given authority to form the future of both our natural and in many cases spiritual descendants. Parents can do it for their children. Pastors can do so for their congregations, and so forth. We provide peace to our descendants in two key ways. First, look out for their benefit. Create an environment where they will enjoy personal fulfillment and growth. Second, speak peace over them and to them. Declare their lives will be blessed and full of abundance. As the person who God has positioned, you have a divine gift to form their future. Stand up today and speak peace to your descendants.

Prayer

Father, I decree peace over my descendants today. I say their future will be full of the peace of God, and I commit to create for them a positive environment of peace. Amen.

Pray and Prophesy

"The Spirit says, know that when you are in the atmosphere of the spirit there is always opportunity to pray in the spirit and prophesy. For I call you to enter that realm often, and from that arena you shall penetrate resistance and change events. "

Prophetic Scripture

And when Paul had laid his hands upon them, the Holy Ghost came on them; and they spake with tongues, and prophesied (Acts 19:6).

The Book of Acts showed us that the Holy Spirit upon people was that they spoke in tongues. In some cases they prophesied. In every account given in Acts of the Holy Spirit's baptism, people spoke in tongues. Two accounts don't say it directly, but further research reveals it. When Paul was baptized in the Holy Spirit in Acts 9:17, it doesn't say he spoke with tongues, but First Corinthians 14:18 says he spoke with them more than anyone. Also, the account of those filled with the Spirit in Samaria doesn't say they spoke in tongues, but when Simon the sorcerer tried to offer them money, Peter rebuked him (see Acts 8:17-21). He told Simon, "You have no part in this matter." The Greek word for *matter* is *logos*, which means something spoken. With all the other accounts of people *speaking* in tongues and prophesying, why would this be different? Plus, how did Simon see it? You can't see a spirit, so there must have been some visible sign. He saw them praying in tongues!

The evidence and the key to the atmosphere of the Holy Spirit is praying in tongues and prophesying. Pray in tongues often in your prayer times and then don't be afraid to launch out and prophesy, just like the believers did in Acts 19:6. It's a spiritual environment that moves things in the realm of the spirit. It's time to pray and prophesy!

Prayer

Holy Spirit, I thank You for the atmosphere of the anointing where I can pray in tongues and prophesy. Even as I pray in the Spirit today, cause me to enter new arenas in prayer with the Holy Spirit. Amen.

Creativity and Inspiration Comes

"Expect to receive creative inspiration for good ideas, says the Spirit. For even as you listen to Me, so shall I impart fresh ideas and the ability to invent, design, and develop new things."

Prophetic Scripture

But there is a spirit in man: and the inspiration of the Almighty giveth them understanding (Job 32:8).

There are certain people in the world we label as either creative or artistic. Then there are others who are always quick to say they are neither of those things. What we need to know is that no matter who we are, all creativity comes from the Lord. He can put in each of us our own version of creativity. Of course, we all have unique and natural talents that we can study to develop, but it's the Lord who adds to and inspires them. Job 32:8 says it is God who inspires and teaches us how to do things. We need to expect inspiration from the Lord in everything we do. The dimension of divine creativity can cause ordinary people to accomplish extraordinary things. It can cause you to come up with ideas on the job that no one considered. It may help you prosper in your own business or add interest to relationships, family activities, or hobbies.

So, if you don't think of yourself as very creative, change your perception of yourself today. Begin to ask the Lord to bring out the creative side that He has given you. Of course, that doesn't mean you need to go sign up for a painting class! Nevertheless, look for God to inspire you in everyday business and see how His Spirit can use you to be a witness to other people. Get ready, because the Holy Spirit is giving you creativity and inspiration.

Prayer

Lord, I thank You that all ideas and creativity come from You. Show me the areas of creativity that You want to bring out of me and help me receive divine inspiration and ideas each day. In Jesus' Name, amen.

The Cloud Has Returned

"The Spirit says, know that I am raising up houses of worship in this hour that shall emulate Heaven. For you shall see, in the months and years ahead, atmospheres of corporate worship where the cloud of glory shall descend once again and the people shall not be able to stand under the cloud."

Prophetic Scripture

...Then the house was filled with a cloud, even the house of the Lord; so that the priests could not stand to minister by reason of the cloud: for the glory of the Lord had filled the house of God (2 Chronicles 5:13-14).

There was a day not many years ago when people talked about the glory cloud filling churches. People testified of when it rolled in, and as it gradually covered each row of people they would fall under the power of God. It would fill the room until everyone was on the floor. I believe if we are not careful, we are on verge of losing that dimension of the supernatural in our worship gatherings. Worship bands have to be careful not to become too professional, just singing the most popular songs. Worshipers must enter in and be willing to linger when the anointing is present.

God is looking right now for people and churches that will allow room for that level of the anointing. Second Chronicles 5:13 says the glory fell when all the singers and musicians came into an undistracted place of unity in their thanksgiving. We need to make more room for the glory to descend upon our worship services once again. Intercede for God to raise up houses of worship who will emulate Heaven so that we can say once again, "The cloud has returned."

Prayer

Lord, I ask You to raise up houses of worship that will emulate Heaven and make room for the glory. Teach me how to become a true worshiper and cause Your Church to say once again, "The cloud has returned." Amen.

It's Time to Exercise!

"It's a time to exercise yourself in spiritual godliness, says the Lord. Even in the same way you exercise your physical person, use these principles for your spirit and you shall enjoy a harvest of fruit that only godliness can bring."

Prophetic Scripture

For bodily exercise profiteth little: but godliness is profitable unto all things... (1 Timothy 4:8).

For most of us, it's challenging to be consistent with exercise. It's not always easy to find the time, and if you are out of shape the routine can be painful! However, the fact we all know is that exercise is good for you and helps you live a more healthy life. It relieves stress and increases energy. Even though the average person doesn't always enjoy consistent exercise, if they commit to it they always feel better.

It is the same with our spiritual routine. Spending time in the Bible and in prayer has its challenges. To be honest, there are times reading the Bible is boring! Sometimes prayer feels dry and you get distracted. In addition to that, we all have busy schedules and keeping a consistent spiritual life will be competed with by other things. Yet a spiritual exercise routine is even more beneficial than natural exercise. First Timothy 4:8 says that while physical exercise is important and does benefit us, spiritual godliness born from our spiritual exercise routine is even better. It has greater power than exercise to keep us not only energized and stress free, but it makes us spiritual powerhouses! Even as you keep making efforts to be consistent in your physical exercise routine, work a little extra on your spiritual one. The results will look good on you, so grab your Bible—it's time to exercise!

Prayer

Father, I ask You to help me develop a strong and consistent exercise routine, not only in the natural things, but spiritually. Continually cause my spiritual muscles to be challenged so I will grow and enjoy the fruit of godliness. In Jesus' Name, amen.

Your Vision Won't Delay

> *"Know that the vision and dream that I have placed in your heart will come to pass. And know that the process toward its fulfillment is preparing you for it. So don't give up, says the Lord. For the things I have put in your heart will not delay."*

Prophetic Scripture

> *For the vision is yet for the appointed time; it hastens toward the goal and it will not fail. Though it tarries, wait for it; for it will certainly come, it will not delay* (Habakkuk 2:3 NASB).

We all have dreams the Lord has put in our hearts that we want to see come to pass. I remember, when we first started in ministry, receiving a prophecy by a prominent minister about how we would have a worldwide ministry and bear much fruit. We were ready, or so we thought, to take on the world! Little did we know that the fulfillment of that vision wasn't going to happen until many years later. In fact, shortly after the prophecy, we took what seemed to be a giant step backward! We were wondering, "Lord, how can this be?" We didn't know that God had an appointed time for the vision He gave us. We first had to walk through the preparation season. Yet all along, the vision was developing right under our noses and we didn't even know it!

Never forget that what seems like delay may not be that at all. Sure, the enemy likes to interfere and slow things down, but God will see to it that the vision happens right on time. Realize that today is getting you ready for tomorrow. You are moving toward your vision, so stay in faith. Surely, the vision comes and won't delay!

Prayer

> *Father, I know the vision You have put in my heart will surely come to pass. I thank You for taking this time to prepare me, for I know the vision shall not delay! Amen.*

You Will Not Faint!

"It is never a time to call it quits with your faith. Yes, there will be times to reassess your battle plan in prayer, but there is never a time to retreat, says God. Stay with the things you have set your hand to this day and determine in your heart you will never faint!"

Prophetic Scripture

If thou faint in the day of adversity, thy strength is small (Proverbs 24:10).

Some battles take longer to overcome than others. It's the ones that take longer to reach victory that tempt you to give up in your stance of faith. Just because a doubtful thought arises in your mind does not mean you have fainted. Many people in Scripture had momentary doubts but still experienced the greatest miracles because they pressed on in faith. Mark 11:23 says that if you tell mountains to be removed and don't doubt in your heart, it will happen. Doubtful thoughts are not doubt from the heart. You can take control of simple thoughts and redirect them back to the Word of God where they can't take root in your heart. Just because you had a bad day or felt discouraged in your faith does not mean you have fainted. Doubt in your heart begins when you start verbalizing fears and doubts to the point where they form your mind-set. People who faint always talk about it first and usually quite often. Some even become resistant to those who try to encourage them to hang in there.

Don't quit on the things you are praying for today. Sure, it's okay to go to God and reassess your battle plan, but the key is stay in there with the Lord and you will not faint.

Prayer

Father, I will not faint on the things I am praying for today. I refuse to give in to any doubtful thought, and I tell my mind to focus on God's Word and His promises. In Jesus' Name, amen.

OCTOBER 8

It Won't Happen Again

"As you embrace your future season, says the Spirit, know that the things that have weighed you down in the past shall not be seen anymore. They are over! So it's a day to say it won't happen again!"

Prophetic Scripture

...Affliction shall not rise up the second time (Nahum 1:9).

The first chapter of the Book of Nahum describes how God will take up vengeance against the enemies of His people. Those enemies are the attacks of darkness that attempt to bring trials into our lives. The chapter describes how God takes vengeance in a furious manner and how even the natural elements quake at His presence when He comes on the scene. It says the mountains melt, the rocks break apart, and He will overrun the darkness with a flood. In this intense descriptive on how God goes after the enemy on your behalf, verse 9 says, "What can you even think to do against the Lord?" There is nothing, so the meaning of the verse is this—affliction shall not rise a second time. God dealt with it so powerfully that it simply cannot come back!

We need to know that God has already risen up against the afflictions of the enemy coming against our lives. He has done so furiously through the sacrifice of Calvary's cross. There is no descriptive act of vengeance more intense than that, because Jesus' blood covers it all. Therefore, our comfort and consolation is that affliction shall not rise up the second time. Rest in that today and believe God today—it won't happen again!

Prayer

Father, I thank You that every trial of affliction has been dealt with by the blood of Jesus. I am protected by the blood, and You have dealt with every enemy so that I can say today, it won't happen again! In Jesus' Name, amen.

Express Yourself

"I look for prayer that is genuine and expressive, says God. For there are unlimited realms of prayer that require different methods to enter them. For even as Elijah expressed himself in fervent prayer, so must you express yourself."

Prophetic Scripture

...The effectual fervent prayer of a righteous man availeth much (James 5:16).

Elijah accomplished many things, but we find a clue that connects his amazing anointing to his prayer life. James 5:16 says that the effectual, fervent prayer of a righteous person availeth much. The Amplified Bible says this fervent prayer "makes tremendous power available." In the Greek, "effectual fervent" is one single word—*energeo*, meaning full of energy, working active, and white hot. Our prayers need to be full of energy—spirit, soul, and body. While there is a place for quiet, calm prayer, there is also a time for expressive prayer where your whole being gets into it. In the verses to follow, it talks about how Elijah was a normal person just like us. He prayed that it would not rain for six months and then prayed again for rain to return. If you read the account in First Kings 18:41-44, you find Elijah threw himself on the ground in prayer with his head between his knees. This indicates a very intense, expressive form of prayer.

While we don't need to pray this way all the time, we also can't eliminate it either. There are different expressions of prayer needed for different things, and we need to be open to them. Some expressions may include walking, laying face down, lifting your voice, and so forth. Just be open because the Lord needs prayer where you will express yourself!

Prayer

Holy Spirit, teach me how to move in different realms in prayer and be open to different expressions so that I may be used effectively in prayer. I thank You that my prayers make great power available! In Jesus' Name, amen.

Strengthen the Teachers

"Even as great false doctrine arises, it's a season to strengthen the teachers who have taught you the good Word of God. Offer them your encouragement, says the Lord, for they are helping you grow and become strong and stable in this endtime."

Prophetic Scripture

Those who are taught the word of God should provide for their teachers, sharing all good things with them (Galatians 6:6 NLT).

All of us who have studied the Bible know the time and effort it takes to extract the depths of revelation hidden in God's Word. We need to appreciate those who have given their lives to bring us the good Word of God. Their countless hours and years of study have given us a priceless wealth of teaching. Because of that, the Bible tells us we should support them and share good things with them. In a day when false doctrine is rampant, we need to express our appreciation to the teachers who have been faithful to present us with sound doctrine. Some of those are national ministries that we watch on television or online. We need to ask God how we can show support to them through offerings or encouraging letters. Other teachers are mentors and pastors who are closer in our lives, and we should express our appreciation to them on an even higher scale because of the closer relationship. We can't forget that those who deliver God's Word, whether on a national or local scale, are on the front lines. They often carry a heavy load in managing ministries and helping people receive a touch from God.

Pray about how you can reach out to the teachers and mentors in your life today. God expects it, and your support does not go unnoticed by the Lord.

Prayer

Father, I thank You for every teacher and mentor You have placed in my life. I ask You to strengthen them and bless their ministry. Show me how I can encourage and support them. In Jesus' Name, amen.

The Glow Is upon You

"Anticipate moments after your times of prayer when those who you least expect will see My presence upon you. Never assume they won't receive your words, for I shall teach you how to draw them in, for the glow of My Spirit is upon you."

Prophetic Scripture

And it came to pass, when Moses came down from mount Sinai with the two tables of testimony in Moses' hand, when he came down from the mount, that Moses wist not that the skin of his face shone while he talked with him (Exodus 34:29).

When Moses spent time with God, the visible presence of God was seen on his face. Of course, Moses didn't realize it until he saw how people around him responded. The Bible says the people were afraid to come near him. However, Moses reassured them by putting a veil on his face as he spoke with them. The Lord has placed a tangible presence of His Spirit on your life. While not everyone can handle the full level of glory that you carry, you need to present it to them in way they can receive. Moses was wise enough to know that he needed to present the glory in a way that made it a little easier for the people. Once he did that they came near him again. He didn't apologize for the glory nor did he explain it away, he just found a way to draw the people in so he could talk with them.

As you talk with people about the Gospel or minister to them in the anointing, engage them in common conversation that will draw them in and make them feel comfortable. As you do, trust from there that the anointing will do the rest to draw them in because the glow of God's presence is upon you.

Prayer

Lord, I thank You that the glory is upon me. Teach me how to present it to people in a way that draws them in, and I trust that Your presence will minister to them in a powerful way. In Jesus' Name, amen.

OCTOBER 12

Sing, O Daughter of Zion

"Sing and shout in this hour, says the Lord. For there is a level of breakthrough and release that only your song will produce. Rejoice today and let My high praise lead you into victorious places!"

Prophetic Scripture

Sing, O daughter of Zion; shout, O Israel; be glad and rejoice with all the heart, O daughter of Jerusalem (Zephaniah 3:14).

There is something powerful about praise; it just does something on the inside of you. It melts away frustration and pain. Praise and shouting have a way of breaking heaviness from your mind. I think that is the reason the Bible is full of verses about singing, shouting, and praising God. When it comes to deliverance, praise is a key to opening prisons in your life like nothing else. It has its own unique way of restoring your joy. Now, the problem is that when heavy weights try to hold you down, you don't always feel like rejoicing. Actually, that is when we feel like praising the least. Haven't you noticed that when you are in a good mood, it's easy to hum a tune, whistle, or sing? Now, when you're sad or upset, it's a whole different ballgame! Yet that is the time to make yourself sing. This is the most crucial time to rejoice. To *rejoice* means to have such exceeding joy that you even spin or dance. In other words, it is joy and it comes over and over again. Sometimes you will have to make yourself do that, but what starts as a forced effort will result in a release of peace and joy. Sing over the things that you are dealing with today. Dance over them and let heaviness melt from your life!

Prayer

Lord, I step into rejoicing today. I shout and sing over all my situations, and I believe that heaviness will leave and be replaced by peace. Thank You, Lord, for the breakthrough of praise that I receive right now! In Jesus' Name, amen.

Your Hard Work Protected

"The Spirit says, take heed that you do not lose what you have worked hard for. For there is a continual river of reward and blessing for the taking, but it's a time to look at each area of your life and reassess your direction in some things. By doing so, you shall prosper and your hard work will be protected."

Prophetic Scripture

Watch out that you do not lose what we have worked for, but that you may be rewarded fully (2 John 1:8 NIV).

The Book of Second John was a letter written to a lady who was a dear friend of the apostle. In the few short verses, he mentions his love for her in the Lord and encourages her to keep that love and hold fast to the word she learned early on. It seems from the letter that she may have been veering off track slightly and needed some admonition from John. In verse 8, he encourages her to watch carefully so that she doesn't let go of everything they had worked for. It seems she was making some decisions that were putting the ministry work they had accomplished together at risk and John wanted her to reassess her direction.

We all need to make occasional adjustments that will keep us from veering off course. Otherwise, we risk losing some things we have worked hard for. That could apply to our personal spiritual walk, ministry, occupation, certain relationships, family matters, finances, and more. We can make these adjustments with the help of the Holy Spirit and quality people in our lives who are willing to tell us the truth, like John did for his friend. Then the things you have worked hard for will be protected and you will enjoy the reward.

Prayer

Lord, show me the areas where I need to make adjustments. I commit to making them as You reveal it. I thank You that my hard work will prosper and I will enjoy the reward from it. Amen.

OCTOBER 14

Purified Thoughts

"Know that love always causes a cleansing of your mind, says the Lord. For even as negative thoughts try to penetrate your thinking this day, sincere love for the brethren will free you from them."

Prophetic Scripture

Seeing ye have purified your souls in obeying the truth through the Spirit unto unfeigned love of the brethren, see that ye love one another with a pure heart fervently (1 Peter 1:22).

The Bible reminds us that there are only two key commandments to be concerned with. Jesus taught them and we see the concept repeated through the New Testament. It's basically this: Love God; love people. The first commandment is love God with all your heart, and the second is love your neighbor as yourself (see Matt. 22:38-40). Why are these the only two important commandments? Because if you love God with everything that is within you, you don't want to sin and do wrong things because you know it hurts His heart. And if you love people, you won't mistreat them or sin with them. This level of love has a profound effect on your mind. Not only does it cleanse your conscience, but when you love others you don't think sinful or unkind thoughts about them. Your mind is washed and uncluttered by offense and sinful intentions. The Word *unfeigned* in First Peter 1:22 means to be sincere. In other words, it isn't a phony love that just hugs people at church and then cuts them down behind their back or lives a double life. It's a love that is expressed by its actions of integrity.

If you have had some trouble with wrong or even sinful thoughts attacking your mind, begin by reminding yourself to love and see how it causes you to have purified thoughts.

Prayer

Heavenly Father, teach me how to love my brothers and sisters in Christ with sincerity. Show me how to love You with all my heart. Wash my mind and cause me to have purified thoughts today. In Jesus' Name, amen.

301

OCTOBER 15

Clues for Hidden Wealth Have Come

"There is wealth and resources hidden in the earth that My Church has not fully tapped into. So it's time to ask Me to show you pieces of hidden wealth in your circle of influence. For even as Abraham and Joseph tapped into the hidden wealth of Egypt, so shall you tap into a portion of the heathen's wealth."

Prophetic Scripture

...And the wealth of the sinner is laid up for the just (Proverbs 13:22).

One of the blessings of the Abrahamic covenant was wealth and financial provision, and we are part of that covenant in Christ. Of course, when you mention the word *wealth*, some automatically assume mansions and fancy cars. No, biblical wealth covers more than finances, because money doesn't solve everything. However, without money the church is limited. As long as the devil can keep the Body of Christ poor and in debt, it limits the effectiveness of ministries worldwide. We need wealth, but wealth from God means something different for everyone. It doesn't mean God is giving everyone a mansion. True financial wealth from God is defined as supernatural provision that enhances and adds to your natural work ethic and occupational efforts. In other words, God takes your particular work efforts and adds to them through supernatural means. God did that with both Abraham and Joseph. Abraham made money in Egypt (a type of secular society). Genesis 13:1-2 says he came up from Egypt and was very rich. Joseph found wisdom from God to store a supply of food before a famine (see Gen. 41).

God is saying that there is a supply of hidden wealth in the earth and He wants to teach you, in the days to come, how to tap into your portion.

Prayer

Heavenly Father, I thank You for the hidden wealth that is in the earth and that You have a portion for me. Lord, I commit that as You provide it for me, I shall always give to Your Kingdom. In the Name of Jesus, amen.

Pray for Marriages

"Pray for marriages this day, says the Spirit. Call out for the protection of the sacred institution of marriage, and also pray for marriages within My Church. For I am looking now for those who will help represent the true meaning of marriage as I have designed it."

Prophetic Scripture

Marriage should be honored by all, and the marriage bed kept pure, for God will judge the adulterer and all the sexually immoral (Hebrews 13:4 NIV).

If there is any institution under attack, it's biblical marriage. Not only are marriages themselves under attack, but also its definition is under attack by secularism. The powers of darkness hate marriage because it represents the union between Christ and the church. Therefore, they are throwing many things at married couples to try and divide them. Things like excess stress, sin, and compromise put strain on marriages. We need to pray for the marriages of the Body of Christ. Secondly, the world is trying to redefine marriage from its biblical definition of being between one man and one woman. They are attempting to go against God's Word by saying that co-partnerships, whether heterosexual or homosexual, are acceptable. We need to go back to Hebrews 13:4, which says marriage, as God defined it, should be honored by all. Married people who honor their marriage covenant don't fight like the world or commit adultery. Those in society, if they honor God's definition of marriage, won't try to change its meaning.

Let's pray for marriages today. If you are married, pray for your marriage and then pray for others. Then ask the Holy Spirit to use His people to stand for the true meaning of marriages so that God's definition will remain sacred in this time.

Prayer

Lord, I pray for the institution of marriage today. Protect it and keep its meaning from being redefined by secular society. I pray for the marriages of the Body of Christ that You would intervene and cause them to be harmonious. In Jesus' Name, amen.

OCTOBER 17

Take It Back!

"The Spirit says, don't let loose of your heritage or those things I have called you to own. See what I have promised and know what I have given you. Let nothing take it away. For I have a heritage for you to own on earth and it's time to take it back!"

Prophetic Scripture

...And the house of Jacob shall possess their possessions (Obadiah 1:17).

When it comes to God we should never assume that a miracle is too late or can't happen. When it seemed Israel lost what they had, God prophesied through Obadiah that they would possess their possessions or "reclaim their inheritance" (Obad. 1:17 NLT). The house of Jacob represents those who are of the Holy Spirit. Jacob in the Bible became Israel in the Old Testament, but in the New he represents the Church, or "house of the Holy Spirit." Prophetically speaking, this verse reveals that God has a plan for His people to reclaim their inheritances that seem to have been lost for a season. Sometimes, we let the devil take them from us. Commonly, our lack of knowledge, lethargy, or even mind-sets cause us to let loose of things in our spiritual heritage. For similar reasons, Israel let go of what God gave them, but the time came for them to take it back.

Look at the things in your life today that you are supposed to have ownership of and take them back. Perhaps it's healing, peace of mind, deliverance, or even business-related things. If so, it's time to reclaim your peace, health, and liberty in Christ. Stand up today and make a decision to take it back!

Prayer

Father, I know that I have a heritage in Christ on this earth that promises certain blessings. I choose today to take back those that have been lost. I reclaim _____ and I say it belongs to me and will be returned right now. In Jesus' Name, amen.

God Gives You a Break

"I want you to rest this day, says the Lord. Rest in your mind and in your soul from all the battles and busy demands of life. For I call you now to take a break and come to complete peace."

Prophetic Scripture

But now the Lord my God hath given me rest on every side, so that there is neither adversary nor evil occurrent (1 Kings 5:4).

When David was king, he spent time fighting many battles. David was always in warfare mode. However, when Solomon took the throne, God gave him rest so he could build the temple. God made it for Solomon as though there was no evil anywhere around him. I am sure there were some evil enemies, but God surrounded Solomon in a cocoon of peace. Literally, God gave him a break. It is easy to live every day feeling caught in a war zone. Sometimes we get caught in that zone simply because we approach every day expecting to face a challenge. Yet God knows there comes a point when you can only take so much fighting. You need a break! Maybe the reason we don't experience those breaks is because we don't expect them. Solomon's name means "peaceful." His name shows that he expected peace. David was a born warrior and God used that characteristic in him to take down the giant and overcome the enemies of Israel. There is a time for warfare; however, there are times when God wants you to be in peaceful mode, like Solomon, so you can focus on building up your life. Smile today—it's time to take a break!

Prayer

Lord, I recognize that You want me to rest and take a break from time to time. Show me how to differentiate between times for war and times for peace. I choose to take a break today, and I ask that You would cover me with peace. In Jesus' Name, amen.

Deliver Yourself

"The Spirit says, know that there is power in self-deliverance. For even as you shake free from the worldly ties that have been weights in your life, so shall you stand up against greater demonic powers with confidence."

Prophetic Scripture

Deliver thyself, O Zion, that dwellest with the daughter of Babylon (Zechariah 2:7).

There is something that happens inside your heart when you overcome something yourself, with the Lord's help of course. Sure, we all need prayer from trusted friends, and we need other believers for accountability in our Christian walk. We certainly don't want to discount the importance of those things. However, when you overcome common bad habits, deficits brought on by your upbringing, or even sin patterns, and you do it from your own resolve with God, it does something to your stamina. No one bailed you out or did anything to help you. It is similar to when you buy a house or something that you worked hard to save money for. You work harder to protect your investment. Self-deliverance is the same. The Lord prophesied through Zechariah that God wanted Zion to deliver themselves from the bondages of Babylon, even though they were still living there. Babylon represents a type of the world. God wanted them to stay free from the worldly culture even though they lived among that culture, and He wanted them to do it with their own internal resolve.

If you have some areas that you want to be free from, like all of us do, and you don't want things that weigh you down to keep holding you back, then make some determined steps for self-deliverance. It will prepare you for great things and boost your spiritual confidence.

Prayer

Lord, I commit to making some steps to further deliver myself from worldly ties. Show me areas where I need to shake free, and I thank You for helping me walk it out so I have confidence for the next level. Amen.

Behold Your City

"Look and behold your city and local surroundings, says the Lord. For there are battles that will only be won through strategic planning and prayer. So study your region more closely now, for your region needs your prayers and voice."

Prophetic Scripture

And when he was come near, he beheld the city... (Luke 19:41).

When Jesus looked out over Jerusalem, He discerned what was going on in the city. He recognized that the city was about to miss its time of divine visitation. Then while looking, He spoke to the city about its current spiritual condition and then began to weep. This account shows us that cities and regions have certain mind-sets and strongholds that are preventing them from receiving the Gospel in certain areas. Often, we don't take the time to discern our region so we can pray strategically for that area's particular needs. In addition, we need to examine our city and region, because it not only helps us pray, but it helps us understand how to reach people in that area. There are ministry models and approaches that work in some territories but not in others. We have to discern the culture and the people who live there.

Whether you are in full-time ministry or a believer who is committed to doing your part to spreading the Gospel, spend some time looking at your city and thinking through how to focus your prayers. In addition, use your knowledge to better minister to people in your circle of influence. With the right strategies in both prayer and ministry, we can be more effective and the Lord will be glorified!

Prayer

Lord, teach me how to take a closer look at my city and region. Help me gain knowledge of the needs and even the strongholds that need to be dealt with so the Gospel can succeed. I commit to do my part to help my region receive the Lord. In Jesus' Name, amen.

Safely Hidden

"Know this day that your old man is gone and Christ is your covering. Your shortcomings and failures are covered, and who you are in Me outweighs what people may say you are in the flesh. So don't let human opinion affect you, says the Lord, for your life is protected and safely hidden."

Prophetic Scripture

For you have died and your life is hidden with Christ in God (Colossians 3:3 NASB).

Although Jesus was the Son of God, people who knew Him tried countless ways to bring him down to something less than He was. When He came back to His hometown, they treated Him like He was nothing more than a carpenter's son whose family they had known for years (see Mark 6:1-6). They downplayed His anointing so much that it limited His miracles. At one point, when Jesus was being pressed upon by multitudes, His friends and family went to get Him out of the situation and went so far to say, "He has lost His mind" (see Mark 3:21; John 7:5). They went to His location and began hollering for Him until He said, "Who are my mother and brothers, but those who do God's will!" (See Mark 3:31–35.) Jesus' mother was in that group! However, Jesus was covered by the anointing and no matter how they tried to belittle Him, His power kept rising.

There will always be people who will only see you after the flesh. They will go back to when you were little and talk about how you haven't changed. Just smile and know that your life is covered in Christ. Your old man is gone and the anointing upon you now will grow until human opinion can't hold it back. You are safely hidden by the anointing today!

Prayer

Father, I thank You that the anointing I have in Christ covers me and makes up for my shortcomings. Help me be confident and learn to live free from fleshly human opinion. I am safely hidden in You. Amen.

Greatness Has Increased

"Yes, it is in My will for you to step into greatness, says the Spirit. Know that I have opened that place of honor for you, and the time to move toward it is now, even right now. Go, for your increase of greatness has begun!"

Prophetic Scripture

Thou shalt increase my greatness, and comfort me on every side (Psalms 71:21).

God has specially designed a place for each of His children to stand in a place of honor and greatness. Yes, greatness and honor are earned, however God will also cause it to rest upon your life. God is the author of greatness, and He will see to it that you will receive due honor for your purity, lifestyle, and commitment to His will. Greatness doesn't mean you have to be famous; it means you receive promotion and honor for obeying God. Your platform of greatness may not be like anyone else's. Stay with your own calling on your road of destiny, and greatness will find you. God will also comfort you along that road as you embrace the hard work that comes with it. Similar to a runner in a race, it takes diligence, practice, hard work, and endurance when no one is noticing you. The greatness of winning the race is only a moment compared to the private work and lifestyle it took to get there. However, the greatness that God gives will be the greatest reward you can receive. Begin to press toward the greatness God has prepared for you and know that greatness will begin to open for you! Move toward your season of greatness today!

Prayer

Father, I receive Your place of destined honor for me. I ask You to help me as I press on the road toward Your will and destiny for my life. Help me to walk in obedience and humility. Anoint me for greatness today, and I thank You, Lord, that I shall be a great testimony unto Your Name! Amen.

His Medicine Arises

"Know that I have brought cures to every fiber of your being, says the Lord. Because you have called upon Me, I have infused you with My medicine and it is permeating every part of you this day."

Prophetic Scripture

But unto you that fear my name shall the Sun of righteousness arise with healing in his wings… (Malachi 4:2).

In Malachi 4:2, the word *healing* in the Hebrew means medicine or cure. The verse is telling us that for those who love the Lord, there is medicine available from the Sun of Righteousness. This of course is talking about Jesus, but likens Him to the natural sun. Because Jesus is likened to the sun here, some translations swap the word *wings* for *rays* as in the rays of the sun. *Wings* literally means extremities. Likening Jesus to the sun, His "rays" are spreading healing or medicine as far as one can imagine. Think of when you stand in the sun and the rays cover every part of you. They envelop you, penetrate your skin, and their warmth is infused into your being. Just the same, Jesus' healing medicine is permeating every fiber of your being the way natural medicine from an IV goes through your system. Think of the Lord's healing power as medicine that is going through your entire system right now touching every organ, the bones, the blood, the immune system, and all your extremities. Every cell, every fiber is being touched by medicine from Jesus, the Sun of Righteousness. Do you know why it is available for you? Because you fear His name; because you love and believe in Him.

If you need any form of healing, just see Jesus infusing you with divine medicine that is going through your body causing a cure today.

Prayer

Lord, I thank You that healing medicine is being infused into me today. That medicine is permeating every part of me, canceling all forms of infirmity, sickness, and disease. Jesus, You are my cure. Amen.

His Voice Is Coming from Heaven

"Today you shall hear My voice. As you put your hand to the tasks before you, so shall I speak. Listen this day, and instruction shall be yours and mysteries from the throne shall be revealed. For you will even hear My perfect will, says the Lord."

Prophetic Scripture

And when the seven thunders had uttered their voices, I was about to write: and I heard a voice from heaven... (Revelation 10:4).

When John received the great heavenly vision on the Isle of Patmos, he experienced the voice of God coming to him in many ways and under a variety of circumstances. On this occasion in Revelation 10:4, he was about to set his hand to the task of recording what he had seen. In other words, it was when he put his hand to the work of God that he heard the voice of God coming out of Heaven in a very divine way. He wasn't trying to hear it, it just came as he was busy doing what he knew to do at that moment. He was immersed in fulfilling the tasks given when God spoke.

If you are seeking to hear the voice of the Lord today, don't spend time exasperating yourself. He wants to speak to you! Like John, focus on the tasks before you and then know that His voice will come. Notice when John heard the voice, he describes it as being from Heaven. When God speaks, you won't have to guess whether or not it's Him. You will know because the revelation will be clear and things will come to you that you couldn't have thought of yourself. Just set your hand upon the day before you, and His voice will come from Heaven!

Prayer

Father, I expect to hear Your voice today. As I focus on the things already before me, I trust Your voice will come to give me divine revelation and make known Your perfect will. In Jesus' Name, amen.

Holy Boldness Rises Up!

"I have called My people to bold, radical faith that rises up when circumstances look their worst. There are those coming who need that secure level of confidence from you, and I will send them your way. So be ready, says the Spirit, for then shall holy boldness from within you rise up."

Prophetic Scripture

The wicked flee when no man pursueth: but the righteous are bold as a lion (Proverbs 28:1).

The anointing of God is attracted to boldness. Boldness is not obnoxious, rude behavior. It is confidence that knows what God will do in adverse situations. According to Proverbs 28:1, the wicked don't have that confidence. When trouble comes into their lives, they are unsure of the outcome. They don't know if they will live or die or if they will keep or lose everything. Their lives hang in the balance. We shouldn't live in that kind of uncertainty because we trust in what God has said He will do in dire situations. When the early apostles were under severe attack in Acts 4, they got together and prayed. Instead of being intimidated, they prayed for even *more* boldness! Acts 4:29 says, "Lord, behold their threatenings: and grant unto thy servants, that with all boldness they may speak thy word." In the verses to follow, the power on their lives got even stronger and even more miracles took place.

If you will take a bold stand for what you believe, the Lord will send you people to minister to who have no hope outside of a miracle from God. So prepare yourself for it and ask the Lord for more boldness, just like the apostles did. Then expect holy boldness to rise up!

Prayer

Lord, I ask You for a greater measure of boldness. Give me the confidence to expect miracles for people who are in desperate situations. Use me to minister to them, and I thank You that I am bold as a lion today! In Jesus' Name, amen.

Your Household Supplied For

"Never fear the future, for I will always supply for your household, says the Lord. Even in times when it seems resources have been reduced and the supply is lean, I will see to it that you always have more than enough."

Prophetic Scripture

And the ark of the Lord continued in the house of Obededom the Gittite three months: and the Lord blessed Obededom, and all his household (2 Samuel 6:11).

When David took the Ark of God to the house of Obededom, he was literally bringing the presence of God. The Ark of God contained God's presence, so once it came into the house of Obededom, it caused his house to come into blessing. Whenever the presence of God enters an environment, you can expect blessing to be there for those who want to receive it.

As a child of God, who has His presence within you and in your house, you can rest assured that your household will be supplied for. Sure, there are challenges we have to overcome in this world's economy. It may look like you are going to lose things, such as a job or home. Perhaps your income is down from where it was a year ago. However, keep relying on God's presence, because even when it looks like blessing is nowhere to be found, His presence will ensure that blessings will come back upon you. God's presence will make up for what you lost, and He will bring back far more than what you originally had. So don't fear your future or worry about how to pay for things. Don't wonder where your bankroll will be one day. The presence of God is with you, and your household will always be supplied for!

Prayer

Heavenly Father, I thank You that Your presence is upon me and in my house. I trust You and know that because of Your presence, my household and family will always be supplied for. In Jesus' Name, amen.

Say Amen!

*"Know that when you say **amen**, it's not just empty words. For I am **The Amen**, and when you say it like you mean it, so shall you affirm what you hear in your heart and it shall be real in your life. So make it a day to say **amen**!"*

Prophetic Scripture

...And all the people said, Amen, and praised the Lord (1 Chronicles 16:36).

Nearly everyone is familiar with the term *amen*. It means "so be it." It is the final word said to affirm the truth. It is said after you hear something you believe in, to affirm where you stand. Israel said "amen" to show their agreement with the Lord. Sometimes those of us who are in church all the time say it and forget its powerful meaning. However, there is more to saying amen than just affirming where you stand; you are literally exonerating Jesus and His Word when you say it from your heart. Revelation 3:14, speaking about Jesus, says, "These things saith the Amen, the faithful and true witness." Here Jesus is referred to as "The Amen." In other words, He is "so be it" or the final Word! So, when you say "amen," you are not just repeating empty words in a religious ritual. You are affirming what you have heard and declaring it to be the truth. You are saying that what you have heard will happen and that you receive it in your own life. Coupled with that, you are lifting up Jesus, who is "The Amen!"

So as you pray today, think carefully of the things you are praying. Then when you say "amen," realize you are declaring that what you have prayed is coming to pass and that Jesus, "The Amen," is above it all! Go ahead, say *"Amen!"*

Prayer

*Lord Jesus, You are "**The Amen**." As I pray right now, I say "Amen" to the things I am asking for and know they will come to pass. Today I say, **amen**!*

Nature Is in Motion

"Let your words change the course of nature this day and set things in motion that need to be changed. For some things have been formed from words spoken over the course of many years, so it's time to reverse their direction and speak new words."

Prophetic Scripture

And the tongue is a fire...and setteth on fire the course of nature... (James 3:6).

James 3 talks about the power of our tongue and how wrong words can have devastating effects. It probably focuses mostly on the negative side of the tongue, because we have a tendency to be more negative with our words than positive. People tend to speak death far more than life. They will discuss sickness far more than the blessings of health. James 3:6 says our tongue is like a fire. Fire has the ability to spread rapidly and eventually affects things not even in its original vicinity. Our words can spread and affect things we didn't even expect or perhaps may never even know about. James 3:6 also says, "and setteth on fire the course of nature." It is saying that our words can literally set nature in motion. If our words can set nature in motion in the negative sense, then they can set it in motion in the positive sense, but those words need time to spread. James also likens our words to the rudder on a ship. Ships can't be turned in one instant. It may take some time to reverse some things with our words, but nature will adjust to them eventually.

So begin to change things that have been formed by words today, whether they were yours or someone else's, and allow nature to be set in motion for blessing!

Prayer

Father, use my words to reverse things that have been set in motion by negative speaking. I ask You to put a watch over my mouth and help me speak the right things that agree with Your Word. I set nature in motion for blessing today. Amen.

Someone Is Mentioning You

"The Spirit says, know that I have raised up people who are praying for you. Stay connected to your fellow believers and pray for them. Then surely you will always know that someone is mentioning your name before the throne!"

Prophetic Scripture

...Without ceasing I make mention of you always in my prayers (Romans 1:9).

What an encouragement Paul's words must have been to the Roman church when they learned that he prayed for them without ceasing! They surely came away from that with the confidence that they were always being brought before God's throne. There is something particularly encouraging about knowing that someone is praying for you. When Jesus was about to go to the cross, He knew the devil was going to come after Peter. He told Peter, "Simon, behold, Satan hath desired to have you...but I have prayed for thee, that thy faith fail not" (Luke 22:31-32). I am sure when Peter faced the shame of knowing he had denied the Lord, he remembered those words. It is probable to say that it was Jesus' prayers and also Peter knowing he had been prayed for that drew him back to the Lord after his sin. It was a lifeline for Peter.

We all walk through things, and just knowing that others are taking the time to think of us and mention our name before the Lord provides a spiritual boost. With that in mind, it is important to then pray for others. Just like their prayers are helping to pull you through, so are your prayers doing the same for them. Let your prayers be a lifeline for someone today and then have peace in knowing that someone is mentioning you.

Prayer

Father, I pray for _____ today. Bless their life and help them receive a breakthrough right now. Draw them closer to You and give them Your peace, and I thank You, Lord, that someone out there is also praying for me today! Amen.

OCTOBER 30

Expect the Unexpected!

"Know that it's the time for greater diversity to be seen in the way My Spirit moves across the land. For miracles that have yet to be seen are descending. So it's time to expect the unexpected at any moment, because I am operating on the earth like you have never seen before."

Prophetic Scripture

And there are differences of administrations but the same Lord. And there are diversities of operations, but it is the same God which worketh all in all (1 Corinthians 12:5-6).

The one key fact we have to always keep in focus about God is that He is supernatural. To eliminate the supernatural is to eliminate God. We have to be careful we don't become so familiar with the miraculous things of Heaven that we treat them as commonplace. Sometimes when we see people get healed at church or the gifts of the spirit begin to manifest, we unconsciously respond as if we have already seen that before. The other thing we inadvertently sometimes do is expect things to manifest a particular way. We think the gifts of the Spirit can only present themselves in a certain fashion. No, they can manifest in many forms and at any moment. If we truly believe the Lord is among us, then we should be ready for Him to move among us. The Holy Spirit is moving across the earth like never before, and we are a part of it! We have only begun to see what God is about to do in this season, so get ready—a fresh wave of the gifts of the Spirit is about to manifest and it's time to expect the unexpected!

Prayer

Holy Spirit, I thank You for the diverse gifts and operations of Your Spirit. I open my heart to them and ask that You would move in my life, my church, my job, and in everything that concerns me. I expect the unexpected today! Amen.

A Ready Answer

"Be ready this day, for it is a time when many from the world shall come to My people with hard questions. They shall call upon you for answers and you shall be there to help them, for I am preparing you with a clear and ready answer, says the Lord."

Prophetic Scripture

But sanctify the Lord God in your hearts: and be ready always to give an answer to every man that asketh you a reason of the hope that is in you with meekness and fear (1 Peter 3:15).

We are the bridge of hope for the lost. We are their connection to Jesus, and they are looking for us to show them the way. We need to be able to answer their questions according to wisdom and according to God's Word. When the Queen of Sheba came to visit Solomon, she came to test him with hard questions, and he was able to answer her questions with wisdom (see 2 Chron. 9:1-12). In addition, when she saw his surroundings she was overwhelmed by how wonderful they were. This story is a picture of the world coming to us to get their questions answered and to see the Gospel genuinely working in our lives.

The world is watching us more than we realize. They want to see if we can answer their tough questions. Give your time to study and ask the Holy Spirit to make you ready for them. The world needs people who can open their mouth and present the Lord in a way they have never seen before. Be ready for them; someone out there needs you! You are their bridge, and God wants to prepare you. They are coming, and God is giving you a ready answer today.

Prayer

Heavenly Father, prepare me to be a bridge that will lead others to Jesus. Prepare me as I prepare myself. Give me wisdom in all I say and fill my mouth with ready answers. In Jesus' Name, amen.

Unfailing Mercy Extended

"See this day that My unfailing mercy sustains you. I have committed My mercy to you so that you may call upon it at any moment. Never think there is a discouragement, failure, or infirmity that My mercy cannot handle, for it extends beyond measure just for you this day, says the Lord."

Prophetic Scripture

It is of the Lord's mercies that we are not consumed, because his compassions fail not. They are new every morning: great is thy faithfulness (Lamentations 3:22-23).

We often read about when people came to Jesus for healing or deliverance, and Jesus commended them for their faith. He often used phrases such as, "your faith has made you whole" or "according to your faith be it unto you." I have often thought Jesus was encouraging them to have faith in His healing power. Of course, undoubtedly that's true. However, as of recent years my personal revelation of faith has extended more to a simple faith in His mercy. If you have faith that He is merciful then you can believe He will heal you. Why do you think blind Bartimaeus cried out, "thou son of David, have mercy" (Mark 10:46-52)? He was believing for healing based on the sheer mercy of the Lord.

If you believe in His mercy, you don't doubt He will heal, forgive, or provide for you. Truly, we simply need confident faith in His unfailing mercy. We can never do enough good deeds to earn it. We are entirely dependent on His mercy for everything. The most powerful part is that His mercy renews itself each morning like new cells that are continually formed in a living organism. Don't fear or condemn yourself today, because His unfailing mercy is being extended to you right now!

Prayer

Lord, I thank You for Your unfailing mercy that is being extended to me. I receive it and know that because of mercy I am forgiven, healed, and provided for today. In Jesus' Name, amen.

Laws Shall Change

"I am raising up My church with a special anointing that shall challenge the legislation of their land. Even laws that were influenced by a spirit of antichrist and have been in place for many decades, some shall change and even be overturned as My people refuse to bow to them."

Prophetic Scripture

Then Nebuchadnezzar spake, and said, Blessed be the God of Shadrach, Meshach, and Abednego, who hath sent his angel, and delivered his servants that trusted in him, and have changed the king's word... (Daniel 3:28).

We recall the three Hebrew boys who refused to obey the king's decree that demanded they bow to a golden idol. Their determined stance angered King Nebuchadnezzar who decided to execute them in a fiery furnace. They were thrown in the furnace only to survive when Jesus showed up in the fire! When they didn't die, the king was so shaken that he gave worship to God, and the Bible says the whole event "changed the king's word." In other words, the original law he made, influenced by evil spirits, was overturned. God anointed the Hebrew boys to stand up to society's pressure. Their bold refusal to compromise their beliefs in order to blend in and protect their own safety caused laws to change.

God is putting an anointing on His people to rise up and challenge established laws and ordinances that clearly defy God's Word. Laws in support of abortion or same-sex marriage need to be continually disputed and we need to take a bold stance and refuse to accept them. Our willingness to make our voices heard and of course, our fervent prayers will cause laws to change in our land!

Prayer

Father, I thank You for the anointing that You are placing upon Your people to challenge the laws that defy Your Word. Use me to be a voice of righteousness that will even cause laws to change. In Jesus' Name, amen.

A Soft Word

"Look this day for ways to respond wisely to others and you shall see the power of a gentle, approving word. For it opens minds and hearts and will cause those you deal with to be favorable to you, says the Lord."

Prophetic Scripture

A soft answer turneth away wrath: but grievous words stir up anger (Proverbs 15:1).

Some people are naturally calm and hardly get worked up about much of anything. Others, who probably comprise a larger portion of the population, find it easier to speak their mind in whatever tone of voice they find necessary in the heat of the moment. Of course, if you're a speak-your-mind kind of person, it is likely that people aren't going to mistake your point. However, just because people know where you stand on an issue doesn't mean they are jumping on board with you. In fact, depending on how you communicated your point, your listeners may withdraw from you simply based on how you spoke to them. While there is a time and place for words to be bold and direct, most of the time soft words that come with an approving tone cause your hearers to be far more open to your ideas and opinions.

Think of those you deal with every day and even those you meet throughout your business day. Look for ways to uplift them, even when you need to say some things that may not always be what they want to hear. Everyone needs to be affirmed and wants to hear a soft word, especially when they are having to face some hard facts. Let this be a day to see the power of a soft word.

Prayer

Heavenly Father, teach me how to speak to people with wisdom and affirmation. Even when truth must be said, give me the ability to use the right tone so that I can gain favor with my listeners. Teach me how to use a soft word. In Jesus' Name, amen.

Say, "It Is Well!"

"The Spirit says, even as you look at your challenges begin to say, It is well! When it would be easy to draw attention to difficulty and despair, say, It is well! Know that each time you say, It is well, you open the way to the miraculous and new life shall enter your soul."

Prophetic Scripture

Run now, I pray thee, to meet her, and say unto her, Is it well with thee? is it well with thy husband? is it well with the child? And she answered, It is well (2 Kings 4:26).

When the childless Shunammite woman gave birth to the baby boy prophesied by Elisha, surely she was elated (see 2 Kings 4:13-26). After the boy grew to be a youth, he was struck with a severe head pain and died. His mother decided to run and find Elisha. When she told her husband she was going to find the man of God, he acted doubtful that she would find him, but her only words were, "It shall be well" (2 Kings 4:23). She finally met Elisha's servant who asked her if she was well. He continued to ask if her husband and child were well. All she would say was, "It is well." She got to Elisha and he realized that she was internally distressed although she said nothing contrary. Immediately, Elisha went to her house and raised the boy from the dead.

While the Bible doesn't say it was her words that caused her miracle, it does draw attention to her constant repetition of the phase, "It is well," spoken in her time of severe trial. Look at your situations today and say, "It is well." The words will flood you with life and open your faith to a miraculous end to the story.

Prayer

Lord, as I look at all my circumstances today, I declare, "It is well." I say it over everything that concerns me and I shall receive miracles. In Jesus' Name, amen.

Create an Altar

> *"The Spirit says, build an altar in your times of prayer. Kneel down and find a place where it is just you and Me, and in that place of sacrifice I will take from your life the things you want removed."*

Prophetic Scripture

> *Then will I go unto the altar of God, unto God my exceeding joy: yea, upon the harp will I praise thee, O God my God* (Psalms 43:4).

The word *altar* comes from a word in the Hebrew that literally means slaughter or sacrifice. In the Old Testament, people built altars and would slaughter their most valuable livestock upon them as a sacrifice to God. Today and in the New Testament, our altars are our places of prayer where we lay our lives down before the Lord and "slaughter" or hand our will over to the Lord. What is powerful about our own personal altar experiences is that when we give the things we hold as "valuable," God uses that sacrificial experience from our hearts to pull out of our lives the things we desperately want to see removed. He takes away the sin habits, the curses, and the things that weigh us down.

As you pray before the Lord, take a moment to create an altar. Perhaps it's just kneeling down in front of a chair or sofa and letting the Lord know that you have come to give Him every part of you. The key is make it something that is meaningful for you. It's a refreshing experience that everyone needs, so take some time and create an altar today.

Prayer

> *Father, I create an altar of sacrifice before You today. I give all of myself to You and ask that You would remove _____ from my life and help me to remain fully committed to You in everything I do. Amen.*

Your Appointments Are Blessed

"Even as you attend each calendared appointment, know that I am sending an angel to go before you who shall set you up for blessing. So don't be concerned with the immediate or apparent results, just trust that your future outcome is in My hands, says the Lord."

Prophetic Scripture

My times are in thy hand... (Psalms 31:15).

Most of us have any number of appointments that we have calendared throughout any given day or week. We have everything—doctor appointments, business meetings, counseling appointments, financial and estate planning, educational appointments, and countless others. We can either be on the facilitating end or the receiving end of these appointments or just there for discussion. Some appointments can be difficult, such as those pertinent to problem resolution or perhaps relating to a medical concern or procedure. As we tackle our various calendared appointments, we need to call upon the Lord to be in the midst of them. Then we need confidence that we do not attend them alone and that angels have been sent to keep charge (see Ps. 91:11-12). Psalms 31:15 says, "My times are in thy hand." Some Bible translations say, "My future is in your hand." In other words, the ultimate outcome of the things we have calendared is being watched over by the Lord, and angels have gone before us so we can be set up and positioned for blessing.

Whatever appointments or meetings are on your calendar for today, have confidence that God will handle the ultimate outcome. Be less concerned with the immediate results, because sometimes we get our eyes too much upon what we can readily see and we lose sight of the good outcome God has in store. Always know that your appointments are blessed!

Prayer

Father, I thank You that You are overseeing all my appointments. I know that angels have been sent to go with me and before me. I place the results in Your hands and know that You are setting me up for blessings. In Jesus' Name, amen.

A Marvelous Sight

"Get ready, says the Lord, for even now I am doing something wonderful for you. For you will be amazed at how I work on your behalf and turn circumstances around suddenly, and you will surely say, What a marvelous sight!"

Prophetic Scripture

This is the Lord's doing; it is marvelous in our eyes (Psalms 118:23).

Psalm 118 is a description of the Lord's defense of His people during times of trouble. Throughout, it gives a prophetic foreshadowing of Jesus. Then verse 23 says, "This is the Lord's doing; it is marvelous in our eyes." In other words, as soon as the revelation of the Messiah was revealed and expounded upon, it caused wonder and amazement. Only God could have come up with it! What we must always remember is that when we are dealing with the everyday circumstances where the Lord is involved, He does things we would have never considered. Therefore, it doesn't pay to sit around for hours musing over how to solve things. Sure, we need to think through decisions and so forth, but what we want to avoid is the human tendency to "think" ourselves into worry or even failure. If we aren't careful, we begin to think of all the situations that seem unsolvable. However, when we focus on the fact that God is involved, even though we may not see it at the moment, we can be assured that His answer is always going to a be a marvelous sight! *Marvelous* means that it causes you to be in awe. It is something you could have never come up with on your own.

Get ready for God to intervene in ways you never imagined, because He will always do something marvelous in your eyes!

Prayer

Lord, I know that You are involved in all my situations, every day of my life. I thank You that I don't have to worry how things will turn out because You are already doing something marvelous in my eyes! Amen!

You Have a New Name

"Speak positively of yourself, says the Lord. For I have purchased for you a new identity. Whatever others have said you are in a negative way, I have changed it and given you a new name that is opposite of it."

Prophetic Scripture

Thou shalt no more be termed Forsaken; neither shall thy land any more be termed Desolate: but thou shalt be called Hephzibah, and thy land Beulah... (Isaiah 62:4).

Often as we go through life, people tend to label us in certain ways based on things such as our personality traits, appearance, or perhaps talents. Some labels we receive aren't always positive. We are also labeled by our mistakes, or even our inabilities and weaknesses. Also, it isn't always others who label us. Out of insecurity, we sometimes label ourselves and thereby form certain negative mind-sets about who we believe ourselves to be. This causes us to limit ourselves and may even prevent us from receiving certain blessings from God or from enjoying all the aspects of life He intends for us. In Isaiah 62:4, God tells Israel that He is changing their label and giving their land a different name. They began with the negative name Forsaken. This is reflective of how life tries to label people. However, in spite of it, God changes their name to Hephzibah and their land to Beulah. Basically, the two terms combined mean that God was married to them and that they were His delight.

Know today that the Lord has labeled you differently than life has tried to label you negatively. Therefore, keep all negative labels out of your vocabulary and rejoice today because you have a brand-new name!

Prayer

Father, I thank You that You have given me a new name today. I repent of all negative labels I have accepted or given myself. I thank You that You have named me after positive things and I am Your delight! Amen.

Ten Thousands of Saints

"Remember, says the Spirit, that those who are called Mine shall stand with Me one day to execute judgment upon the wickedness of the world. Even ten thousands of My saints shall come with Me. So stand with Me now regarding the issues, so you are prepared to stand with Me on that day."

Prophetic Scripture

...Behold the Lord cometh with ten thousands of his saints (Jude 14).

As saints, we are being positioned to stand with Jesus to execute judgment on the evil of this world someday. Jesus is going to return and we will be at His side. Jude 15-19 describes the behaviors that will receive these judgments. It's sobering to think that we will be standing at Jesus' side to bring His righteous government upon this world. According to verses 20-22, we are to remain busy in the meantime preparing ourselves. Jude gives us four things that we are to be doing. We are to be building ourselves up by praying in the spirit (verse 20), keeping ourselves connected to the love of God (verse 21), showing mercy to those whose faith/walk with God is wavering (verse 22), and sharing the Gospel so as to save others from hell while remaining uncontaminated by the world. That means we are going to have to make some determined decisions not to become entangled by the world's ungodly principles. We can't soften worldly ideals to make them somehow palatable or let them influence how we think or operate.

You are one of God's ten thousand saints being prepared. As part of that preparation, it's time to stand by His side even now as one of His ten thousand saints. Let's get ready because He is coming!

Prayer

Lord, thank You for the honor that I will have one day to stand with You to execute Your righteous judgments on this world. I choose to stand with You now and ask that You would help prepare me. In Jesus' Name, amen.

Jesus Standing Before You

"Call out for what you desire this day and don't give up. Call out to Me for the manifestation of the healing anointing. Call out and I will stand right there before you, and I will minister to you and even put healing virtue in your hands, says the Spirit of the Lord."

Prophetic Scripture

And Jesus stood still... (Mark 10:49).

In Mark 10:46-52, the blind man cried out to Jesus in such a way that it was almost to the point of embarrassment. People kept telling him to quiet down, but when they did he cried out even more. I am sure if those people are like most modern-day folks, they probably thought, "What is wrong with this crazy man?" However, his crying out was nothing more than a determination to obtain from Jesus what he needed. He wasn't going to take no for an answer; he was determined to get a hold of the power inside Jesus. He was willing to throw all caution aside in order to get Jesus' attention. But it was this very determined approach that made Jesus do something that probably not everyone expected Him to do. In spite of everyone telling the blind man to quiet down, Jesus suddenly stopped. The Bible says, "And Jesus stood still." Then Jesus stood right before the blind man and gave him what he came for—his eyesight.

If you really want to see the Lord manifest for you, it takes this kind of determination that will keep calling out to the Lord until you receive. The Lord looks for faith and determination from those who will not leave without the thing they need. Keep calling out to Him. Jesus is standing before you.

Prayer

Lord Jesus, I call out to You! I call out for healing power to manifest upon me. I refuse to live without what I need, and I thank You that You are standing before me to provide it. Amen!

No More Disappointment

"Look to this next season of your life as a season of fulfillment, says the Lord. Declare it your season of abundance and blessing. Say from your lips, 'No more disappointment' and then expect the things that once disappointed you to be no more."

Prophetic Scripture

Instead of the thorn shall come up the fir tree... (Isaiah 55:13).

Whenever the Lord used the Old Testament prophets to speak to Israel, He often encouraged them to be hopeful and see that the past season of disappointments would soon become a season of blessing and fulfillment. He spoke through the prophet Isaiah and told them, "Instead of the thorn shall come up the fir tree" (Isa. 55:13). The word *thorn* in this verse means to prick. It represents something that grows that you didn't want or expect, and it pricks at your life. Thorns also speak of disappointment, like when you are expecting a crop or a beautiful plant to emerge, but up comes a thorn-covered weed! Yet God is saying in this verse that instead of those disappointing thorns, start expecting the fir tree. The fir tree in ancient Israel was a plant used for making musical instruments, which are key for worship. So put it all together and you can see God prophesying a season when, instead of expecting those disappointing thorns, you can begin to expect things to emerge that will reflect a season of blessing which causes praise and worship to just bubble up from within!

Know that God always has a season of blessing woven into His prophetic timetables for your life. However, they begin with a prophetic declaration that expects it to come to pass. It's time for you! See this season as one of fulfillment when disappointment will be no more!

Prayer

Father, I know You want me to embrace a season of blessing. I choose to expect blessing over disappointment, and I declare that my season of fulfillment is upon me. I declare, no more disappointment! In Jesus' Name, amen.

Have Courage

"The Lord says, for I am moving in situations concerning you where it may seem right now as though nothing is changing according to your natural eye. So have courage this day and don't be fearful, for I am walking in your midst."

Prophetic Scripture

For they all saw him, and were troubled. And immediately he talked with them, and saith unto them, Be of good cheer: it is I; be not afraid (Mark 6:50).

When Jesus appeared to the disciples walking on water, they didn't initially recognize Him. They thought He was a ghost! Instead of seeing Jesus in the midst of them, they quickly assumed something negative or even demonic was at work, and they became afraid. Many times, we look at our circumstances and instead of seeing Jesus, we assume negative things are happening and thus we let go of our courage. Yet it's when we can't see it that the power of God is most often producing something supernatural. When the disciples couldn't see Jesus walking among them, it was the very moment when He was there doing something miraculous! He had to remind them not to be fearful, but instead to "be of good cheer." That also means "have courage!" Instead of fearing that something other than Jesus was at work, they needed to have courage that Jesus was at work!

Whatever situations you are dealing with today, don't assume that just because it doesn't appear anything is happening that Jesus isn't working a miracle. Those are the very times we need to have courage and keep our words and thoughts in line with God. Instead of wrongly assuming that nothing is happening, we need to be confident that a miracle is in the making. Have courage—Jesus is in your midst today!

Prayer

Lord, I thank You that You are always with me and working something miraculous on my behalf. I have courage that even when I cannot see it, supernatural things are happening and You are there with me! Amen!

NOVEMBER 13

You Are a Bridge

"Seek ways to be a bridge with those who may be different from you or those who you may not always feel connected with. Know that if they are following Me in integrity and truth, there is great benefit when you uplift and promote the good they are doing for Me, says the Lord."

Prophetic Scripture

If it be possible, as much as lieth in you, live peaceably with all men (Romans 12:18).

One of the beautiful things about the Body of Christ is that we are all different. It reflects an actual physical body with different parts, shapes, and functions. However, as different parts of Christ's Body, sometimes we don't always see eye to eye or appreciate the importance of the other parts of the Body. Due to many factors, we can all have a different approach to ministry, church, Scripture, and even prayer. Some pray loudly, while others are more quiet. Some preach in a mild-mannered way, while others shout. In any given setting, factors such as these can cause us to misunderstand one another or not appreciate one another's value.

Instead of being critical, choose to be a bridge. We can be a bridge by realizing that while someone may not be our personal flavor, they may be the right flavor for someone else. We can be a bridge by focusing on the areas where we are similar instead of different. We can also be a bridge by not over-emphasizing our differences and blowing them out of proportion. The key is we need to live in peace where we are able and know that this endeavor has great benefits for all of the Body of Christ. Always remember—you are a bridge.

Prayer

Lord, teach me how to be a bridge with my fellow members of the Body of Christ. Help me not become critical of those who I don't understand or who are different from me. Teach me how to live in peace whenever possible. Amen!

Supervisors Honored

"Make a point this day to show honor to those you give an account to. Show support to your supervisors, leaders, and authorities. For know that as you do so, you are sowing for yourself a future of favor and peace."

Prophetic Scripture

Let as many servants as are under the yoke count their own masters worthy of all honour, that the name of God and his doctrine be not blasphemed (1 Timothy 6:1).

The Bible gives many examples of how to treat our bosses or those we answer to on many various levels. Whether it be our boss at work, department supervisors, parents, pastors, or similar authorities, we are to show respect because of the fact that they play some current role in our success. Perhaps you feel you have a boss or supervisor who is out to get you somehow or who is just difficult to work with. Perhaps they are hard to deal with simply because life has been hard on them. Maybe there are some areas where you need to step up your support of them. Sometimes those who lead or supervise just need to feel supported and appreciated by those who they are given the responsibility to govern. We can never see all the factors that bring people to where they are today. You may very well find that a little extra touch of support is all they need. It positions you for favor when you might have otherwise felt unappreciated or even been mistreated in some way. Your purpose isn't to manipulate them, but rather be obedient to God's Word and to represent the Christian faith through love. Ask the Lord to give you ideas of how to support and honor your supervisor, boss, or leaders. It is rewarding, and you will be so glad you did!

Prayer

Father, I commit to show You honor by honoring those You have put in position to supervise over me. Teach me key ways to show them support as the Bible teaches so that I may be a good example as a Christian. In Jesus' Name, amen!

There Is a Way Out

"The Spirit says, when you are feeling tested and tempted beyond measure, always remember I have created a way out even when it seems there is no escape. Stay close to Me and I will ease the burden and temptations that put excess pressure upon you!"

Prophetic Scripture

There hath no temptation taken you but such as is common to man: but God is faithful, who will not suffer you to be tempted above that ye are able; but will with the temptation also make a way to escape, that ye may be able to bear it (1 Corinthians 10:13).

The devil never plays fair. He doesn't relent in his attempts to defeat you. He kicks you when you are down to make you feel there is no way out. He wants you to think you are powerless to overcome by shooting every defeating thought imaginable into your mind. He will use all sorts of things to lure you away from God and His Word. He will tempt your flesh relentlessly! However, the Holy Spirit always has a way out of temptation. Sure, there may be those moments or periods of several hours where you are having to fight thoughts almost every minute. Don't give up. Just stay close to the Lord, stay connected to other believers, and keep casting down those thoughts. Be on guard regarding your weaknesses. If you do those things, the Spirit of God will begin to take over and the pressure will ease. Remember, the Bible says God will not allow the temptation to become greater than you can bear (see 1 Cor. 10:13). So stand up strong and see that the Lord has provided your way out today!

Prayer

Father, I thank You that You always provide a way out of temptation. I take control of my thoughts today and press in close to You. I know that You will ease the pressure of every temptation against me! In Jesus' Name, amen.

Yes, I Will!

"The Spirit says, know that I am always willing. I am willing to give, provide, and answer all your needs. So, when you ask, listen for Me to say, 'Yes, I will!'"

Prophetic Scripture

...I will; be thou clean...I will come and heal him (Matthew 8:3,7).

Have you ever noticed that when people came to Jesus with their needs, He never turned them away or gave them no for an answer? When they sought Him for healing, He always gave them an emphatic "yes!" In Matthew 8:2-13, when both the leper and centurion came to Him, Jesus responded to their requests for healing by saying, "I will!" You don't find any account in the Bible when people came to Jesus for healing or deliverance that He told them no. That is because Jesus came to do His Father's will (see John 6:38). He came to reveal the heart of the Father though the things He did (see John 14:9). Acts 10:38 says, "How God anointed Jesus of Nazareth...who went about doing good, and healing all...." Jesus' actions were a demonstration of the Father's will for people.

Jesus has not changed; through the power of Calvary's cross, He is still revealing the heart of the Father just as He did on the shores of Galilee (see Heb. 13:8). The needs of people today are no different from those back in the days of the Bible. We are mistaken to think God only healed and delivered people back then, but then stopped that kind of activity today. The Bible is our example, and from it we see that God's heart for you is to be completely well and supplied for. So go to Him with your need today; He is saying, "Yes, I will!"

Prayer

Father, I thank You that Your will for me is healing and deliverance. You are more than willing to supply my needs, and You demonstrated through Jesus that You are saying, "Yes, I will!" In Jesus' Name, amen.

Further Than You Realize

"Be encouraged, says the Lord, for you are further than you realize in your spiritual growth and in the calling I have placed upon you. Others will see it even more readily than you, so watch as they begin to call upon you for assistance and spiritual insight. Then shall you realize how far you have come!"

Prophetic Scripture

...And the seed should spring and grow up, he knoweth not how (Mark 4:27).

Physical growth is hard to detect. Growing from childhood into adulthood isn't something you observe in the mirror. Healthy growth is so gradual you don't notice it. Rather than actually observing the growth process, you simply live out the results of growth. The results of growth are seen when perhaps you are given more responsibility, buy different sized clothes, or know a little bit more than last year.

Spiritual growth is the same. Many times, we don't see ourselves growing in the Lord. In the parable of the farmer in Mark 4:27, he plants seed but doesn't actually observe the growth process. He doesn't know how it grows; it just happens. All he knows is that one day he is enjoying the crop that came from that growth process. Like the farmer, if you have planted the right "seed" you will experience a good crop. By putting God's Word in your heart and staying close to the Lord, you don't know how it happens, you just grow! Eventually, you see the results of that growth because people will begin to notice the fruit growing on the tree of your life. While you may not see it, you are growing and have probably come much further than you realize.

Prayer

Father, thank You for helping me grow and for leading me in how far I have already come. I know that many shall receive from the fruit that will continue to grow in my life. In Jesus' Name, amen.

A Gift Indescribable

"Know that the gift of grace is so expansive you cannot describe it with words. It's causing you to receive many gifts from Heaven that are designed just for you. So be ready, for gifts shall appear in your life in various unexpected places and will leave you blessed beyond words, says the Lord!"

Prophetic Scripture

Thanks be to God for his indescribable gift! (2 Corinthians 9:15 NIV)

When something is indescribable it means that there are not enough words or volumes of books to fully illustrate it. The word *indescribable* simply means you cannot describe it! The majority of the time, the word is used in the positive sense, meaning that something is too wonderful for words. This is the best way to describe God's grace. It is so wonderful, you can't describe it. That is how Paul spoke about it in Second Corinthians 9:14-15. Of course, we know that grace in its simple form means favor. While you can't fully describe it, it is a favor from God that treats you as royalty. Try for a moment to imagine being so specially favored that everywhere you go there are gifts, blessings, and surprises waiting for you. Think of it as being like an honored guest or VIP receiving the red-carpet treatment. What even makes us more speechless about grace is that God gave it when we didn't deserve it! God showers us with favor when we didn't do a single thing to earn it.

Because of the indescribable gift of grace upon you today, you can expect blessings to appear in your life on a regular basis. It doesn't matter if you feel worthy to receive them, it is simply because of grace, God's indescribable gift!

Prayer

Lord, I thank You today for the indescribable gift of grace. You gave it when I didn't deserve or earn it. I know that I have been favored by You and many blessings are being poured out upon my life! In Jesus' Name, amen.

Face the Giants

"Don't run from situations that would try to intimidate you, says the Lord. For the things that you run from will only continue to plague you again and again. So rise up and face the giants in your life, for you are well able to overcome them!"

Prophetic Scripture

...Let us go up at once, and possess it; for we are well able to overcome it (Numbers 13:30).

When Israel had the opportunity to go up and possess the land the Lord gave them in Numbers 13, instead of welcoming the opportunity they shied away from it. They saw some giants in the land and were terrified to face them because they looked bigger and stronger. However, these enemies were certainly no bigger than the enemies they had faced previously back in Egypt. So it would appear that they had developed some kind of fear pattern that continued to plague them, and it kept resurfacing each time they faced a new challenge. Instead of being ready to face the giants, they responded in defeat. Caleb was the only one, besides Joshua, who was ready to go into the land and face the enemy (see Num. 13:30). He recognized they were able to do it!

This pattern of responding to challenges and enemies in fear, exhibited by Israel, is the same pattern we deal with today. The things you don't address today will follow you into tomorrow. If you have been afraid to face the giants in your life, they will resurface in your future until you deal with them. Don't let the giants of your past follow you anymore. Recognize that you are well able to face every giant today!

Prayer

Father, I ask that You would help me to deal with every giant that has tried to plague my life. Help me identify them and then face them head-on so that I can embrace my future with freedom! In Jesus' Name, amen.

Who Am I to You?

"Know that I love you uniquely, says the Lord. You are distinct from others and I enjoy hearing revelation that comes up from within your own heart, communicated in your own words. And even as you speak of Me this way, so shall divine revelation continually increase upon you."

Prophetic Scripture

He saith unto them, But whom say ye that I am? (Matthew 16:15)

We have often heard the saying, "Be a voice, not an echo." This simply means to be a person who imparts fresh information and doesn't just repeat what was heard from someone else. While there is nothing wrong with repeating or sharing things you receive from others, there still needs to be the dynamic in your life where revelation is personally received from your own walk with God. When Jesus asked His disciples who people thought He was in Matthew 16, many of them gave answers. They could all easily chime in and repeat what they heard the public say about Jesus. It wasn't until He narrowed the question by saying, "But who do you say I am?" that it got quieter. He asked the question to all of them, but instead of getting multiple responses this time, only Peter answered by saying He was the Christ.

We cannot live only on revelation from others or what we hear them say about Jesus. We need to obtain revelation for ourselves as we pursue the Lord. God wants to feel the affection we have for Him as we dig for our own unique nuggets of revelation. Jesus asks all of us, "Who am I to you?" Let Him have the pleasure of hearing it from your heart and no one else's today.

Prayer

Lord, I ask You to give me my own personal revelation of You that is deeper than what I have known thus far. While I welcome helpful impartation from others, help me learn of You in the unique way that is personal between You and me. Amen.

Impossible Mountains Bow to Grace!

*"Though it seems some mountains have not moved and have faced you for a long time, don't stop speaking **grace** to them! Know that every mountain in your life must bow to grace, so shout **grace** unto the mountains before you even now, says the Spirit of Grace!"*

Prophetic Scripture

Who art thou, O great mountain? before Zerubbabel thou shalt become a plain: and he shall bring forth the headstone thereof with shoutings, crying, Grace, grace unto it (Zechariah 4:7).

When you feel nothing can move your mountain, you have to keep shouting grace! When it seems you can't overcome an obstacle, just shout grace. Grace is the way and it makes impossible mountains move. Grace makes up for the failures in our lives. It makes up for our inabilities and shortcomings. When you speak grace, you are speaking ability to what you cannot accomplish on your own. We have heard it said many times, "Grace means I can't, therefore God must!"

Look at some of the mountains in your life today. Perhaps it's debt. Look at debt in the eye today and say, "I can't fix debt by myself, but God's grace will move debt out of the way!" Look at sickness and realize that though you may not be able to find healing by natural means, God extends healing grace. When circumstances are greater than what it seems you can emotionally bear, shout grace! While you may not have answers right now for the tough things you are facing, shout *grace, grace!* For impossible mountains are moving this day and they are bowing down to *grace!*

Prayer

*Dear Lord, I thank You that mountains move to the sound of **grace**. Impossible situations cannot stand up to the power of God's favor undeserved. So I shout this day **grace** to all my circumstances and **grace** shall see me through. In Jesus' Name, amen.*

Bring the Children

"The Spirit says, bring children before My throne. Bring the children into My Kingdom. Reach out to the children and tell them of Me, for it is through the anointing upon children and young people that I shall move and shall even save a generation yet to come."

Prophetic Scripture

Suffer little children, and forbid them not, to come unto me; for of such is the kingdom of heaven (Matthew 19:14).

Children have several character qualities that are particularly powerful when it comes to spiritual things. They have an innocent version of faith that blindly trusts the words they hear. They don't have to analyze things, nor do they need an excessive explanation in order to be convinced. Because of this quality, Jesus wanted the children to be brought to Him. Undoubtedly, it was their sweet, tender innocence He loved. However, it was surely more than just that alone. He wanted the children to be brought to Him because it will take the faith of children for the Gospel of the Kingdom to spread and for miracles to manifest in the earth. The Lord knows that children hold a measure of faith that the success of the Gospel depends upon. It will be children who will have the blind, unaltered kind of faith that will save a future, degenerate generation from sure destruction. It's children that make up the Kingdom of Heaven.

Make a point to pray for the children and the youth today. In addition to prayer, also allow God to use you in doing your part to bring children into the Kingdom. Perhaps it's your own kids and teens, or it's other children you have opportunity to minister to. Just do your part and bring the children to Jesus.

Prayer

Lord, I pray for the children and young people today. Help me draw children into Your Kingdom and not neglect any young person whom You have given me opportunity to minister to. Show me how to bring the children to You. Amen.

Shortage Becomes Excess

"Watch Me increase the excess now, says the Lord. For where you felt like there was just barely enough to get by, I shall provide not only enough, but more than enough so that your shortage becomes excess in this time."

Prophetic Scripture

Blessed shall be thy basket and thy store (Deuteronomy 28:5).

So many people live paycheck to paycheck and it seems they have barely enough money to make it until the end of every month. In a world where recession has been rampant, some have suffered from lost wages or even job losses. Savings have dwindled and for many people have disappeared altogether. One of the key prophecies God spoke to Israel through the mouth of Moses was that if the people would keep trusting God in hard times, God would see to it that restoration hovered over their storehouse. This was speaking of excess resources that are set aside for future use. God was preparing Israel to not be moved by circumstances that didn't seem to be going like they wanted. He wanted them to know that no matter what, even when resources were lean or hard to find, He would see to it that blessing would return to their savings and storehouse.

God wants to pour excess into your life even when it seems that there is not enough provision to go around. We have to believe it simply because God is supernatural. It's excess in the middle of shortage that shows the glorious power of God in action. We need to expect that kind of outpouring because we serve the Lord who turns shortage into excess!

Prayer

Father, I know that You are the God of excess in times of shortage. You bless my savings even when resources seem low. I ask You to fill my storehouse and cause blessing upon it right now so that I have more than enough! In Jesus' Name, amen.

Gather Together

"Know that the time and season is upon the earth when it is more important for My people to gather together. Worship together, learn together, and love each other. For as you assemble together, there is healing in your gathering that shall protect you against the time to come."

Prophetic Scripture

Not forsaking the assembling of ourselves together, as the manner of some is; but exhorting one another: and so much the more, as ye see the day approaching (Hebrews 10:25).

These days many people are making church attendance and time with fellow believers less of a priority. Some are replacing church attendance with online or television ministry. Others are simply not prioritizing Christian fellowship. However, we need time around our fellow members of the Body of Christ on multi-faceted levels. Church attendance is important because you are able to simply receive ministry, while small group sessions offer more of an interactive setting. We simply cannot survive without staying connected to God's people and gathering together with them. Sure, no fellow Christian is perfect, nor is any church or group leader perfect. We are all people with flaws, but God has still chosen us to be the life source for each other. This will become even more necessary as the world we live in grows darker with each passing day. So no matter how busy you are, make church a priority and make time to be with fellow Christians. Gather together where you can exhort others and they can exhort you. It keeps us all on the straight and narrow and gives us a breath of fresh air after we face the world every day. There is healing and protection when we gather together.

Prayer

Lord, I thank You for the Body of Christ. Thank You for the believers who You have put in my life for a divine purpose. I pray and ask Your blessing upon them and I commit to gather together with them. Amen.

Our Eyes Are on Thee

"Never be fearful when it seems you have nowhere to turn. For natural solutions are limited in their ability, but I am never limited to them. So, just keep your eyes steadfastly upon Me for I am already performing miracles in your midst."

Prophetic Scripture

...Neither know we what to do: but our eyes are upon thee (2 Chronicles 20:12).

The famous story of King Jehoshaphat who was attacked by an army that outnumbered him gives us a constant reminder that we cannot put our eyes on natural solutions in tough situations (see 2 Chron. 20). Jehoshaphat was attacked by the Ammonites, whose army was much larger than his own. He immediately knew he didn't have the military might to retaliate. It looked like certain death, and he didn't have anywhere to turn other than to rely solely upon the Lord.

Everyone has faced something challenging when they simply didn't know where to turn. Every option seemed like no option at all. While we should rely on the Lord in all things, these are times when we need an unwavering confidence. The Bible says that Jehoshaphat and all of Judah stood before the Lord. They didn't do anything else but pray because there was no point in doing anything else! They stood before the Lord and said, "Lord, we don't know what to do, but our eyes are upon you" (see 2 Chron. 20:12). When they did so, God gave them direction and He stepped in with a miracle and caused the army of the Ammonites to begin killing their own soldiers! Now, how does that happen? It's God! So make a habit in your life of just standing before the Lord and simply saying, "Lord, my eyes are upon thee!"

Prayer

Father, I make a determination to rely upon You even more. I look to You for answers to all my needs, and in all situations I declare, my eyes are upon thee! In Jesus Name, amen.

Keep Pursuing Your Dreams

"Even though there are times when you may feel faint, it's the time to keep pursuing hard after your dreams, says the Lord. Even when it seems resources and open doors are limited, stay with the things that I have truly put in your heart, for those dreams will come to pass."

Prophetic Scripture

And Gideon came to Jordan, and passed over, he, and the three hundred men that were with him, faint, yet pursuing them (Judges 8:4).

God gives everyone a dream for their future. Some are short-term and others are lifelong dreams. Many times the process to realizing those dreams is challenging and takes far longer than anticipated. Perhaps you have become weary in pursuing your dreams. A good biblical example of someone who was weary but kept pursuing was Gideon and his 300-man army. The Bible says his men were "faint, yet pursuing" (Judg. 8:4).

If you are feeling weary, there are some principles that may help. First, decide if your dream is truly from God. If so, there will be confirmations from others and circumstances will begin to align leading up to it. If these factors exist but there's still a hold up, ask the Holy Spirit to guide you to the reasons. Perhaps there are some areas holding you back that need adjustment. We all need to reassess our direction sometimes. It could also be a timing issue and nothing more. The key is that once you know your dream is from God, keep pursuing it with passion. Determined pursuit creates success. Sure, you may feel faint sometimes, but that's often when you are the closest to breakthrough, so keep pursuing your dream today!

Prayer

Heavenly Father, I know that You have put a dream in my heart regarding _____. I will not give up on the things You have given me to do and to become. Give me strength, I pray, and help me to keep pursuing my dream! Amen.

Enjoy the Fruit of Your Labor

"I want you to be rewarded for the hard work you do in life, says the Lord. So do not let unnecessary things attack your time, your finances, nor allow occupational stress to prevent you from enjoying the fruit of your labor, says the Lord."

Prophetic Scripture

And also that every man should eat and drink, and enjoy the good of all his labour, it is the gift of God (Ecclesiastes 3:13).

One of life's tragedies is to work hard and never get ahead. Some people are working as hard as humanly possible, yet something always steals their opportunity to appreciate the results of their efforts. Some people work so hard they are literally workaholics who can never seem to turn off the business day. Others work hours upon end, but never seem to improve their financial position. Then there is yet another group who can't seem to be free of the mental stress created by their work life. However, it's God's will for every hard-working person to enjoy the fruit of their labors. This means something different for everyone. For most people it simply means being able to comfortably pay their bills and still have resources remaining to enjoy some simple pleasures in life. It could also mean enjoying some much-needed time off or simply being able to be mentally free from focusing on work.

There comes a point when we all need to put the demands of life aside and simply enjoy life. God created the world in six days, then looked around and took a full day to appreciate His work. The Lord wants you to enjoy the fruit of your labor too. It's a gift from Him!

Prayer

Father, I know that You want me to enjoy the results of my hard work. Help me deal with the areas that want to steal my ability to do so. Thank You, Lord, for the gift of enjoying good things in life. In Jesus' Name, amen.

Remember Those in Adversity

"The Spirit says, be considerate of those in situations of suffering and hardship. Even those who are abused and mistreated, consider them in prayer and even when there is opportunity to help them, for I will honor your remembrance of them."

Prophetic Scripture

Remember them that are in bonds, as bound with them; and them which suffer adversity, as being yourselves also in the body (Hebrews 13:3).

One of the beautiful things about being a Christian is that we have the love of God in our hearts. We are to be the most caring, thoughtful, and considerate people anywhere. People should look to us for strength and encouragement during hard times. Not only that, but the Lord expects us to have heartfelt compassion for people during their hardships. There are scores of people who live abused, imprisoned, or in impoverished circumstances. Some are just everyday people who are going through tragic situations. We must be careful not to get so busy that we overlook the suffering of others, especially that of our fellow believers. When we see others suffering from adversity, we also must be careful not to unfairly judge them or draw conclusions about their situations when we don't know all the facts that led up to their present situation.

The Bible teaches us to remember those in adversity. Think of someone today you can pray for. You don't have to know all the details surrounding their situation, nor do you need to even know them personally—just pray. When God brings someone across your path that you know is suffering in some way, love them and reach out to them. God will honor you for remembering those in adversity today.

Prayer

Lord, I pray for those in adverse situations right now. I specifically pray for _____. Help them through this difficult time, Lord, and touch their life with peace. Show me what I can do to offer strength for those who You put in my path. In Jesus' Name, amen.

Early Harvest Is upon You!

"Some harvests take time to grow, says the Lord. For I have reserved some harvests to come upon you before their time, when you don't expect them. Then rejoice and know that an early harvest is upon you!"

Prophetic Scripture

Behold, the days come, saith the Lord, that the plowman shall overtake the reaper, and the treader of grapes him that soweth seed... (Amos 9:13).

Both in the natural and spiritual realms, there are seasons reserved for planting and others for harvesting. Everything on earth is built upon the seed and harvest principle (see Gen. 8:22). Farmers plant seeds for natural harvests while we plant harvests for life through our choices. When it comes to the Kingdom of God, we reap spiritual harvests by sowing "seeds" into the things pertaining to God's Kingdom. Not all these seeds are financial, but can be seeds of mercy, love, patience, right words, and so on. These seeds have a growth season and then eventually produce a harvest. Yet when it comes to God, spiritual harvests can transcend normal time. While there are established times for when harvests normally come, God can cause supernatural harvests to appear before their expected time. According to Amos 9:13, there is a type of harvest that can come so quickly that the harvest itself is maturing even before the seeds are fully planted.

There are supernatural harvests from God that come into the lives of everyone. Have you ever received a blessing that came quicker than you expected? That is a supernatural or "early" harvest. Know that God has planned some harvests in your life to come sooner than expected. Expect them at any time and know that times for an early harvest are always upon you!

Prayer

Lord, I thank You for seasons of early harvest that are established for me. I call them to manifest by faith. I see good things coming upon me that I didn't even expect. Thank You, Lord! In Jesus' Name, amen.

Turn Your Back!

"The Spirit says, enticements from the world shall increase in this time. For they shall come through media, co-workers, and even close family and friends. Be on the alert, and when subtle persuasions are before you, quickly turn your back upon them!"

Prophetic Scripture

My child, if sinners entice you, turn your back on them! (Proverbs 1:10 NLT)

The reason many people fall into temptation is because they give the source of it access to them. Of course, most temptation starts out subtly and then slowly gains momentum. Some looks completely innocent at the onset, but then grows. This modern-day world with the addition of so many media outlets has more enticements to present than ever. They are almost coming at lightening fast speeds! Some enticements don't come via the media, but come through people we trust who we wouldn't expect to be a source of temptation. That is why we have to be in our Bibles and stay on the alert every single day so we are able to discern when sinful persuasions are being presented. While we don't need to live in fear, we do need to live on guard.

The Bible teaches us to turn our back on enticements from the world regardless of their source (see Prov. 1:10). While we shouldn't be rude to those who may be presenting worldly or sinful things, we do need to turn our back on what they present. We can do it kindly, but we must be resolute or the devil will keep trying to use that area to find an opening in your heart until he slowly breaks you down. Follow the Lord and stand strong against these enticements. Quickly turn your back on them today!

Prayer

Lord, I turn my back today on all enticements of sin. Cause me to have an awareness from You to know when subtle temptation of any form is being presented. I thank You, Lord, that I shall overcome temptation in Jesus' Name! Amen.

DECEMBER 1

Your Lips Are Sealed

*"Watch negative words about yourself or even others. For it's often through
negative words thoughtlessly spoken that negative circumstances are formed.
So ask Me to place a seal over your lips this day so that the negative is not
formed through you, says the Lord."*

Prophetic Scripture

Set a watch, O Lord, before my mouth; keep the door of my lips (Psalms
141:3).

We can all think of things we have said without thinking. When it
pops out of your mouth, you find yourself saying, "Where did
that come from?" In addition, we have all spoken things we either didn't
mean or have spoken our conclusion about something or someone
based on limited information. We live in a world where everyone has
an opinion about everything. We even share these opinions on internet
blogs and social networking sites. Because of this, we have to be so
careful we don't just let unfounded opinions or words that we will
later be sorry for come thoughtlessly flying from our mouths. Negative
words, either about ourselves or others, can produce negative situations
we didn't expect. We have to be so careful with what we say, particularly
those things we say thoughtlessly.

According to Psalms 141:3, we can ask the Lord to put a watch over
our words that will help us not speak things on a whim that don't need
to be said. The Holy Spirit within will stop you right as you are about
to jump out and say something that may either damage your own life
or someone else's. Never forget that words, once spoken, are difficult to
reverse, so ask the Lord to seal your lips today.

Prayer

*Lord, put a watch over my lips today. Seal them so that I will only speak
words that will build up, not tear down. I repent of negative words spoken
and I ask You to help me protect my future and that of others by speaking
things that edify everyone. In Jesus' Name, amen.*

DECEMBER 2

See This Lamb!

"Never take your focus away from the Lamb of God and what He has taken upon Himself on your behalf. For in those times when you would feel inadequate and your weaknesses are prevalent before you, look to Heaven and see this Lamb!"

Prophetic Scripture

The next day John seeth Jesus coming unto him, and saith, Behold the Lamb of God, which taketh away the sin of the world (John 1:29).

When John the Baptist made the statement, "Behold the Lamb of God, which taketh away the sin of the world," he wasn't just saying that Jesus had arrived. Everyone in Israel would have understood what it meant when he used the word "lamb." They knew that a lamb was slain upon an altar and used as a sacrifice for sin. So they should have understood that when John referred to Jesus as the Lamb, it meant God was putting His Lamb, Jesus, upon an altar. Had their ears been tuned to it, they may have also noticed that John didn't say this Lamb was only going to cover sin, but this Lamb would remove sin. He was, in effect, telling them that no matter what shortcomings or weaknesses were in their lives, they could look to this Lamb and their sins would be taken away.

We cannot stop looking to the Lamb of God. Whenever we are feeling weak or seem burdened by our own shortcomings, we need to see the Lamb of God once again, who has taken our sins away. When we look at the Lamb, we are reminded of the Lord's mercy, who makes up for our failings. No matter what seems to be lacking in your life today, just see this Lamb!

Prayer

Heavenly Father, I see the Lamb of God today. I am reminded of what Jesus, the Lamb, did for me. He took all my failures upon Himself and all my shortcomings are made up for and my sins forgiven as I see this Lamb! Amen.

You Can Trust Again

"Even as you think this day of those you trusted and how some betrayed or let you down, know that I am removing scars that entered your heart through them. Even in areas where you've been apprehensive to trust people, I will give you the assurance so that you can trust again, says the Lord."

Prophetic Scripture

For it is not an enemy who reproaches me, then I could bear it; nor is it one who hates me who has exalted himself against me, then I could hide myself from him. But it is you, a man my equal, my companion and my familiar friend (Psalms 55:12-13 NASB).

Everyone has been betrayed by someone they trusted. What makes betrayal so painful is that it doesn't come through casual acquaintances. It comes from people close to us, and the level at which betrayal can scar a person's heart depends upon how much was invested in the relationship. Without even knowing it, many people have scars from which they have never been fully healed. It's why some don't go to church anymore—because they were hurt by a church. Some who've been through a painful divorce have a hard time believing they could trust someone in marriage again. Still others have cut out nearly all close relationships because of broken trust.

David described his own experiences with betrayal in Psalm 55, but he found healing by recognizing the hurt and calling upon the Lord. Living scarred by broken trust is not God's will for our lives. We need the Holy Spirit to heal these areas so we don't view everyone through our hurt. Believe that the Lord is giving you a new assurance today so that you can freely trust again!

Prayer

Lord, I ask You to heal my heart of all scarring that entered my life because of betrayal or broken trust. Help me recognize the areas in my soul that need healing and cause me to freely trust again. In Jesus' Name, amen.

You Shall Finish Greater!

"The Spirit says, I beckon you to the finish line. For your finish to this year is destined to be far greater than when you began. So press into it now and know that because I am with you, you shall finish in victory!"

Prophetic Scripture

Better is the end of a thing than the beginning thereof... (Ecclesiastes 7:8).

Every runner who competes in a race comes prepared and ready. Before they ever get to the track, they get themselves psyched up and ready for the big event. Everyone gathers and excitement is in the air as the runners all line up on the track and shoot off the starting block. Once the race begins, the runners must keep pressing hard for the finish line because they each want to see the result they hoped for at the beginning. However, for the winner that finish-line experience suddenly becomes far greater than the adrenaline experienced at the beginning of the race. He realizes that his determined press toward the finish was well worth it.

This picture depicts many people's calendar year. We begin the race with excitement, but as the year progresses we wonder how we will finish. Like a winner, we need to keep seeing the finish line we pictured for ourselves at the beginning of the year. We can't give up now. There is still a finish-line experience ahead of us that is far greater than our beginning. Sure, we might be a little out of breath right now as the year draws to a close, but we need to keep pressing to the end. The Spirit of God is there helping you finish this year in victory, so know that it shall be far greater than how you began!

Prayer

Father, I know that You are anointing me to finish my race and destiny for this year. Help me get a refreshed view of the glorious finish you have in store for me, and I know that I shall finish it with victory! In Jesus' Name, amen.

DECEMBER 5

Rejoice Evermore!

"Let it be a day to rejoice, says the Lord. Rejoice for your healing, rejoice for your blessing, rejoice over your family, and rejoice for tomorrow. For even as you offer up cheerful rejoicing shall good things be attracted to you."

Prophetic Scripture

Rejoice evermore (1 Thessalonians 5:16).

First Thessalonians 5:16 is one of the shortest verses in the Bible, but it really packs a punch. It's telling us to keep a cheerful attitude all the time. In fact, the word *rejoice* in the Greek means cheerful. God wants us to have a cheerful demeanor in all circumstances. Of course, we know that this isn't always easy to do. Sometimes we feel just the opposite, especially when things don't go just like we wanted. So why would the Lord tell us to be cheerful all the time if it wasn't that easy? Probably because God knows that a cheerful approach changes things. First of all, it has a tremendous effect on you personally. Cheerfulness helps you overcome tough times. It gives you the mental wherewithal to rise above things. Second, cheerfulness also makes people like being around you more. That in itself offers encouragement and strength. Another thing cheerfulness does is brighten up the atmosphere. It's like opening the blinds and letting the sun shine into the window. However, I am convinced that God wants us to be cheerful for yet another reason. That is because rejoicing and cheerfulness is exactly the opposite of everything the devil is. When we rejoice, the devil just cannot hang around! Without the devil hanging around, we open the way for good things to be attracted to us. Go ahead and try it and see what rejoicing all the time will do for you today!

Prayer

Lord, I rejoice today! I rejoice over every situation that concerns me, especially over _____. As I rejoice, every demon has to flee, and I thank You, Lord, that good things shall come my way. In Jesus' Name, amen.

His Anger Is No More

"Never think that I am directing My anger toward you, says the Lord. Know that because of the blood of Christ, I have offered you My open arms instead. So never fear opening your heart to Me, for when you do, instead of judgment, My love for you will be found."

Prophetic Scripture

To me this is like the days of Noah, when I swore that the water of Noah would never again cover the earth. So now I have sworn not to be angry with you, never to rebuke you again (Isaiah 54:9 NIV).

Many people's picture of God is that He is so angry that He can hardly wait to strike everyone He meets with lightening. When someone does something wrong, you will often hear folks joke that you should get away from them before the lightning strikes! Even as Christians, who have a pretty good understanding that God loves us unconditionally, we struggle to believe that God isn't up in Heaven at times half disgusted by some of our actions. That isn't to say that sin doesn't disappoint God; it's just that God has chosen to see us through the blood of Jesus. When He sees that blood, there is nothing to be disappointed or angry about. Instead, the Lord offers His open arms. Because of Jesus' blood, God's anger has been abated, so instead of trying to hide from Him when you make mistakes, go to the Lord and open your heart. When you do, His love will be found and you will find that His anger is no more.

Prayer

Father, I thank You that because of the blood of Jesus You are not angry with me. Thank You for forgiveness and that Your open arms of love are reaching out. I give everything to You and rest in Your love today. Amen.

Amazed by One Word

"Listen for Me to speak a word to your heart this day. For as you listen for Me to speak, My Word shall illuminate in your heart and you will be amazed by one word from Me."

Prophetic Scripture

...But my heart standeth in awe of thy word (Psalms 119:161).

Maybe you have heard it said, "One word from God changes everything." Really, when it comes to our success, a word from the Lord is all we need. Whether it's from the Bible, a prophet, or a word spoken to our hearts by the Holy Spirit, one word from God is the very fuel that sets us on course. When you have a word from God, you have concrete direction. It gives you the confidence on where you're headed and that the outcome is going to turn out right. You recognize the moment that word from God comes because it's like a light bulb going off and you find yourself amazed by it. It feels like a lifeline and it sets your mind free. It feels like the very thing you needed to hear, and you are so in awe because of it that you want to tell somebody.

Listen for God to speak one word today. If you are in a situation where you need some fresh direction, start carefully tuning your ear to the Lord and expect Him to talk to you. He may speak a Scripture during your prayer and study time. He may illuminate a word in your heart as you go through the day. However it comes, just know that God wants to speak, and you will always be amazed when you receive that one key word from Him.

Prayer

Lord, I tune my ear to listen to You today. I ask You for one key word that I can use that will set me on the right path concerning _____. I thank You for speaking and I am always in awe of Your Word. Amen.

Your Conscience Is Clean

"Because you have been washed in the blood of Christ, your conscience is now purified and you need not live in guilt and shame. So keep looking to the blood, for it makes your conscience new and clean, says the Lord."

Prophetic Scripture

Just think how much more the blood of Christ will purify our consciences from sinful deeds so that we can worship the living God... (Hebrews 9:14 NLT).

When we were born again, the Lord did an overhaul on our conscience. The blood of Jesus imparted within us a new set of principles and ethics. Things we once believed to be acceptable we suddenly didn't want in our lives anymore. Jesus' blood upon our hearts also continues to keep us in check. It's that something inside us that makes us take pause before we choose our actions. Thank God for His Spirit that has given us a pure conscience that wants to do right.

However, not only did God's Spirit within change our sense of right and wrong, it also delivered us from the shame of wrongdoing and it continues to do so every day of our Christian lives. His blood washed us from those feelings of guilt and condemnation regarding our sins of the past. It also continues to wash our consciences from the guilt and shame of recent mistakes. The beauty is that each time we look to His blood, it restrains us from further wrongdoing, but it also continually flushes our minds from resurfacing guilt. Keep your eyes on the blood of Jesus today. It will restrain you and wash your mind. His blood makes your conscience clean.

Prayer

Lord, I thank You that the blood of Jesus has given me a clean conscience. I look to the blood today and thank You that it restrains me from wrongdoing and frees me from guilt and shame. Amen!

A Word Over Your House

> *"Declare a word of Scripture over your house this day, says the Lord. For even as you declare it shall it be placed into motion in the realm of the spirit. And each time you speak it, shall it grow and then be birthed into manifestation for you."*

Prophetic Scripture

> *And thou shalt write them upon the posts of thy house, and on thy gates* (Deuteronomy 6:9).

We have to remember that the Bible is the Word of God. That means it's the very utterance spoken from God's mouth. In Deuteronomy 6:9, when God told Israel that they needed to write His words over the posts and doors of their homes, it was because that Word was to become the very utterance from God that would shape their home lives. Not only were the words posted over their houses as a commitment to a certain standard of living, it was also a declaration for the future they wanted to see manifest.

Think of a Scripture you want to become reality over your household. Perhaps everything looks opposite right now, but you can become the force that upholds it by the word you declare. Of course, it can be difficult to keep that word upheld when it seems that things are not lining up. However, remember, God told Israel to write it upon the posts. Now that doesn't necessarily mean you have to hang a literal sign. What it really means is to lift a continual standard over your house through what you believe and speak every day by faith. Eventually, if continually upheld that word will become reality in the atmosphere of your home. Let today be the day to speak a word over your house!

Prayer

> *Father, I speak _____ as the Scripture written over my house today. I believe that it shall come to pass no matter what it looks like now. I declare this word shall manifest over the future of my household. In Jesus' Name, amen!*

Tear Up Your Lists

"The Spirit says, think this day of those whom you can still recall the things they did to hurt you. Take the list of their faults that exists in your mind and tear it up, says the Lord, so that the list no longer has the power to hurt you."

Prophetic Scripture

… Love…takes no account of the evil done to it [it pays no attention to a suffered wrong] (1 Corinthians 13:5 AMP).

Often when people hurt us, we develop subconscious mental lists of their faults. Most of the time, we don't deliberately formulate these lists, but when someone mentions that person's name an entire host of hurtful memories suddenly resurfaces. When First Corinthians 13:5 says that love doesn't take account of the hurtful things done to it, it is saying that love doesn't keep lists of the faults of others. Of course, the devil will always make sure there are plenty of people available to hurt you, especially in the areas where you are the weakest. This makes it even harder to tear up those lists and the hurt keeps resurfacing. Eventually, if we are not careful we form our future outlook and actions based on some of the hurts from these lists without even realizing it.

The only way to be free is to tear up your lists. Perhaps you may even consider creating a literal list of those who hurt you. Declare that you forgive them, then finish by actually tearing up the list. If we don't tear up these lists, whether literally or figuratively, they will always have the power to come back and hurt us. Ask the Holy Spirit to help you tear up your lists today so you can be free!

Prayer

Father, I choose to tear up every mental list today regarding those who hurt me. I will not relive these hurts in my mind. I forgive each person who hurt me and ask You to forgive me for every person I hurt also. Amen!

Hold On Tight!

"Keep closely focused on the things you have learned from Me this year, says the Lord. Don't let them slip away in the year to come, for they will be of great value and will propel you victoriously into the next season of your life."

Prophetic Scripture

Therefore we ought to give the more earnest heed to the things which we have heard, lest at any time we should let them slip (Hebrews 2:1).

Sometimes we take in things, such as sermons we've heard, Bible verses we have read, or even life lessons learned, and we forget them in a few short days, weeks, or months. Sometimes they fade and lose their value as new experiences come along. However, as you look back on your year, it's a good time to reflect on some of the key things God taught you. Recount the key Scriptures that stood out to you this past year and hold on tight to them! Perhaps, it was an anointed sermon that changed your life. Don't let it fade from view; hold on tight to it and make it work in your life for next year. The Bible says we are to give even more, not less, earnest heed to the things we have heard. We must take careful effort not to let these important impartations in our lives slip out of sight (see Heb. 2:1). They may be the very things intended by the Holy Spirit to prevent wrong circumstances in the months and years to come.

Take the revelations you have received this past year seriously. Make a list of the key things and implement them in your daily living. They will be the very things that will propel you into victory for the upcoming year. It's time to hold on tight!

Prayer

Holy Spirit, I ask You to help me recall every key thing You taught me this past year. Help me implement these things in my life so that I may embrace my upcoming year in victory. Amen!

DECEMBER 12

He Knows Your Heart

"Know that I see the secret chambers of your heart. I see the thoughts, intentions, feelings, and even the parts that you cannot understand about yourself. And also, what others do not seem to understand about you, I the Lord know and understand your heart."

Prophetic Scripture

Search me, O God, and know my heart: try me, and know my thoughts (Psalms 139:23).

The workings of the human soul and spirit can be a complex thing. The inward dwelling of the Holy Spirit conflicts at times with our own fleshly behaviors, which are compounded with a wide range of emotions. On top of all that is the intellectual part of us that is often complicated by the need to sort through the advice and input of others. Then we have memories and lifelong habits learned from childhood in the mix. All of this can create a wide range of feelings and potential misunderstandings, either for ourselves or others. It can leave some people unable to know exactly what they want from life and even less able to communicate the things truly important to them to other people. It all sounds very daunting, but there is one key solace. The Lord knows and understands our hearts! He gets in the middle of our thoughts and helps sort them out. He can impart within us the divine ability to make sense of things. More importantly, because He understands our hearts, we never have to worry that no one cares how we feel. The Lord cares. We don't have to feel confused by our own mixed-up feelings. All we have to do is rest in the fact that the Lord knows our hearts, and that alone will give us peace.

Prayer

Father, I thank You that I live in peace because You know my heart. Help me in the areas where I need to have a heart change. Also, help me to always communicate my heart to others, when it's needed, in a way that pleases You. Amen.

Your Ministry Will Be Fulfilled

"I am helping you fulfill everything I have called you to do, says the Lord. For the gifts that I have given to My people shall not become null and void. So say this day that your ministry shall not be fruitless, but that it shall be fulfilled."

Prophetic Scripture

And Barnabas and Saul returned from Jerusalem, when they had fulfilled their ministry... (Acts 12:25).

It is important to remember that just because we are in God's will doesn't mean that life is a bed of roses and there won't be setbacks. In fact, often when you are in God's will that is when everything is against you. There are seasons in life when it seems you are not getting ahead with whatever God has called you to do. Perhaps it's full-time ministry or a marketplace type of ministry. Either way, we all have a call upon our life to do something constructive for God's Kingdom. Yet there are times when it feels like you aren't getting anywhere. When Paul and Barnabas began to travel together in ministry, they certainly weren't strangers to setbacks. Paul's very entrance into ministry invited immediate opposition. But notice that even with setbacks, Acts 12:25 says they didn't return back to Jerusalem without first fulfilling their mission and bearing fruit because God saw to their success.

If God put the gift and calling in you, it will not come back without bearing fruit. God will cause your ministry to touch somebody, somewhere at just the right time. Sometimes we just need to take our eyes off all the natural things that make ministry seem unsuccessful. Instead of believing in those things, we simply need to keep on saying that our ministry will be fulfilled!

Prayer

Lord, I believe that the ministry that is in my heart is from You. I know it shall touch lives. So I say today that my ministry will not become void, but it will bear fruit and be fulfilled! In Jesus' Name, amen.

DECEMBER 14

Forget the Pain!

"It is time to forget your season of pain and embrace your season of fruitfulness, says the Lord. Even as Joseph named his firstborn Manasseh, it was his declaration that he had forgotten his years of hardship. So must you declare that your years of struggle and toil are behind you now!"

Prophetic Scripture

And Joseph called the name of the firstborn Manasseh: For God, said he, hath made me forget all my toil, and all my father's house. And the name of the second called he Ephraim: for God hath caused me to be fruitful in the land of my affliction (Genesis 41:51-52).

No matter what hardships you have been through, God always has a plan to move you forward to a new chapter. Whether your hardships are from your distant past or they just occurred yesterday, God is always beckoning you to put that season of toil behind you. Notice in the verses above when Joseph called his firstborn son Manasseh, it was because God had made him forget all his hardship and all his father's house. Why *all* his father's house? That is because to him, the years he spent growing up held a lot of bad memories and hurts. Maybe your upbringing was filled with similar memories. Well, it's time to move from that place and open a new chapter. It is your Ephraim chapter, which in the Hebrew means double fruitfulness! (See Genesis 41:52.) Even negative experiences from this week will lose their ability to keep you down when you choose to forget your struggles. It's time to forget the pain and dwell instead on the blessings of tomorrow and wonderful fruit God is producing in your life!

Prayer

Heavenly Father, I thank You that today I give "spiritual birth" to Manasseh by choosing to forget the hurts of yesterday. I declare this is now my season of Ephraim—my season of double fruitfulness—and it is a new chapter in my life. Thank You, Jesus! Amen!

None Makes You Afraid

"Never fear potential harm from lawbreakers or those with criminal intent. For My angels are walking with you and they dwell on all your property. They keep a close eye on your goods so that none can make you afraid."

Prophetic Scripture

And they shall no more be a prey to the heathen, neither shall the beast of the land devour them; but they shall dwell safely, and none shall make them afraid (Ezekiel 34:28).

Everyone knows that crime is on the rise. People work to protect themselves in various ways from becoming potential victims. We protect ourselves from robbery by installing security systems. We protect ourselves from identity theft or internet crimes through various online services. We look over our shoulder in a dark parking lot and teach our children about the dangers of talking to strangers. Of course, this isn't to say we shouldn't do these things. We do need to live prudently and wisely in this world. However, what we as believers have to trust in first and foremost is the Lord, so that we don't succumb to fear. Think of how many times God's angels kept Israel from would-be attackers. The Lord opened the prison doors for Peter on two different occasions when a criminal government would have murdered him (see Acts 5:17-19; 12:1-17).

We have to understand that God's angels are watching over us to keep us from falling prey to these things (see Ezek. 34:28). Perhaps if you have been victim of some form of petty or even more serious crime, the Lord wants to give you the renewed confidence not to be afraid. His anointing is over you today so that no lawbreaker will cause you harm and none shall ever make you afraid.

Prayer

*Lord, You are my protection from every form of crime. I declare I will **never** be hurt by a lawbreaker or criminal. I am protected and kept safe because Your angels are watching over my life and property. In Jesus' Name, amen.*

Gifts Everyday

"If you will look diligently for them, says the Lord, you will see that I have daily gifts and blessings to give you. Search for them and you will find them, for gifts from Heaven are yours and are being heaped upon you every day."

Prophetic Scripture

Blessed be the Lord, who daily loadeth us with benefits, even the God of our salvation. Selah (Psalms 68:19).

Sometimes we don't see the gifts God brings us every day because we either don't look for them or we overlook them. We can unintentionally be going along each day not seeing the good things that happen as special gifts from the Lord. However, they are gifts from Him that we need to cherish and appreciate. Psalms 68:19 says that the Lord daily loads us with benefits. That means there are gifts of God coming into your life every single day! Notice that verse doesn't just say the Lord daily *gives* you benefits. It says that He daily *loads* you with benefits. That means there is more than one gift to be on the lookout for each day! I love how the verse ends with *Selah*, which means pause and reflect on it. In other words, if you will take time to notice, what God gives is so amazing it's almost hard to fathom.

Begin noticing the simple things and thank the Lord for them. The more you practice searching for and appreciating the Lord's daily gifts and benefits, the more you will find them. Then watch them get bigger from there. When you see things as gifts from the Lord, it releases greater things upon you because gifts are yours every day!

Prayer

Lord, I thank You for the daily load of benefits that You give me. Help me not to overlook a single one of them. You are the God who never runs short of goodness and blessing, and I reflect on that with a grateful heart today. Amen.

DECEMBER 17

Their Words Have No Power

"Know that the unjust words and accusations that are made against you have no power unless you give them power through fear, says the Lord. So let your life in Me prove their lies false, for I have already said their words have no power."

Prophetic Scripture

No weapon that is formed against thee shall prosper; and every tongue that shall rise against thee in judgment thou shalt condemn. This is the heritage of the servants of the Lord, and their righteousness is of me, saith the Lord (Isaiah 54:17).

Everyone has critics. In fact, some critics will not only criticize but will outright lie. While not one of us will please or make friends with everyone, we can live above our critics and accusers. Whether it's the kid in the schoolyard being teased by peers, the divorcee accused by a former spouse, or even the preacher being criticized by listeners, we can't let accusations get us down. It's tempting to answer every lie and criticism out of fear someone will erroneously believe a lie about you. While there are times to speak up, the majority of the time we just need to trust that God won't allow their false accusations to prosper. Sure, they may affect a few others, but in the larger scheme of things, these accusers are only ruining themselves.

Your godly heritage as a believer is that God defends your righteousness through Him. The miracle is that while you are being criticized and accused, God keeps moving you toward success while the lies said of you diminish and ultimately have no lasting effect on your life. So remember today that what they are saying right now may seem irreparable, but their words have no power!

Prayer

Lord, I thank You that my godly heritage is that You are defending my righteousness in You. The words and lies of critics and false accusers cannot prosper, and their words have no power to harm me. In Jesus' Name, amen.

The Lord Remembers You

"Never assume that what seems to be a barren season won't change in one moment of time. For I have been listening intently to your prayers, and you will surely birth much spiritual fruit and many prophetic destinies because I, the Lord, have remembered you."

Prophetic Scripture

...And the Lord remembered her (1 Samuel 1:19).

When Hannah prayed desperately for a child, it probably seemed like a long barren season. Hannah's barren season resembles our own prayer experiences when it seems we aren't birthing any answers to the things we are praying for. Of course, one of the key things Hannah did that caused her to eventually give birth to the prophet Samuel was that she continued praying when it didn't appear to be working (see 1 Sam. 1:12). She continued to trust the Lord and call out to Him. Many people would have given up and believed the lie that God somehow quit listening to their prayers because it appeared nothing was any different. What if Hannah had been like some of us and given up? The earth would have lost out on the blessing of one of the most prominent prophets of the Bible. Her persistence brought forth a prophetic destiny that changed a nation. However, her persistence first got the attention of the Lord, and First Samuel 1:19 says of Hannah, "and the Lord remembered her." What was God remembering? Surely, He remembered Hannah's persistent prayers and unwillingness to accept barrenness as the final answer.

Keep pressing into God in prayer for the things you are trusting Him for. Don't give up today, because the Lord your God remembers you.

Prayer

Father, I come before You like Hannah did in continual, persistent prayer. I pray today about _____. I thank You that because You remember me it will come to pass and I will see the fruit of it brought forth into the earth. In Jesus' Name, amen.

DECEMBER 19

Send Prosperity!

"There is an anointing upon you this day for advancement, says the Lord. It shall cause you to push forward quickly because My Spirit has sent an endowment of prosperity upon you now!"

Prophetic Scripture

Save now, I beseech thee, O Lord: O Lord, I beseech thee, send now prosperity (Psalms 118:25).

In Psalms 118:25, the word *prosperity* means to advance and push forward. When the psalmist was calling out for the Lord to send prosperity, he was saying, "Lord, we beg of you, push us forward and cause us to advance successfully now!" He was expressing to the Lord his feeling that the next step going forward was going to require a supernatural "push" by the Spirit of God. Sometimes our next step requires a supernatural thrust from the Lord to help propel us to keep moving forward. Notice how the psalmist begins the verse by saying, "Save now." He was revealing that the next step toward success needed a God-intervention for it to even be possible. He needed God to literally force his feet forward.

Sometimes, we need God to place an endowment upon us for that kind of advancement. Of course, that need for advancement can mean any number of things. Prosperity can certainly include a much-needed advancement in the area of finances; however, the need is different for everyone. The important thing is knowing that if the psalmist could call out to God for divine prosperity to be sent in his situation, so can we. In whatever area you need to prosper or advance, ask the Lord to give you a divine endowment of power to push forward. Expect it to manifest, and know that the Lord is sending prosperity now!

Prayer

Lord, I ask You to send an anointing for prosperity upon me right now. Cause me to push forward and advance in those areas where it looks impossible. I receive a divine intervention of prosperity upon my life today! Amen.

Focus on the Good

"The Spirit says, what might happen if you only focused upon the good things around you this day? Eliminate from your thoughts all the negative things and focus only on the good. Then, surely, you will even see good multiply all around you."

Prophetic Scripture

Finally, brethren, whatsoever things are true, whatsoever things are honest, whatsoever things are just, whatsoever things are pure, whatsoever things are lovely, whatsoever things are of good report; if there be any virtue, and if there be any praise, think of these things (Philippians 4:8).

Human nature easily focuses on the negative things of life because it's what has a tendency to steal our attention. For example, in a classroom there could be 29 excellent students, but it's that one disobedient child who demands the teacher's attention. Another example is when someone mistreats you. Everyone you met that day could have treated you like royalty, but your mind wants to zone in on the mean one. When it comes to paying bills, every bill could be paid, but it's that one that you didn't have enough money for that gets you. I believe the reason Philippians 4:8 was written is because we have to make a conscious effort to emphasize the good. If we don't, our minds will do just the opposite and we start to think everything is going downhill when that is the farthest from the truth!

Consider making a short list today of all the good things that happen. It will change your perspective and help you realize that when you focus on the good, the good things are far outweighing the bad. You will even find that the good things are not only abundant, but actually multiplying all around you!

Prayer

Father, I make a conscious effort to focus on the good things in my life today. I choose not to give my attention to the negative things, and I thank You that good is going to multiply all around me! Amen.

Surely God Is in Thee

"Expect the world to see Me in you, says the Lord. Expect them to see My power displayed through you. Be prepared now, for many will come your way who will declare that surely God is in thee!"

Prophetic Scripture

…Surely God is in thee; and there is none else, there is no God (Isaiah 45:14).

Understand that if you walk with God it is more evident than you may realize, especially to the world who doesn't know God. People are spiritual beings and their human spirit can feel and recognize the presence of God. They may not always want to encounter God's presence, but they know when it's there. Some may act like they don't notice, refuse to acknowledge, or even try to downplay it. Some will mock or resist. Isn't that what happened in Acts 2 when the Holy Spirit fell? Some mocked and accused the newly Spirit-filled believers of being drunk (see Acts 2:13). There is no doubt, with the kind of power that was displayed, that they felt a genuine supernatural presence. Sure, some will downplay God's presence in you, but others will seek you out. Some will ask for prayer because they know somehow that you have a connection with God. When people need God, they know who to look for!

Everywhere you go, expect people to feel God upon you. It doesn't even mean you always have to say or do anything. It's simply that you walk with God and it will be evident. People are desperate today and are looking for God, so be prepared—many are coming and will say, "Surely, God is in thee!"

Prayer

Holy Spirit, I thank You that Your presence fills me and it is evident to those I meet. Let them see You in me and upon me. Draw those to me who are hungry to encounter Your presence, and I will connect them to You! Amen!

Say You Are Strong!

"Don't allow your weaknesses to govern you, says the Spirit. Look at them and say that you are strong. Even tell your physical frailties to receive strength, for it's time once again for the weak to say, I am strong!"

Prophetic Scripture

...Let the weak say, I am strong (Joel 3:10).

When God instructed the people of Judah to make war in the Book of Joel, one of His key instructions through the prophet was for the weak to begin to proclaim strength. That is because when you say it, you begin to believe it, and eventually strength comes. Many people today are dealing with numerous forms of weakness, especially physically. They deal with countless nagging ailments. Sometimes when we feel weak, we give in because it's easy to do. Most people won't deny their tired bodies the opportunity to go to bed! Of course there is time for rest; however, the devil wants to get us feeling weak all the time so we slowly decline. This can happen spiritually, emotionally, or physically. We have to resist this tendency and war against these feelings of weakness and frailty. Some people are so weak that they feel helpless to stand up to the devil's attacks. You may be saying, "That's me! I am just too weak to rise up!" Well, the best way to overcome it is to begin saying you are strong. Most anyone can lie there and speak! You may not feel like you are strong, but you have to begin to say it by faith. This is how God instructed Judah to rise up. Eventually, they put on strength for weakness simply by saying it was so. Overcome all your weaknesses today and begin to say, "I am strong!"

Prayer

Lord, I declare today that I am strong in every area of my life. I can overcome my weaknesses because Your strength comes into me. I speak to every frailty and say I am strong! In Jesus' Name, amen.

Your Loved Ones Spared

"Even as I spared Lot because of righteous Abraham, so shall I spare your loved ones from harm if you will call out to Me on their behalf. Know that I will hear your prayer for them because your righteousness is before Me, says the Lord."

Prophetic Scripture

And it came to pass, when God destroyed the cities of the plain, that God remembered Abraham, and sent Lot out of the midst of the overthrow... (Genesis 19:29).

When God overthrew Sodom and Gomorrah, He spared Abraham's nephew, Lot, and his family who were living there. God took Lot into consideration simply because of Abraham who was righteous. God didn't save Lot because of Lot's own walk with God. In fact, there must have been some serious worldliness in Lot's life for him to tolerate living in these sinful cities. It was such a wicked environment that when two angels visited Lot's home prior to the overthrow, the men of the cities wanted to have homosexual relations with the angels. Lot stood up against them but was still deranged enough to offer his two virgin daughters instead! No, it wasn't Lot's own lifestyle that spared him. Lot was spared because of Abraham's relationship with God. Now that doesn't mean because you are born again that your loved ones are automatically saved. What it means is that when you call out to the Lord for your family, God hears your prayers and places a covering upon their life so they can be set up to encounter God in a salvation experience.

Like Abraham, call out for your loved ones. Your walk with God and your prayers are causing them to be spared so they can be given every opportunity to receive the Lord.

Prayer

Lord, I pray for my loved ones today. I pray specifically for _____. I ask You to protect them from harm and cause them to be positioned to have a genuine encounter with You. In Jesus' Name, amen.

Multitudes Rejoicing

"Look now, says the Spirit, for you are about to see a sweep of worship across the globe when entire multitudes will gather in stadiums and arenas to worship and lift up My Name. Yes, they will gather to praise in mass numbers because of the miraculous things they have seen and heard!"

Prophetic Scripture

And when he was come nigh, even now at the descent of the mount of Olives, the whole multitude of the disciples began to rejoice and praise God with a loud voice for all the mighty works that they had seen (Luke 19:37).

When people see miracles they get excited. That is because people don't want to encounter a man-made, powerless version of the Gospel. They want to experience the real Gospel that is full of the kind of power that transforms lives in a supernatural way. The real Gospel manifests in the same way it was through Jesus who performed miracles, signs, and wonders. People followed Him because their physical needs were met through the power of God. They got healed and set free. On one occasion in Luke 19:37, the multitude of disciples that followed Jesus was so excited for the miracles they had seen they broke out into a mass worship event! They lifted up their praise with a loud voice.

As we continue to present the power of the true Gospel the same way Jesus and His disciples demonstrated it, people will gather to worship God on a mass scale. We have been trying so hard to get them into church, but it will be hard to keep them out of church! The Lord is moving and it's the season now to see multitudes rejoicing!

Prayer

Father, I ask You to help those of us in Your Church to present a powerful, miraculous Gospel worldwide. Even as miracles blanket the earth, cause us to draw people and let us be ready to handle the time when we will truly see multitudes upon multitudes rejoicing! Amen.

Give What You Have

"Because you carry My miraculous power within you, says the Lord, give it away. Give what you have to those who need it and I will back you with the anointing as signs and wonders are performed through your hands."

Prophetic Scripture

Then Peter said, Silver and gold have I none; but such as I have give I thee: In the name of Jesus Christ of Nazareth rise up and walk (Acts 3:6).

When Peter and John encountered the crippled man at the Gate Beautiful, he thought they were going to give him money. According to Peter, it appears he didn't have any money because he said, "Silver and gold have I none." Perhaps Peter didn't have any cash on him, but consider that Peter may have been saying something far more profound. Perhaps Peter wasn't just trying to say he didn't have any literal cash. Most people have at least a couple coins. What if Peter was instead trying to communicate to the man, "I could give you money, but instead I am going to give you something that I have which is more effective than money!" Peter then gave the very thing he knew he carried which was far more powerful than money. Peter gave the power of God!

Sometimes we are so busy giving to people in the natural that we aren't giving them what we really have, which is the anointing! Sure, giving natural things such as money and physical substance is important, but we can't neglect giving people God's power. You carry the very power of God within you, so think of how you can give what you have today and present the power of God to someone who needs it!

Prayer

Lord, I know that I carry Your miraculous power within me. Show me how to give what I have to someone who needs it. Teach me how to present the anointing accurately and effectively so people may experience signs and wonders. In Jesus' Name, amen.

Rewarded in His Will

"Many have become distracted by all the world has to offer, and it has caused some to walk away from My best for them. So remember that as you stay with Me, you will be rewarded for living continually committed to My will."

Prophetic Scripture

And the world passeth away, and the lust thereof: but he that doeth the will of God abideth forever (1 John 2:17).

There are rewards for living in a continual pursuit of God's will. Jesus never said it was an easy road. In fact, He said the road that leads to God's will is straight and narrow, while the road leading away from God is crooked and twisted (see Matt. 7:13-14). On the straight road, there isn't a lot of wiggle room before you veer off. In other words, this road isn't always a fun party. It requires doing the same consistent things every day, over and over again. While this narrow road requires the most discipline, it also provides the most peace and security because you know exactly where you are headed. There aren't a bunch of surprise curves and blind corners to navigate, like you find on the road that leads away from God. That road offers all sorts of pleasures, but it offers no stability and will eventually disappear. However, by staying on the road to God's will, you know that you are headed straight into His perfect plan which lasts forever.

Too many people these days are getting on the wrong road that offers no happy ending. While it may not always be popular, stay on the road to God's will because it lasts forever and eventually you will enjoy the lasting reward it brings.

Prayer

Lord, I commit myself to live in pursuit of Your will. Keep me on the right road and I choose to discipline myself to follow You on the straight and narrow path. I thank You, Lord, that I shall enjoy the reward it brings. Amen.

The Scriptures Opened

"The Spirit says, even as you read My Word this day, I will open the Scriptures to you that you might understand the depths of the Spirit and even receive prophetic revelation that will be the next step for your future."

Prophetic Scripture

Then opened he their understanding, that they might understand the Scriptures (Luke 24:45).

One of the most powerful ways to receive revelation that will propel you into a successful future comes from the Bible. While reading the Bible can offer meaningful thoughts, it takes Holy Spirit inspiration for the Scriptures to be opened to you. Many people read the Bible. It is almost a poetic piece of literature for some. This is the reason people from all sorts of backgrounds print Bible verses on wall art or greeting cards. It has a meaningful, poetic tone that makes people feel in touch with God somehow. However, it takes a real relationship and baptism with the Holy Spirit's fire to cause the Scriptures to be completely opened to you. It's what causes you to read the Bible in such a way that the words begin to jump off the pages with transforming power. This is what happened when Jesus met the disciples on the Road to Emmaus in Luke 24. While they had already had previous encounters with the Lord, on this occasion Jesus opened the prophetic truths from the Scriptures and caused its words to hit home and change their lives on a whole new level.

The Holy Spirit within is opening the Scriptures to you today. If you meditate on His Word, He will cause the verses to be expounded upon in your heart so they can form your future. Get ready for the Scriptures to be prophetically opened today!

Prayer

Holy Spirit, I ask You to open revelation from the Scriptures to me. Help me understand what I read. I thank You that divine truths from Your Word will come alive and will propel me powerfully into my future! Amen.

The Lord Sees You

"Be on guard against emotional walls, says the Lord. For though it would be tempting to close out the world when you think you have been misunderstood, know that I am the God who always sees you."

Prophetic Scripture

And she called the name of the Lord that spake unto her, Thou God seest me… (Genesis 16:13).

When Hagar, Sarah's maid, became pregnant by Abraham, she became an outcast. It was a scheme by Sarah who thought herself too old to have a baby. She told her husband to sleep with her maid so she could raise the child and call it her own. Of course, when Hagar became pregnant Sarah was angry and cast her out. Hagar then fled to the wilderness and sat by a fountain of water on the road to Shur (see Gen. 16:7). This was prophetic in that a fountain of water always represents revelation from the Holy Spirit, while *Shur* in the Hebrew means *wall*. It reveals that when Hagar was on the road to putting up her own emotional walls, that was when a fountain of revelation from God appeared. It caused her to receive the revelation that God is always watching, even during your deepest frustrations. She then called the Lord, "The God who sees me." Right when she was about to give in to putting up emotional walls, the Lord intervened.

We can all be tempted to put up emotional walls when we feel misunderstood. However, we need to resist it because that is when God is about to reveal Himself. It's when you realize that God has been watching the entire scenario and helping you all along. He is always involved, because He is the God who sees you!

Prayer

Lord, You see every frustration and misunderstanding I have ever been through. I choose not to put up emotional walls because I know that You will always give me revelation during those times. You are the God who sees me! Amen.

Keep Preaching!

"Though the world would resist with vehemence, keep preaching, says the Lord. Keep teaching and declaring My Word wherever you go and don't stop. While some may reject, others will hear, so whatever you do in this season, keep preaching, says the Spirit of Grace!"

Prophetic Scripture

Preach the word… (2 Timothy 4:2).

There are countless things today trying to silence the voice of the Church. Some want to make the truth of the Gospel message sound as if it's nothing more than some extreme cult that wants to spread hate toward other world religions. They are against the idea that the only access to God is through Jesus Christ and promote that anyone who believes such is completely intolerant. When some attest that other world religions also offer a way to God other than Jesus, Christians are expected to embrace it even though Jesus said, "I am the way" (John 14:6). Christians who don't agree are labeled hateful and intolerant. All of this pressure is a ploy by the devil to intimidate and silence the Church. So how should we respond? Keep preaching the truth!

We are in a time when we need to make some hard decisions. We need to keep preaching the truth of God's Word in spite of the pressure. If we don't, we may lose a generation to a watered-down version of Christianity and secularism. The Bible is becoming less palatable to the present generation, so we must keep preaching it amidst resistance or even persecution. The early apostles kept preaching and it increased God's grace upon them. It will take all of us in this season to reach the world. So wherever your sphere of influence might be, just keep preaching!

Prayer

Father, I choose to keep sharing and preaching Your Word. Give me the boldness and confidence to declare Your Word in my circles of influence. Send me to those who will hear it, that they might encounter You. Amen.

Your Year Crowned with Good

"Get ready, says the Spirit, for I am surrounding your year with My goodness. So expect to see my goodness in all things and in every situation. For even as you do, the things that held you back in the past shall be no more."

Prophetic Scripture

You crown the year with a bountiful harvest; even the hard pathways overflow with abundance (Psalm 65:11 NLT).

God always wants our future to be bright. According to Psalms 65:11, God's intention is to surround us with abundance and blessing. It says He crowns our year with a bountiful harvest. In the Hebrew, the word *crown* means to surround. God wants your year surrounded with good things from Him. Of course, the Lord knows that there are plenty of things in this world that try to prevent us from feeling like we are experiencing God's goodness. There are things that try to steal our peace, health, provision, joy, and much more. Jesus said that we would experience tribulation in this world but that He has overcome it (see John 16:33). So in other words, while there are many forms of tribulation that try to enter your life, God always has a divine plan for you to come out of it into abundance. His desire is for you to experience His goodness in such a way that even the most difficult experiences from last year or even the last several years will begin to turn around. Psalms 65:11 says, "even the hard pathways overflow with abundance" (NLT).

This is the picture that we need to expect for the upcoming year. We need to expect God's goodness to surround our year with good!

Prayer

Father, I thank You that my upcoming year shall be surrounded with goodness. I expect to experience Your goodness. I take authority over the things that would try to steal that and thank You that my hard pathways from the past shall be filled with abundance. In Jesus' Name, amen.

It's Not Relevant!

"The Spirit says, know that the past is no longer relevant to your future. Your past mistakes, problems, and even the things that didn't turn out like you hoped are now over. So as you look at the year to come, say of the past, It's not relevant!"

Prophetic Scripture

Blotting out the handwriting of the ordinances that was against us, which was contrary to us, and took it out of the way, nailing it to his cross (Colossians 2:14).

We often let past problems and mistakes form our outlook and approach to the future. Many people think they can't enter the future without the past looming over them like a dark cloud. They expect their future to be hindered or altered somehow because of it. However, God can take the problems of the past, reshape them, and make it so they aren't relevant to our future. Colossians 2:14 says Jesus took the incriminating evidence against us and nailed it to the cross. The verse says, "and took it out of the way." In other words, Jesus has taken our sins, failures, weaknesses, and problems out of our way so we are able to say of the past, "It's not relevant!" You don't have to make your past relevant to your future. It doesn't have to be a factor in formulating your outlook and actions for the upcoming year. If you need to repent and come clean in some areas, then do it now so you can leave last year in last year! Then start expecting something new and wonderful to be on the horizon. Start saying of your negative past, "It's not relevant!"

Prayer

Lord, as this year comes to a close, I repent of all sins. Forgive me and reshape my future. I thank You that Jesus took my sins, weaknesses, frustrations, and problems out of the way. I look for a bright new year to come, and I say of my negative past, "It's not relevant!" In Jesus' Name, amen!

About Brenda Kunneman

For more information about Hank and Brenda Kunneman, One Voice Ministries, or to receive a product list for books and audios or for information on speaking engagements, please go to www.hank andbrenda.org or write to:

One Voice Ministries
5351 S. 139th Plaza
Omaha, NE 68137 USA
Phone: 402-896-6692
Fax: 402-894-9068

Visit Hank and Brenda Kunneman at their Website: www.hankand brenda.org

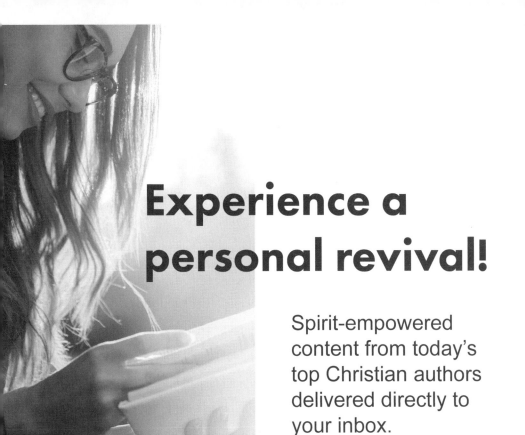